# English in the World

# English in the World

## Teaching and learning the language and literatures

Papers of an International Conference
entitled 'Progress in English Studies'
held in London, 17–21 September 1984
to celebrate the Fiftieth Anniversary of
The British Council
and its contribution
to the field of English Studies
over fifty years

Edited by

## *Randolph Quirk and H. G. Widdowson*

Associate Editor: Yolande Cantù

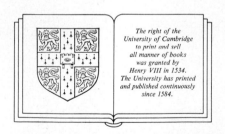

The right of the
University of Cambridge
to print and sell
all manner of books
was granted by
Henry VIII in 1534.
The University has printed
and published continuously
since 1584.

## Cambridge University Press

Cambridge
London   New York   New Rochelle
Melbourne   Sydney
*for*
The British Council

Published by the Press Syndicate of the University of Cambridge
The Pitt Building, Trumpington Street, Cambridge CB2 1RP
32 East 57th Street, New York, NY 10022, USA
10 Stamford Road, Oakleigh, Melbourne 3166, Australia

© The British Council 1985

First published 1985

Printed in Great Britain
at the University Press, Cambridge

Library of Congress catalogue card number: 84–28590

*British Library cataloguing in publication data*

English in the world: teaching and learning the
language and literatures: papers of an international
conference entitled 'Progress in English Studies' held in
London, 17–21 September 1984, to celebrate the fiftieth
anniversary of the British Council and its contribution
to the field of English studies over fifty years.
1. English language – foreign countries
I. Quirk, Randolph   II. Widdowson, H. G.
III. British Council
428.2'4      PE2751

ISBN 0 521 30483 0 hard covers
ISBN 0 521 31522 0 paperback

219160

**WD**

# Contents

Contents

# Foreword

The year 1934, when the British Council was founded, did not of course mark the beginning of the spread of our language and culture to other parts of the world. One might perhaps see the Pilgrim Fathers as the first British Council mission, or, as was suggested by an overseas delegate, Robinson Crusoe as the first English Language Officer. But 1934 did mark the start of a determined effort to promote an enduring understanding and appreciation of Britain in other countries through cultural, educational and technical cooperation. Our operational budget has increased – from £5,000 to over £180 million today – but our task remains essentially the same, based on the principles of reciprocity and mutual respect.

Over the same period the Council's involvement in English Studies has likewise grown under the encouragement and guidance of eminent scholars – from such renowned figures as Ifor Evans, Daniel Jones and J. R. Firth in earlier days, to such equally notable figures of today as Randolph Quirk, Henry Widdowson, and the many members of our English Teaching Advisory Committee.

To mark the Fiftieth Anniversary of the Council's active involvement in progress in English Studies, we invited forty-two leading figures from thirty-eight overseas countries, twenty from the UK and ten from our own ranks to spend a week together discussing major current issues in this field. It was felt that the event in itself was a fitting tribute to our achievements (although many delegates were kind enough to add warm verbal tribute as well). But it was also hoped that such a galaxy of experts might provide helpful insights into current problems and pointers to future developments.

There was always a risk of our attempting too broad a canvas, that such wide-ranging topics as information and educational technology, teacher training, methodology (including ESP), literature teaching and linguistic standards would split the participants into a number of small non-overlapping camps. And Professor Sinclair has drawn attention to some of the obvious omissions, with Dr Davies deploring the absence of a session devoted to teaching and evaluation. But the obvious genuine enthusiasm emanating from the many comments I have received from participants, orally and in writing, make it clear that the Conference was in fact overwhelmingly successful. This was due to a number of factors – the manageable size of the group, the uniquely high level of expertise for so small a gathering, and the academically admirable and convenient setting of the University of London Senate House.

Some of the many important issues to emerge from the Conference were:

1 The need to bring a sense of realism to information technology, and to let a new and richer approach to classroom methodology lead developments in computer-assisted language learning.

2 The renewed emphasis on the *education* of teachers, as distinct from training, with *two* main papers referring to the INSET programme.

3 A strengthening of the move towards learner-centred teaching – how to get more out of the learner rather than how the teacher transfers 'information' *to* the learner.

4 The insistence on the plural form 'English literatures' – referring not only to what is produced in countries where English is traditionally the native language, but also where it has the status of second language.

5 The obvious will to remarry those divorcees, language teaching and literature teaching, who parted company on such bad terms in the sixties.

6 The fascinating ferment in the development of 'Englishes' world-wide (and the discussion of what Clifford Prator once called the British 'heresy'), as countries which have adopted English look less and less to countries in which English is spoken as the native language for the setting of linguistic norms, and local variations like Indian English and Nigerian English are increasingly seen as underpinning national independence. And yet, paradoxically, the notion of 'standards' is vigorously if tacitly asserted: witness, as Professor Quirk points out, the common denominator of the BBC World Service of London; All India Radio of Delhi; the *Straits Times* of Singapore; and the *Japan Times* of Tokyo.

Let me stress that this volume should in no sense be seen as a valedictory Festschrift. The British Council has no intention of reducing its involvement in the promotion of English Studies. It will continue to do all it can to help those who wish to acquire a knowledge of the English language for a variety of purposes – to gain access to a world of new technology or the international market place; to help those who wish to develop English as the language, or one of the languages, through which their own culture and values can find expression, and through which we in our turn can get to know and understand them better; and to help those who wish to learn English in order to get to know *us*, our language, culture and literature.

In conclusion, I wish to say how greatly indebted I am to all those who worked so hard to make the Conference a success: the main speakers, those who chaired the sessions, the commentators, rapporteurs and reporters; the Vice-Chancellor of the University of London for allowing us to use his splendid premises; all the members of our English Teaching Advisory Committee, particularly its Chairman Henry Widdowson,

Professor Sinclair and Peter Strevens; the Bell Educational Trust for their generous contribution to the cost of the Conference; and to those members of my own staff responsible for its organization, the preparation of the papers and mounting the associated exhibition.

Sir John Burgh
Director-General
The British Council
October 1984

# Acknowledgements

The Editors gratefully acknowledge permission to quote from works in copyright:
'Considering the Snail' from *My Sad Captains* by Thom Gunn, reprinted by permission of Faber & Faber Ltd; from *Moly* and *My Sad Captains* by Thom Gunn, copyright © 1971, 1973 by Thom Gunn, reprinted by permission of Farrar, Straus & Giroux, Inc. 'The Unconquered', copyright © 1943 by W. Somerset Maugham, from *Creatures of Circumstance* by W. Somerset Maugham, reprinted by permission of A. P. Watt Ltd, The Executors of the Estate of W. Somerset Maugham; and Doubleday & Company, Inc. Preface by Arthur Waley to *Monkey* by Wu Ch'êng-ên, translated by Arthur Waley, reprinted by permission of Allen (George) & Unwin Publishers Ltd.; and Harper & Row, Inc. *The Country and the City* by Raymond Williams, reprinted by permission of Chatto & Windus Ltd and The Hogarth Press Ltd; and Oxford University Press, Inc.

The Editors would also like to acknowledge their great indebtedness to Yolande Cantù, without whose dedicated work the publication of this book would not have been possible.

# Abbreviations

| | |
|---|---|
| AUPELF | Association des Universités Partiellement ou Entièrement de Langue Française |
| CAI | Computer-Assisted Instruction |
| CALL | Computer-Assisted Language Learning |
| CDCC | Council for Cultural Co-operation (part of the Council of Europe) |
| CIEFL | Central Institute of English and Foreign Languages (Hyderabad) |
| CILT | Centre for Information on Language Teaching and Research |
| DTEO | Direct Teaching of English Operation (British Council) |
| EAP | English for Academic Purposes |
| EFL | English as a Foreign Language |
| ELC | English Language Centre |
| ELT | English Language Teaching (to speakers of other languages) |
| ENL | English as a Native Language |
| EOP | English for Occupational Purposes |
| ESL | English as a Second Language |
| ESP | English for Specific Purposes |
| EST | English for Science and Technology |
| ETIC | English Teaching Information Centre (British Council) |
| FLT | Foreign Language Teaching |
| GA | General American |
| GE | General English |
| INSET | In-service Teacher Education and Training |
| IT | Information Technology |
| L1 | First Language |
| L2 | Foreign or Second Language |
| LDC | Lesser Developed Country |
| LSP | Language for Specific Purposes |
| R&D | Research and Development |
| RE | Research English |
| RELC | Regional English Language Centre (Singapore) |
| RP | Received Pronunciation |
| TESOL | Teachers of English to Speakers of Other Languages (the organization) |

# THEME I   THE ENGLISH LANGUAGE IN A GLOBAL CONTEXT

## a)   The English language in a global context

Randolph Quirk

In this 'global context', I want to address the controversial issue of *standards*, so let me begin by recalling one of the best-known statements of a standard for English. In *The Arte of English Poesie* (1589, reputedly by George Puttenham who died in the following year), the creative writer is advised that one form of English is more highly regarded than all others. In consequence, one should follow 'the usuall speach of the Court, and that of London and the shires lying about London within lx. myles, and not much above'. No variety of English is 'so courtly nor so current'.

That view dates from the time when Shakespeare was a young man and when English was not in global use but only 'of small reatch, it stretcheth no further than this Iland of ours, naie not there over all' (Richard Mulcaster in 1582). The language was in those years known almost exclusively to native speakers and there were perhaps as few as seven million of them.

The contrast with the position of English four hundred years later is extraordinary: now in daily use not by *seven* million people but by seven *hundred* million – and only half of them native speakers of the language. No longer 'of small reatch' but a language – *the* language – on which the sun does not set, whose users never sleep. For between 1600 and 1900, speakers of English pushed themselves into every part of the globe (more recently, to lunatic deserts far beyond the globe), so that at this present time, English is more widely spread, and is the chicf language of more countries than any other language is or ever has been.

But that is only part of the contrast between the 1580s and the 1980s – and not the most striking nor, in the present connection, the most relevant. In the 1580s almost no one who was not actually brought up speaking English ever bothered to learn it. Now English is in daily use among three or four hundred million people who were not brought up speaking it as their native language. Most of them live in countries requiring English for what we may broadly call 'external' purposes: contact with people in other countries, either through the spoken or the written word, for such purposes as trade and scientific advance. They are people for whom English remains a foreign language (though usually the chief foreign language) whether they live in a country with a highly developed tradition of English teaching, such as the Netherlands or Yugoslavia, or in a country where English teaching is less well developed such as Spain or Senegal. We refer to these countries as *EFL* countries, and it should be noted that their use of English is in no way confined to contacts with English-speaking countries: a Korean steel manufacturer will use English in negotiating with a Brazilian firm in Rio.

But there are many millions of people who live in countries where English is equally not a native language but where English is in widespread use for what we may broadly call 'internal' purposes as well: in administration, in broadcasting, in education. Such countries range in size from India, struggling with economic development of a huge and various population in a huge and various territory, to Singapore, tiny by contrast, and economically thriving. By reason of the sharply different and much wider role of English in these countries, where the language is usually designated in the constitution as one of the 'national' languages, along with indigenous ones, it is inappropriate to regard English as merely a foreign language. The practice has grown up of referring to English in these circumstances as a 'second' language and to the countries concerned as *ESL* countries. That great Indian university institution in Hyderabad, which specializes in training expert language teachers, interestingly proclaims this distinction in its official title: CIEFL – the Central Institute of English *and Foreign Languages*. Not, we notice, English and *other* foreign languages. English is not a 'foreign' language in India, though the proportion of the population making competent use of it is in fact far smaller than that in several advanced EFL countries such as the Netherlands.

Finally, in contrast with these EFL and ESL countries, we can complete a terminological triad by marking off those countries such as the UK, the US, Australia, and South Africa, where English is a native language: the *ENL* countries. And, it may be remarked, English is a global language in each of these three categories: there are ENL, ESL, and EFL countries all round the world.

But the coming into existence of this threefold manifestation of English by no means completes the list of essential distinctions between the 1580s and the 1980s. When there was only ENL and that for only seven million people, it was possible – as we have seen – to recommend a single model or standard. And in specifying it as he did, the author of *The Arte of English Poesie* went on to say that in this 'we are already ruled by th'English Dictionaries and other bookes written by learned men'. Few today would suggest that there was a single standard of English in the world. There are few enough (not least among professional linguists) that would claim the existence of a single standard within any one of the ENL countries: plenty that would even deny both the possibility and the desirability of such a thing. Recent emphasis has been on multiple and variable standards (insofar as the use of the word 'standard' is ventured): different standards for different occasions for different people – and each as 'correct' as any other.

Small wonder that there should have been in recent years fresh talk of the diaspora of English into several mutually incomprehensible languages. The fate of Latin after the fall of the Roman Empire presents us with such distinct languages today as French, Spanish, Romanian, and Italian. With the growth of national separatism in the English-speaking countries, linguistically endorsed not least by the active encouragement of the anti-standard ethos I have just mentioned, many foresee a similar fissiparous future for English. A year or so ago, much prominence was given to the belief expressed by R. W. Burchfield that in a century from now the languages of Britain and America would be as different as French is from Italian.

As it happens, I do not share this view. We live in a very different world from that in which the Romance languages went their separate ways. We have easy, rapid, and ubiquitous communication, electronic and other-wise. We have increasing dependence on a common technology whose development is largely in the hands of multi-national corporations. Moreover, we have a strong world-wide will to preserve intercomprehen-sibility in English.

It so happens that when Burchfield made his prediction I chanced to be reading a book by that great Oxford linguist Henry Sweet, who had made precisely the same prediction just a hundred years ago: 'in another cen-tury . . . England, America, and Australia will be speaking mutually unintelligible languages'. Sweet's forecast (which, given the circum-stances and received knowledge of his time, had a greater plausibility than Burchfield's) proved dramatically wrong because he overestimated the rate of sound change.

We can err, likewise, if we unduly emphasize a difference between the present and the 1580s in respect of variation within English. Variety and variability were well acknowledged in Shakespeare's time (and they are certainly well attested in Shakespeare's own writing). In part, the problem has been the failure to make explicit which aspects of English were to be regarded as susceptible of standardization. Gradually, it came to be felt that individual lexical items could be dubbed 'standard' as opposed to, say, dialectal (though Caxton's hesitation between *egges* and *eyren* was to be paralleled for many a generation of printers); that there was a standard grammar (though *writ* and *wrote* could both for long be of it); that above all there was a standard spelling (though this admitted a wide range of variation until fairly recently and even now embraces such things as both *judgment* and *judgement*).

Always least liable to be categorized as standard or non-standard was pronunciation: reasonably enough, since standardization was predomi-nantly occasioned by the need to provide long uniform print-runs of books and papers on which pronunciation had no bearing. But with the advance of mass broadcasting in the 1920s, managers of the new medium were faced with the oral analogue of the issue that had confronted Caxton and others in the late sixteenth century. And an analogous decision was taken: there would be generalized use of a single accent, assumed to be admired by or at any rate acceptable to the greatest number of the most critical section of the public. In the US an educated Midland was selected which came to be referred to as 'network English': in the UK the minority voice of the public schools ('RP') was selected and this came to be referred to quite often as 'BBC English'. In fact, in each case, it was something more: by having been thus selected for nationwide broadcasting, each was implicitly regarded in its respective domain (American or British) as the *standard* pronunciation.

But broadcasting did not merely thus dramatically extend the scope of potential standardization: it also made overt that there was indeed more than one single standard of English. Of course, it had always been known that Americans spoke differently from the British (just as Yorkshiremen spoke differently from Cornishmen); but this knowledge did not of itself raise the question as to which – if any of these – was standard. Moreover, since in neither the US nor the UK was the selected accent that of anything like the majority of speakers (though more nearly so in the case of network American English), there was a further implication: the standard language is inevitably the prerogative of a rather special minority. This last aspect has of course had its own reverberations: in the US, a competitor for the rank of standard in accents has been New England ('Harvard'), and this has been far more obviously a minority mode of speech than 'network'. We shall come to other reverberations below.

Meanwhile, the early twentieth century also saw the rise of another development: the professional teaching of English world-wide to those for whom it was not a native language. I adopt this cumbersome periphrasis so as to embrace the peoples of both the EFL and the ESL countries as we now (but did not then) distinguish them. At first this was almost entirely (as it remains predominantly) a British activity. The accent that John Reith adopted as the voice of the BBC was the one already identified by Daniel Jones as the 'Received Pronunciation' appropriate to teach to non-native learners. Textbooks rapidly disseminated this standard, together with the congruently hieratic lexicon and grammar, on a world-wide basis. Unchallenged for more than a generation, certainly till long after the recognition at home in the ENL countries that at least one other standard existed (and in a far more populous and wealthy country), America's dramatically extended involvement after 1945 both in West Europe and the Orient rapidly confronted foreign learners with what seemed like a sharply polar choice. The fact that the choice is neither sharp nor polar (especially in the hieratic lexicon and grammar), that the

differences between American English and British English are smaller
than the differences within either, is understandably obscured for the
non-native learner by the national necessity for the government agencies
concerned to package the language teaching with clearly distinguished
cultural, institutional, regional, and political support-components,
British or American as the case may be. Our own *Grammar of Contemporary English* and associated books are still in a minority in demonstrat-
ing that a single educated and universally acceptable variety of English
can be described as a unity, yet catering for the features which lie to a
greater or lesser degree outside this common core.

But the reluctance to speak of, still less command, a single standard of
English is not merely sensitivity to the proclaimed institutionalization of
at least two major standards, British and American. As I indicated earlier,
the very notion of standard has itself become suspect: most signally
within the educational establishment of the ENL countries. The printed
announcement for a book published this summer on *The Art and Craft of
Lexicography* (the publisher is Scribner, the author Sidney Landau) states
that among the topics considered are 'Such vexing questions as what constitutes "standard" English', and the writer's acknowledgement that this
question is indeed vexing is betrayed by putting sceptical quotation marks
around the word *standard*.

There are in fact good historical, even good linguistic reasons for
reaction against the whole received notion of standards in language. In
the hands of narrow, unimaginative, unsympathetic, authoritarian
teachers, the wielding of a heavy standard has been known to bludgeon a
natural (and surely desirable) self-respect and local pride into a snobbish
self-contempt. Such insistence on standard English is suspected of stifling
creativity in whatever particular variety of language is most natural to a
particular youngster. Moreover, the academic linguist – with the whole
spectrum of a society's language activity in his field of vision – has been
at pains to explain that there isn't a single all-purpose standard for
language any more than there is for dress. Linguists have of course been
known to go further and to cock a snook at fashionably unfashionable
élitism by implying (or even stating) that any variety of language is as
'good', as 'correct' as any other variety. And with the linguist's preoccupation in the last couple of generations not so much with written as with
spoken language (where standardization is particularly recent and particularly controversial), it is the rich variety – even personal variability –
of speech that has seemed naturally enough the aspect of language that is
in need of contemporary emphasis.

Nonetheless, understandable as all this is, I hold that the stated or
implied orthodoxy of regarding the term 'standard' as fit only for
quotation marks is a *trahison des clercs*. It seems likely, indeed, that the
existence of standards (in moral and sexual behaviour, in dress, in taste

5

generally) is an endemic feature of our mortal condition and that people feel alienated and disoriented if a standard seems to be missing in any of these areas. Certainly, ordinary folk with their ordinary common sense have gone on knowing that there are standards in language and they have gone on crying out to be taught them. And just as certainly, the *clercs* themselves are careful to couch even their most sceptical remarks about standard language in precisely the standard language about which they are being sceptical. Disdain of élitism is a comfortable exercise for those who are themselves securely among the élite.

I believe that the fashion of undermining belief in standard English has wrought educational damage in the ENL countries, though I am ready to concede that there may well have been compensating educational gains in the wider tolerance for an enjoyment of the extraordinary variety of English around us in any of these countries. But then just such an airy contempt for standards started to be exported to EFL and ESL countries, and for this I can find no such mitigating compensation. The relatively narrow range of purposes for which the non-native needs to use English (even in ESL countries) is arguably well catered for by a single monochrome standard form that looks as good on paper as it sounds in speech. There are only the most dubious advantages in exposing the learner to a great variety of usage, no part of which he will have time to master properly, little of which he will be called upon to exercise, all of which is embedded in a controversial sociolinguistic matrix he cannot be expected to understand.

The English language works pretty well in its global context today: certainly the globe has at present no plausible substitute. But let me underline my main point by giving four examples of English working best in the global context. They are the BBC World Service of London; All India Radio of Delhi; the *Straits Times* of Singapore; and the *Japan Times* of Tokyo. They represent oral and printed media, and they represent ENL, ESL, and EFL countries. And there are several outstanding features in common to these and to the scores of analogous examples that might have been selected. They all use a form of English that is both understood and respected in every corner of the globe where any knowledge of any variety of English exists. They adhere to forms of English familiarly produced by only a minority of English speakers in any of the four countries concerned. And – mere accent alone apart – they observe as uniform a standard as that manifest in any language on earth.

# Commentator 1

Graeme Kennedy

There is a delicious irony in Professor Quirk's clear, forthright and stimulating paper. In 1968 Clifford Prator published a paper in which he lambasted what he called 'The British heresy in TESL', arguing that the acceptance and encouragement of local varieties of English by the British was detrimental to global communication. The heresy he criticized has since, of course, become widely orthodox and is probably now the conventional wisdom, especially among those who study the nature and use of language. Professor Quirk's paper reflects, in many respects, the position Prator advocated, namely, the desirability of a global standard. However, since the orthodoxy has changed, it might be argued that Professor Quirk articulates a new British heresy. You simply cannot win.

The issue of standards in countries where English is a native language is fundamentally an attitudinal and especially an aesthetic one. The standard or standards which emerge are those of the groups which have power and prestige in the economy, entertainment, the media, the arts and so on. In a global context, however, the question of intelligibility comes in. It is very easy to use English internationally and not be understood. In fact, one sometimes wonders how the putative number of speakers of English throughout the world is arrived at, particularly when one goes beyond the bounds of familiarity with an extremely limited range of functions. As a speaker of ENL I have had enough experience of communicative difficulties in other countries to find myself in considerable sympathy with Professor Quirk's argument for the recognition of a global standard.

What I am less sure of, however, is whether that is within the bounds of the possible. In particular, I would take issue with him over the statement that there is 'a relatively narrow range of purposes for which the non-native needs to use English (even in ESL countries)'. Whenever there has been careful research on the use of English in an ESL context, an organic complexity has been revealed in functional range, use and purpose. Singapore is one example. Surely it is what the users of the language do, not what a small élite would like them to do which counts in the end.

Since English is so much the world's language, international popular culture may be a more powerful determinant on norms than so-called standards, whether or not they have official or educational sanctions. I suspect that in the final analysis, the vast majority of users of English tend to adopt local varieties, regardless of the admonitions of English teachers. As Professor Quirk has suggested, even in the case of ENL countries, such admonitions may have had, as a primary effect, a lowering of self-esteem rather than a change in language behaviour.

I therefore wish to ask this question. Although standards of English may be adopted or encouraged, can they influence significantly the directions English moves in and the use of English in a global context?

# Commentator 2

David Crystal

I very much agree with Professor Quirk's emphasis on standard English. I am sure this is the nub of the matter. What concerns me, however, is the way in which all discussion of standards ceases very quickly to be a linguistic discussion, and becomes instead an issue of social identity, and I miss this perspective in his paper. The social origins of the notion of 'standard' are evident in dictionary definitions of the term, e.g. 'something established by authority, custom or general consent as a model or example' (*Longman Dictionary of the English Language*). Society indeed confers or sanctions the status of standard on something, as Professor Quirk has clearly indicated, and it thereby acquires the secondary sense of 'a degree of quality or worth', which in turn leads to the pejorative uses of 'non-standard' and 'sub-standard'. The term renews its connection with society whenever there are arguments about usage, though often the social assumptions remain below the surface. For example, at a local level, the arguments used by teachers when correcting a child's written English are often couched in purely linguistic terms: you shouldn't use *ain't* – why? – because it isn't standard English. But this is to identify the problem, not to explain it, and any follow-up question of the sort 'But why do I have to write/speak standard English?' leads inevitably to social reasoning (the need to pass exams, to get a job, to qualify as a member of a profession, and so on).

The same principle applies globally, only now the question of identity becomes more difficult. Consider the range of items which can be used to fill the slot in the kind of question frames a social psychologist might use: 'If he speaks English, he must be . . . '. Depending on where you live, so the answer might be 'British / American / an imperialist / an enemy / one of the oppressors / well-educated / a civil servant / a foreigner / rich / trying to impress / in a bad mood . . . '. There is a long list of possible clozes, and not all make pleasant reading. This conference is concerned to evaluate progress in English studies, in which case we must not forget those areas where the spread of English is bad news, and where people are antagonistic towards the language, for a variety of social, economic or political reasons. How would the slot be filled in parts of Francophone Canada, for example? Or in parts of Wales, Scotland and Ireland? Or, these days, in different parts of India? Or amongst certain groups in South Africa, or West Africa, or indeed in any area where language planning policies are having to take seriously the identity demands of minority groups? The question is not so much *do* people use English internationally, but in what state of mind, with what attitude, do they use it? Are they proud of it, or ashamed of it? Do they see it as a strength or as a weakness? Who do they see themselves as being identified with, when they use it, and are they happy to be so identified?

These questions can all of course be applied to any one variety of the language, as well as to the language as a whole. Thus we may ask them of RP, of network American, or of any regional or class variety. We may ask them of standard English within England, as Professor Quirk points out. But before all this, we need to ask them of the 'single monochrome standard' which is the theme of his paper. The many questions, in effect, reduce to one: should not the quantitative view of English in the world be supplemented by a rigorous qualitative view – a pragmatic or ergonomic view – in which we recognize levels of acceptance, acquiescence and antipathy amongst those who have come to use the language; and in the end is not this view of far greater importance for those involved in world English teaching and research than a simple awareness of the unity and spread of the standard language? I see two questions here. However, let me cut them down to one. Professor Quirk's final paragraph began: 'The English language works *pretty well* in its global context today'. My question comes from the kind of sociolinguistic viewpoint I have been outlining, and it is simply this: 'How pretty is pretty?'

# b) Standards, codification and sociolinguistic realism: the English language in the outer circle

Braj B. Kachru

## 1 Introduction

It is perhaps not coincidental that the fiftieth anniversary of the British Council looks back on a span of fifty years which has witnessed a linguistic phenomenon of unprecedented dimensions in language spread, language contact, and language change. It is particularly noteworthy since these phenomena can be seen in relation to the diffusion and internationalization of one language, English, across cultures and languages. This anniversary, therefore, is an appropriate milestone to review the past, and to gaze into the crystal ball for future linguistic and other indicators.

Earlier research, especially after the 1950s, provides some perspective about the international diffusion of English, the attitudes towards it and other languages of wider communication, its formal and functional characteristics, and its impact on major world languages. We now have both satisfactory and not-so-satisfactory case studies of what has been termed the *nativization* of English, and the *Englishization* of other world languages.[1]

However, the sociolinguistic aspects of English in its international context are still not well understood; they have not even been fully researched for a variety of attitudinal, theoretical, and logistical reasons. Attitudinally there is a conflict between perceived linguistic norms and actual language behaviour. Theoretically, linguists are still conditioned by a monolingual model for linguistic description and analysis, and have yet to provide a framework and descriptive methodology for description and analysis of a bi- or multilingual's use of language and linguistic creativity. In logistical terms, such an investigation entails enormous empirical work by researchers who are multilingual and to some extent multicultural as well. I shall elaborate on these points later.

What further complicates the task is the sheer magnitude of the spread of English, the variety of global contexts in which English is used and the varied motivations for its acquisition and use in the erstwhile colonial regions after the political phase of the Colonial Period. There are also some who believe the Post-Colonial Period has ushered in a phase of *decontrol* of English, as it were, from earlier, reasonably well-accepted standards. The impression now is that with the diffusion of and resultant innovations in English around the world, universally acceptable standards are absent. In addition, the situation becomes even more involved due to the lack of a precise methodology for understanding and describing English in the international sociolinguistic contexts.

The aim of this paper is to discuss some implications of the global diffusion of English, focusing in particular on the issues of standardization and codification of the linguistic creativity and innovations in its institutionalized non-native varieties. But before I come to that, a digression is desirable to outline the main concentric circles within which the world varieties of English are presently used.

## 2   Three concentric circles of world Englishes

The initial questions about the universalization of English are: What is the major stratification of use due to the internationalization of English? And, what are the characteristics of such stratification? The spread of English may be viewed in terms of three concentric circles representing the types of spread, the patterns of acquisition and the functional domains in which English is used across cultures and languages. I have tentatively labelled these: the *inner* circle, the *outer* circle (or *extended* circle), and the *expanding* circle. In terms of the users, the inner circle refers to the traditional bases of English – the regions where it is the primary language – the USA (pop. 234,249,000), the UK (pop. 56,124,000), Canada (pop. 24,907,100), Australia (pop. 15,265,000), and New Zealand (pop. 3,202,300).[2]

The outer (or extended) circle needs a historical explanation: it involves the earlier phases of the spread of English and its institutionalization in non-native contexts. The institutionalization of such varieties has linguistic, political and sociocultural explanations, some of which I shall discuss later.[3]

The political histories of the regions where institutionalized varieties are used have many shared characteristics: these regions have gone through extended periods of colonization, essentially by the users of the inner circle varieties. The linguistic and cultural effects of such colonization are now a part of their histories, and these effects, both good and bad, cannot be wished away.

Numerically, the outer circle forms a large speech community with great diversity and distinct characteristics. The major features of this circle are that (a) English is only one of two or more codes in the linguistic repertoire of such bilinguals or multilinguals, and (b) English has acquired an important status in the language policies of most of such multilingual nations. For example, in Nigeria it is an official language (Bamgboşe, 1982); in Zambia it is recognized as one of the state languages (Chishimba, 1983); in Singapore it is a major language of government, the legal system, and education (Platt and Webber, 1980; Lowenberg, 1984); and in India the Constitution recognizes English as an 'associate' official language, and as one of the required languages in the Three Language Formula implemented in the 1960s (Kachru, 1982a and 1983a).

In functional terms the institutionalized varieties have three character- istics: first, English functions in what may be considered traditionally 'un-English' cultural contexts. And, in terms of territory covered, the cross-cultural spread of English is unprecedented among the languages of wider communication used as colonial languages (e.g., French, Portuguese, Spanish), as religious languages (e.g., Arabic, Sanskrit, Pali) and as language varieties of trade and commerce (e.g., pidgins or bazaar varieties). Second, English has a wide spectrum of domains in which it is used with varying degrees of competence by members of society, both as an intranational and an international language. Third, and very import- ant, English has developed nativized literary traditions in different genres, such as the novel, short story, poetry, and essay.[4] In other words, English has an extended functional *range* in a variety of social, educational, administrative, and literary domains. It also has acquired great *depth* in terms of users at different levels of society. As a result, there is significant variation within such institutionalized varieties.

The third circle, termed the expanding circle, brings to English yet another dimension. Understanding the function of English in this circle requires a recognition of the fact that English is an international language, and that it has already won the race in this respect with linguistic rivals such as French, Russian and Esperanto, to name just two natural languages and one artificial language. The geographical regions charac- terized as the expanding circle do not necessarily have a history of coloni- zation by the users of the inner circle (Ituen, 1980). This circle is currently expanding rapidly and has resulted in numerous performance (or EFL) varieties of English (Kachru and Quirk, 1981).

It is the users of this circle who actually further strengthen the claims of English as an international or universal language. This circle encompasses vast populations of such countries as China (pop. 1,015,410,000), the USSR (pop. 262,436,000), and Indonesia (pop. 151,720,000). A partial list of other countries, where such performance varieties of English are used includes: Greece (pop. 9,898,000), Israel (pop. 415,000), Japan (pop. 119,420,000), Korea (pop. 8,961,500), Nepal (pop. 15,769,000), Saudi Arabia (pop. 19,188,000), Taiwan (pop. 18,590,000), and Zimbabwe (pop. 7,539,000).

The outer circle and the expanding circle cannot be viewed as clearly demarcated from each other; they have several shared characteristics, and the status of English in the language policies of such countries changes from time to time.[5] What is an ESL region at one time may become an EFL region at another time or vice versa. There is another difficulty: countries such as South Africa (pop. 25,770,000) and Jamaica (pop. 2,223,400) are not easy to place within the concentric circles since in terms of the English-using populations and the functions of English, their situation is rather complex. I have, therefore, not included these in the above lists.

During the last fifty years, the spread of English has been characterized by several political and sociolinguistic factors which deserve mention. At present, English is fast gaining ground in the non-Western countries, and the mechanism of its diffusion, by and large, is being initiated and controlled by the non-native users. This situation is very different from what it was before the 1940s. English is used as an additional language – often as an alternative language – in multilingual and multicultural contexts. In a socio-economic sense, a large number of English-using countries fall in the category of 'developing' nations; their needs for the use of English are determined, on the one hand, by considerations of modernization and technology, and on the other hand, by linguistic, political, and social 'fissiparous tendencies', to use an Indian English expression.

These regions are geographically distant from English-speaking nations of the inner circle, and this factor has serious implications for the learning and teaching of English. A significant number of such nations are quite different in their religions, beliefs, cultural patterns, and political systems from the countries where English is the primary language.

As an aside, one might add here that all the countries where English is a primary language are functional democracies. The outer circle and the expanding circle do not show any such political preferences. The present diffusion of English seems to tolerate any political system, and the language itself has become rather *apolitical*. In South Asia, for example, it is used as a tool for propaganda by politically diverse groups: the Marxist Communists, the China-oriented Communists, and what are labelled as the Muslim fundamentalists and the Hindu rightists as well as various factions of the Congress party. Such varied groups seem to recognize the value of English in fostering their respective political ends, though ideologically some of them seem to oppose the Western systems of education and Western values. In the present world, the use of English certainly has fewer political, cultural, and religious connotations than does the use of any other language of wider communication.

These three circles, then, bring to English a unique cultural pluralism, and a linguistic heterogeneity and diversity which are unrecorded to this extent in human history. With this diffusion, naturally, come scores of problems concerned with codification, standardization, nativization, teaching, and description – and, of course, a multitude of attitudes about recognition of various varieties and subvarieties. The diversity, both in terms of acquisition and use of English, and in terms of different political, social, and religious contexts is, for example, evident in the following ten major English-using nations of the world.[6]

| | |
|---|---|
| USA | 234,249,000 |
| UK | 56,124,000 |
| India | 27,920,000 |
| Canada | 24,907,000 |
| Australia | 15,265,000 |
| Bangladesh | 3,786,000 |
| Nigeria | 3,564,700 |
| Pakistan | 3,528,800 |
| Tanzania | 789,480 |
| Kenya | 714,000 |

## 3  Speech community and speech fellowships of English

The preceding background is relevant for several reasons: first, in a theoretical sense, one faces a dilemma now in defining an 'ideal speaker–hearer' for English (Chomsky, 1965: 3), and in explaining what constitutes its 'speech community'. Are all users of English in the above mentioned three circles part of a single English-using speech community? If not, what are the differences?

It is evident that linguists, language planners, and language teachers have never had to confront a question of these dimensions before, with so many theoretical, applied, and attitudinal implications. Answers to such questions are relevant to the description, analysis, and teaching of English. Furthermore, an answer to this question is basic to our discussion of the standards, codification, and norms of English. Prescriptivism – even of a mild form – must be based on some linguistic pragmatism and realism.

Before I further elaborate on this point, let me go back to the concept 'English-using speech community'. It is now being realized that the term 'speech community' – a cardinal concept in theoretical and applied linguistics – needs some modification. In pedagogical literature this term has acquired a special status for providing a 'norm'. In linguistic literature, a speech community is generally seen as an abstract entity consisting of 'ideal speaker–listeners'. Here, of course, the focus is on *la langue*.

Whatever the theoretical validity of this term and its traditional uses, the present global spread and functions of English warrant a distinction between a *speech community* and a *speech fellowship*, as originally suggested by Firth (1959: 208). The distinction identifies, as Firth says, 'a

15

close speech fellowship and a wider speech community in what may be called a language community comprising both written and spoken forms of the general language'.

I believe that the term *speech fellowship* brings us closer to the real world of English users, their underlying distinct differences, and also their shared characteristics. One might find that the genesis of each such speech fellowship in English is unique, or there may be typologies of general patterns of development.

We certainly find such distinct patterns of linguistic and sociolinguistic development in the speech fellowships who use what Quirk *et al.* (1972: 26) have termed 'interference varieties'. In the last fifty years such varieties of English have become

> . . . so widespread in a community and of such long standing that they may be thought stable and adequate enough to be institutionalized and regarded as varieties of English in their own right rather than stages on the way to a more native-like English.

What we see here, then, is that the non-native English-using speech fellowships are using Englishes of the world in their divergent *situations* and *contexts* and with various linguistic and ethnic *attitudes*. Let me explain what I mean by these three terms: *situation* includes the linguistic, political and sociocultural, and economic ecology in which the English language is used. *Context* refers to the roles of participants in these situations and to the appropriateness of varieties of language used in these roles. And *attitude* is specifically used here for the overt and covert attitudes toward a language, its varieties, and the uses and users of these varieties.

## 4   Types of English-using speech fellowships

In a normative sense, then, the speech fellowships of English around the globe are primarily of the following three types:

1 *Norm-providing* varieties (the inner circle): these varieties have traditionally been recognized as models since they are used by the 'native speakers'. However, the attitudes of the native speakers and non-native speakers toward such native varieties are not identical. One might say that traditionally the British variety was generally accepted as the model, and it is very recently that the American model has been presented as an alternative model. There is, however, still resistance toward accepting Australian or New Zealand varieties. The history of the battle of attitudes toward native English is an interesting story itself (see Kachru, 1982d and 1984a).

2 *Norm-developing* varieties (the outer circle): in regions using these varieties there has been a conflict between linguistic norm and linguistic behaviour. They are both endonormative and exonormative.
3 *Norm-dependent* varieties (the expanding circle): this circle is essentially exonormative.

I should, however, mention that in pedagogical literature, in popular literature (e.g., in newspapers) and in power élite circles only the inner circle varieties are considered 'norm makers': the other two are treated as the 'norm breakers'. Even in the inner circle only a specific élite group is considered as 'norm makers' or as models for emulation. We see this attitude for example, in the writing of Newman (1974 and 1976) and Safire (1980) whose work has significant impact on the 'linguistic etiquette' of the general public (see also Eble, 1976, and Baron, 1982, especially pp. 226–41).

In this paper, I am primarily concerned with the outer circle, which includes the institutionalized varieties (Kachru, 1982d: 38–9). However, as discussed earlier, it is evident that these categories are not necessarily mutually exclusive. Grey areas between the latter two do exist and we might as well recognize them.

## 5   Descriptive issues and prescriptive concerns

The questions and controversies which have emerged as a result of the universal spread of English during the last fifty years may be reduced to four types. These questions repeatedly occur in theoretical literature, in applied and pedagogical discussions, and in the training of professionals. The first question concerns the codification of English (e.g., Who controls the norms?). The second relates to the innovations which are formally and contextually *deviant* from the norms of the users of the inner circle (e.g., What types of innovations and creativity are acceptable?). The third question is about the pragmatics of selecting a norm (e.g., What are the factors which determine a norm for a region?). And finally come the issues surrounding the *de-Englishization* of the cultural context of English in the institutionalized non-native varieties (e.g., What are the parameters for the acculturation of English?). I will now discuss these and related questions under four labels: codification, innovation, de-Englishization, and the non-native bilingual's creativity.

First, the question of codification. In spite of the attitudes expressed and the vehement debates of linguistic purists, English actually has no authoritative channels of linguistic regulation other than the indirect ones: dictionaries, social attitudes, educational preferences, and discrimination in professions on the basis of accent.[7] However, the need for

17

some standards in written and spoken English for intranational and international intelligibility is well recognized (see e.g. Nelson, 1982 and 1984; Smith, 1983).

A second often discussed question, innovation, is an offshoot of the question of codification, since codification does imply standards for innovation. In the case of English, there are two types of innovations: those initiated by the users of the inner circle, and those which are essentially initiated by the users of English in the outer circle. An innovation in the outer circle, then, refers to the linguistic formations which are contextually and/or formally distinct from language use in the inner circle. In the literature, various pejorative labels have been used for such innovations, including 'mistakes', 'errors', 'peculiarities', 'linguistic flights', and so on. It is only recently that studies of sociolinguistic appropriateness have been undertaken which encompass the discoursal level, speech acts, and functionally determined regional variation.[8] In this case, then, codification implies determining the bounds of such innovations or creativity – in other words, 'allowable' deviation from the native norms.

At the formal levels, one is thus able to provide a schema for 'error gravity' as has been done from native speakers' perspectives in the case of several non-native varieties of English. The concept of 'error' or 'error gravity' has some use in morphologically or syntactically 'deviant' constructions. However, a serious problem arises when one turns to the functional characteristics of such varieties because the formal deviations cannot be isolated from their functions. As several studies have demonstrated, in discussing their characteristics the term *transfer* (or *interference*) is handy. The degree and function of transfer may be seen as a *cline*: a cline of competence, lectal range, and domain assignment to English. Functionally, then, we find at least three marked varieties of Englishes on this cline:

a)  educated variety (acrolect): not to be confused with ambilingualism or 'native-like' competence;
b)  semi-educated variety (mesolect);
c)  bazaar variety (basilect).

Within each variety, of course, further distinctions are possible, and an educated speaker may switch between one or more varieties, or mix varieties with other languages. Consider for example, the following functionally appropriate innovations from Africa (A), South Asia (SA) and Southeast Asia (SEA).

1  Contextually determined collocations: *tiffin carrier* (SA: 'a carrier for a snack or a light meal'), *Himalayan blunder* (SA: 'a grave or serious mistake'), *military hotel* (SA: 'a non-vegetarian hotel'), *waist-thread* (SA: 'a ritualistic thread worn around the waist'), *communal question*

(SA: 'a question related to Hindu-Muslim relationships'), *bush child* (A: 'child born out of wedlock'), *funeral beer* (A: 'beer brewed and drunk after a funeral'), *grave diggers* (A: who are 'cousins of the dead person, traditionally responsible for digging the grave'), *tight friend* (A: 'a close friend'), *backward class* (SA: 'deprived groups'), *small room* (A: 'a toilet'), *co-wife* (A: 'the second of two wives'), *minor wife* (SEA: 'a mistress'), *knocking-fee* (A: 'a bribe'), *chewing-sponge* (A: 'a twig for cleaning the teeth'), *been-to-boys* (A: 'been to England'; cf. SAE: '*England-returned*'), *cop-shop* (A: 'police station'), and *snatch boys* A: 'pickpockets').

2 Hybridization: *kraal family* (A: 'family sharing the same enclosure'), *lobola-beasts* (A: 'enemies who use bride-price as a means of exploiting while feigning friendship'), *swadeshi hotel* (SA: 'a native, vegetarian restaurant'), *lathi charge* (SA: 'use of bataan for control' [by police, etc.]), and *lovemuti* (A: 'a charm to entice people to love').

3 Idioms (all from African varieties): *like a bushfire in the harmattan, like a yam tendril in the rainy season, where there is dew there is water, wisdom is like a goat skin – everyone carries his own, like a lizard fallen from an iroke tree, like pouring grains of corn into a bag full of holes, to eat each other's ears* (to talk privately), *to whisper together* (to talk privately), *to have no shadow* (to have no courage), and *to have no bite* (to have no courage).

4 Comparative constructions: *as honest as an elephant, as good as kitchen ashes,* and *lean as an areca-nut tree* (all from South Asian varieties). In addition, consider for example, *roaring silence* as used in Southern Africa, or *pin-drop silence* used in India, both meaning 'dead silence'.

The third question about the pragmatics of selecting a norm has been in the forefront since English developed its transplanted native varieties (e.g., in Australia and the USA), and non-native varieties (e.g., in Africa, South Asia and Southeast Asia). These issues have been discussed in detail from various perspectives in, for example, Baron (1982, especially pp. 7–40), Finegan (1980), Kachru (1976, 1982d and 1984a) and Strevens (1982a and 1982b).

The question concerning de-Englishization is related to the functional deviation and raises wider – and frequently debated – issues. One might ask: What relationship is there between language and culture? To what extent is a language acculturated in a new context in which it functions? And attitudinally important: How do native speakers of a language, e.g. English, react to such a situation? The innovations above sentence level take us to more interesting aspects of the linguistic creativity in the outer circle: the organization of nativized discourse strategies, registers, and speech acts (see Kachru, 1983b; Y. Kachru, 1983; Chishimba, 1983;

Magura, 1984; Lowenberg, 1984). In such innovations, there are clear relationships between the linguistic patterning of the text, transfer of underlying culturally determined strategies, and culturally intended effects.

These questions are important since, with its diffusion, English ceases to be an exponent of only one culture – the Western Judaeo-Christian culture; it is now perhaps the world's most multicultural language, a fact which is, unfortunately, not well recognized. The present multicultural character of English is clearly revealed in its uses around the globe, especially in creative writing. In the writing of, for example, Cyprian Ekwensi, Gabriel Okara, Amos Tutuola, and Chinua Achebe, English represents the Nigerian culture; in Alan Paton, it represents South African culture; in R. K. Narayan, Raja Rao and Salman Rushdie, it represents South Asian culture; in James K. Baxter, Witi Ihimaera and Frank Sargeson, it represents New Zealand culture; and in Edwin Thumboo, Ismail Sharif, and Fadzilah Amin, it represents Southeast Asian culture. In other words, English is now the language of those who use it; the users give it a distinct identity of their own in each region. As this transmuting alchemy of English takes effect, the language becomes less and less culture-specific (see Kachru, 1985b).

This takes me to the fourth aspect, the world-wide literary and other types of creativity in English. This includes, for example, aspects of creativity by its non-native users which are appropriate in the contexts of: (a) creative writing (short stories, novels, poetry, etc.); (b) regional uses (newspaper, legal, administrative, etc.); (c) international and interpersonal uses (social interaction, letters, obituaries, etc.); and (d) the visual and spoken media (radio, television, etc.). To give just one example here, India is now the third largest book producing nation in English after the USA and the UK. This fact cannot be ignored in discussing the diffusion of materials produced in English.

## 6  Typology of innovations

In several earlier studies, attempts have been made to analyse both formal and functional characteristics of such innovations. Due to limitations of space, I will not discuss these here. However, on the basis of variety-specific (e.g., Singaporean, Indian) or region-specific studies (e.g., African, Southeast Asian, South Asian), tentative typologies have been suggested about the shared characteristics of the institutionalized non-native varieties.[9] Again, I must avoid a digression here and not go into the details. The main claims of such studies are:

1 The sociolinguistic context of language use determines such innovations and language change.
2 The productive linguistic processes used for such innovations are shared with other such varieties, though the lexical realization in each variety may be different (e.g., hybridization, context-dependent modes of reference and address, degrees of politeness, and strategies reflecting such deference).

What an outsider, then, views as an extreme linguistic divisiveness in the outer circle of English, in reality is not so alarming and unusual. A surface judgement of this phenomenon is actually misleading; there is an underlying pattern and a shared direction in the linguistic nativization of English.

## 7 Prescriptivism and innovations

When we talk of prescriptivism in terms of innovations, we are primarily thinking of formal (lexical, phonological, syntactic), contextual, and discoursal deviations. What prescriptivism implies, then, is that with the spread of English we also expect the learners to acquire norms of behaviour appropriate to the users of the inner circle. The expected behaviour pattern characterizes what one might call an 'educated Englishman' (or American). This hypothesis is based on the assumption that language spread entails spread of cultural and social norms, or what has been termed in pedagogical literature an 'integrative motivation' for language learning. This hypothesis certainly is not fully applicable to the users of the institutionalized varieties of English. It is also doubtful that in a serious sense such integration was the aim of introducing English in the far-flung colonies. In any case, the present uses of English have clearly shown that an initially Western code has acquired numerous non-Western cultural incarnations and messages.

In understanding the present spread of English – and in looking for possible answers to our questions – what guidance can the other past and present languages of wider communication provide? Perhaps very little. We have already seen that the diffusion of English differs substantially from other languages of wider communication in terms of the vast territories it has covered in its spread, the depth of its penetration into different societal levels, and the range of functions allocated to it. In the West, the earlier spread of Latin and Greek was restricted to only selected regions. The spread of Arabic, Sanskrit, and Pali outside their traditional territories was again geographically and functionally constrained: these were basically languages of religion.

The other languages of colonization – Spanish, French, Dutch, and Portuguese, to name just a few – have not come close to the spread of

English. Only one artificial language, Esperanto, gained some users and acceptance, but its present 100,000 speakers around the world, and its 10,000-odd publications after almost one hundred years of existence provide no threat to English.

The past cannot, therefore, guide us in terms of providing equivalent situations, but it does reveal some tendencies which are associated with languages of wider communication. These lessons are (1) that the spread of a language invariably results in increased variation both in its functions and in terms of proficiency; (2) that the displacement of a language from its traditional locale entails new acculturation; and (3) that the attempts at codification in such contexts may be psychologically uplifting for the purists, but the actual results of these attempts are very limited.

## 8   Arms of codification

Since the past provides no insights, given the present international sociolinguistic profile of English, what are the possible arms for such codification, that is, if codification (or standardization) is the main concern? I shall consider four types here in order of their importance.

First, *authoritative codification*: this entails a recognized codification agency for English, such as the ones established for Italian in 1582 (Accademia della Crusca, in Florence), for French in 1635 (Académie Française), for Spanish in 1714 (Real Academia Española), and more recently, for Hebrew and for Bahasa Indonesia. As we know, the attempts made for English, in Britain in 1712, and in the USA in 1780, did not succeed (see e.g. Baron, 1982).

Second, *sociological* (or *attitudinal*) *codification*: this requires strengthening a rigorous 'accent bar' as discussed by Abercrombie (see Kachru, 1984a). The term 'accent' must be interpreted here in a wider sense and extended to other linguistic innovations and 'deviations'.

Third, *educational codification*: this refers to determining codification by instruments of education – dictionaries, the media, teacher's attitudes, and indirect references to 'proper' and 'acceptable' use of language. This type of codification is, of course, related to sociological codification, and has always been present in the case of English (see e.g. Kachru, 1981).

Finally, *psychological codification*: this has been used in ancient times for languages such as Sanskrit, where a hymn if not recited in the prescribed manner would result in the wrath of the gods and 'get the reciter [of a hymn] destroyed by god Indra [the chief Vedic god, also the god of rain and thunder]' (see Kachru, 1984b). In this case, language is associated with a specific 'power' and that power diminishes if the authoritative norms for its use are not obeyed. However, in the case of

English, the psychological pressure is not God-induced, it has other, more worldly channels, but still the psychological pressure or power is felt.

What, then, are the choices for responding to the present complex international dynamics of English? The first choice seems to be to recognize the present variation in English in terms of the three circles and the variation within each circle. Such recognition will help in developing appropriate theoretical approaches, in initiating applied research, and in producing relevant pedagogical materials for each situation. This will also mean reconsidering claims for the universal applicability of particular methods and approaches for teaching and learning English.

The second choice is to adopt various authoritative means for controlling the 'divisiveness' and multiplicity of norms. This would naturally entail undertaking corpus planning with reference to the innovations and creativity, and status planning with reference to the varieties within a variety. This, as we know, is not an easy task. But, then, 'purists' have always had visions of doing it.

The third choice is to recognize the concept 'speech community' of English as an abstract concept, and the 'speech fellowships' as the actual norm-producing linguistic groups. In a way, such norms are specific to speech fellowships and do not apply to the whole speech community. The intelligibility of English among members of a speech fellowship and across speech fellowships will depend on several sociolinguistic parameters: age, education, role and so on. The types of variation that we find in the native varieties cannot be overlooked in the case of the non-native varieties of English. Consider, for example, the following observation made by Ida Ward almost half a century ago about English in Britain (Ward, 1929: 5).

> It is obvious that in a country the size of the British Isles, any one speaker should be capable of understanding any other when he is talking English. At the present moment, such is not the case: a Cockney speaker would not be understood by a dialect speaker of Edinburgh or Leeds or Truro, and dialect speakers of much nearer districts than these would have difficulty in understanding each other.

In Ferguson and Heath (1981), we see that in the USA the situation is even more complex. Hence, there is no reason to expect homogeneity in the multiethnic and multilinguistic societies of Africa, South Asia, Southeast Asia or the Philippines.

Is this, then, a picture of desperation in which one throws up one's hands and proclaims that the battle is lost? The answer depends partly on the depth of a person's linguistic cynicism. Let me indulge here in a non-linguistic observation: the mental make-up of the English-using nations is not such that they will accept linguistic codification from above. The users in the inner circle will most likely not accept the formal authoritative means which they rejected more than two hundred years ago. Such users will continue to rely on subtle psychological, attitudinal, and sociological codification. But more important, resistance to even such subtle codification has already developed, as we have seen, in many non-native English-using countries.

Nevertheless, despite this resistance to deliberately imposed norms, what is emerging in the diverse native and non-native English-using speech fellowships is an *educated variety* of English (or, shall I say, educated varieties of English) which is intelligible across these many varieties. This point leads me to Daniel Jones's cone-shaped concept of a speech community. It is actually a cone of variation; as one goes up on the scale, an extended level of intelligibility is acquired.

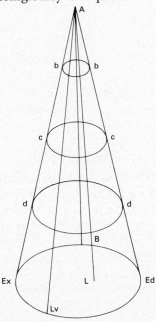

As I have stated elsewhere (Kachru, 1984a: 70):

> there is a pragmatically refreshing side to all these situations. What appears to be a complex linguistic situation at the surface, in Britain, in America, in Africa, or in South Asia, is less complex if one attempts to understand it from another perspective. In his cone-shaped diagram (reproduced in Ward, 1929: 5 *et seq.*), Daniel Jones has graphically shown that 'as we near the apex, the divergences which still exist have become so small as to be noticed only by a finely trained ear' (Ward, 1929: 6). Ward rightly provides the argument of 'convenience of expediency' (p. 7), suggesting that 'the regional dialect may suffice for those people who have no need to move from their own districts.'
> In this I find a clear case of parallelism between the native and institutionalized non-native varieties of English. Intelligibility is functionally determined with reference to the sub-region, the nation, political

24

areas within the region (e.g., South Asia, Southeast Asia), and internationally. True, educated (standard) Indian English, Singapore English, Nigerian English, or Kenyan English is not identical to RP or GA (General American). It is different; it *should* be different. Do such educated varieties of non-native Englishes create more problems of intelligibility than does, for example, a New Zealander when he or she talks to a midwestern American?

What is needed, then, is to move from linguistic authoritarianism of the 'native-speaker says' variety to a speech fellowship-specific realism. In such an approach, pedagogical prescriptivism is valid; so is the concern for acquisitional deficiencies, but with the realization that the functional and sociocultural distinctiveness of each speech fellowship cannot be arrested. In other words, the need is for an attitudinal change and linguistic pragmatism; these are not easily attainable and require sustained effort and supporting research.

## 9 Collaborative research on international Englishes

This takes me to my final major point: I believe that the time is more than ripe now for an international institute for the study of and research on English across cultures. I am not suggesting an academy for 'correcting, improving and ascertaining the English tongue', as did Jonathan Swift in 1712, but a research centre which has the functions of a clearing-house, archive, think tank, and a graduate teaching programme.

Is this a Utopian idea? What would be the organizational structure of such an institute, and its launching base? Is it financially feasible to undertake such an enterprise? These and related questions naturally crowd one's mind. The idea of such an institute has been discussed informally for the last five years. I believe that we should now discuss it more seriously and also take some initiative in this direction.[10]

Broadly speaking, the institute should have the following components:

I    Archives for English across cultures
II   Graduate teaching programmes
III  Research programmes
IV   International exchange programmes

Let me elaborate on these components one by one. The first component, comprising the archive, may include source and research materials of the following types:

1 *Empirical studies*: resource and background studies, e.g., sociolinguistic profiles of English in the inner circle, the outer circle and the expanding circle. These include profiles of the composition of English-using speech fellowships, the status of English in the language policies of different English-using countries, functional domains of English in

ESL regions, and attitudinal studies concerning varieties and varieties within varieties.

2 *Functional domains*: types of Englishes as they have developed in terms of various culture-specific roles of the language: localized norms, variational (lectal) range within local norms, and types of language contact and their impact (e.g., borrowing, 'mixing').

3 *Formal studies*: the characteristic formal features of nativized uses of English from various text-types, including registral (e.g., administrative, newspaper, legal), interactional (e.g., non-native norms for interaction in English) and creative (e.g., localized literatures in English).

4 *Survival registers*: studies of what may be termed *international* survival registers of English with their localized variants, e.g., medical, legal, *Seaspeak*, and aviation.

5 *Pedagogical studies*: comprehensive cross-cultural data for the teaching of English, including methods for the teaching of the English language and literature at various educational levels; curricula for the English language teaching specialists; and texts, teaching aids, and supplementary materials.

6 *Resource materials*: these include background materials of the following types – major agencies for the coordination of training and research within each region (e.g., the Regional English Language Centre (RELC), Singapore; the Central Institute of English and Foreign Languages (CIEFL), Hyderabad); resources and research appropriate for each English-using region, specifically regional surveys of English (e.g., aspects of literature or language); and surveys and critical studies of the development of literatures in English (see e.g. Narasimhaiah, 1976).

The second component concerns the graduate training programme. I am not suggesting that a new graduate programme be initiated. We need to extend the focus of current curricula leading to Master's degrees in English studies. In such courses a graduate student clearly has to be exposed to the internationalization of English and its linguistic, sociolinguistic, literary, and pedagogical implications. Ideally, such a curriculum should include the *multicultural* and *multinorm* contexts of the World Englishes, and the consequences of these varied contexts for teaching methods, discourse and stylistic strategies, pedagogical materials, cultural contexts of texts, and lexicography.

The third component involves research programmes, and this cannot be isolated from the above two components. In a way, this component may be seen as an extension of the curriculum for graduate teaching programmes. The research should be seen in terms of the priorities established in the agenda for the first component.

The last component aims at providing for international exchange of researchers in the field of English studies. The goal is to establish serious links for interaction among scholars in the field. This may be a step toward collaborative research among the centres. One hopes that the well-established data banks for description and analysis of English will make their resources available to such an institute. The insightful work done at such centres as the following may, then, be made available for shared research undertakings: Survey of English Usage, University College, London; the Standard Corpus of Present-day Edited American English, Brown University; data available at Stanford University, California; RELC, Singapore; CIEFL, Hyderabad; lexicographical projects in the West Indies, South Africa, and so on.

I envisage that a project of this nature will be an extension of one of the present centres of TESL training and research. The reorganization and extension of an existing centre will be easier than establishing an altogether new one. The other components discussed above may be added to such a centre as a collaborative undertaking with English-using countries.

This paper, of course, is not a blueprint for such a centre; it is rather an articulation of an idea. More important, this is not an idea for the codification of English – even if it were possible – but a suggestion for initiating collaborative efforts between the native and non-native users of English for monitoring, as it were, the direction of change in English, the uses and usage, and the scope of the spread and its implications for intelligibility and communication. I believe that it is through such collaborative attempts that a clearer picture of the forms and functions of English will emerge.

By the term 'collaborative' I do not imply simply collaboration between the British Council or other British institutions and interested agencies in the USA. Such an undertaking will be globally collaborative in the sense that those who use the English language in Africa, in Asia, and elsewhere, must feel that they are a part of this undertaking. They must realize that at one level, there is a stake in maintaining an international standard for English, and, at another level, there is a need to describe the uses of English with reference to diverging English-using speech fellowships. If there is concern for standards, the collaborating countries must contribute toward maintaining and staffing such an international institute.

## 10   Will-o'-the-wispish concerns v. linguistic pragmatism

The above outline is, of course, programmatic, but the idea behind it deserves some attention: my main suggestion is for a collaborative effort, for exchange of ideas, and for the establishment of a think tank where

27

concerned scholars can discuss the shared issues and their implications. But with this outline, all the bees are not out of my bonnet. A number of other issues and concerns emerge, particularly within the context of the post-1950s developments. I shall merely mention some of them here.

First, in terms of exporting English language (and literature) experts, we are witnessing a new phenomenon: the users of the institutionalized varieties are now not only 'norm-developing', as I have discussed earlier, but also function as the channels for the diffusion of their respective norms to the expanding circle of English (EFL contexts). This function is performed in various roles: as teachers of English, as engineers, as doctors, and so on. Sri Lankans, Malaysians, and Indians, to name just three outer circle speech fellowships, are now involved in academic planning and teaching of English in, for example, Egypt, Saudi Arabia, Iran, the Gulf countries, and Southeast Asia, in addition to their own countries. The figures, for example, for the export of teachers of English and mathematics from South Asia are impressive. One only has to take a look at the faculty lists of the universities and colleges in the above EFL regions. Moreover, this import of non-native educators of English does not apply only to the expanding circle of English, but also to several countries which belong in the outer circle, where English has been institutionalized (e.g., Singapore, Malaysia, Nigeria, Kenya). The need for these expatriates as teachers and professors is immense and fast increasing. There is at present, as Cooper (1984) observes in Israel, a 'hunger' and 'indecent passion' for acquiring English. But this is not restricted to Israel.

The teaching of English has, therefore, become everybody's business: it has developed into an international commercial enterprise and every English-using country is capitalizing on it in its own way.

The second issue has pedagogical implications. In the international context one must ask: What does the term *communicative competence* mean for English? In other words, competence within which context or situation? The question is especially applicable to the institutionalized varieties of English.

The third issue takes us to the core of some recent paradigms of research in second language acquisition, particularly with reference to English. A number of key concepts in this research deserve a serious second look, including the concepts 'error analysis', 'fossilization', and 'inter-language'. The universal use of the term *error* for all divergences from native-speaker norms was incorrect and diverted attention from serious sociolinguistic research for at least two decades, until such research in 'error analysis' came to a dead end. We are only now, as it were, recovering from it (for a discussion, see Lowenberg, 1984).

The fourth key issue relates to the models and methods used for research on institutionalized varieties of English. I have discussed this issue elsewhere (cf. Kachru, 1985a), but let me reiterate a few points here.

It is useful to consider, for example: What is the state-of-the-art of research on non-native Englishes? What have been the approaches used for such research? What would be the useful lines of research to follow? The answers to these and related questions are vital for the study of direction and change in the English language. Until very recently the dominant paradigm for such research was what I have termed the *deviational* model. It is only recently that other approaches have been used, such as the *contextualization* model, the *interactional* model, and the *variational* model.

The fifth issue takes me to TESL and TEFL as a profession and as an area of enquiry. Let me stick my neck out a little farther now and ask, for example: Has our profession realized its responsibilities within the changed new contexts in which English is used? Has it incorporated the insights with which the long tradition of teaching, learning, and non-native creativity in English has provided us? It seems to me that the answer is 'no'.

One interpretation of this situation is that the current approaches to TESL reveal indifference to the pragmatic context of the present status of English as a world language. A harsher interpretation is that our profession has not been able to shake off the earlier evangelical and rather ethnocentric approaches to its task. One might add, then, that this ostrich-like attitude is not the correct response to the international ecology of English. What is needed is both attitudinal change and professionalism based on pragmatism and linguistic realism.

## 11 Conclusion

If this paper has given the impression that I am a linguistic cynic lamenting that we have come to a state of linguistic helplessness, that impression is wrong. If I have given the impression of preaching linguistic anarchy, that impression is wrong as well.

My position is that the diffusion of English, its acculturation, its international functional range, and the diverse forms of literary creativity it is accommodating are historically unprecedented. I do not think that linguists, pedagogues, language planners – and, if I might include the purists here – have ever faced this type of linguistic challenge before. I do not believe that the traditional notions of codification, standardization, models, and methods apply to English any more. The dichotomy of its *native* and *non-native* users seems to have become irrelevant. We may talk of 'standards' for our linguistic satisfaction, but we seem to be at a loss to explain what we mean by them, and equally important, how to apply them. I do not think that in discussing standards for English, the sociolinguistic reality of each English-using speech fellowship can be ignored.

In my view, the global diffusion of English has taken an interesting turn: the native speakers of this language seem to have lost the exclusive prerogative to control its standardization; in fact, if current statistics are any indication, they have become a minority. This sociolinguistic fact must be accepted and its implications recognized. What we need now are new paradigms and perspectives for linguistic and pedagogical research and for understanding the linguistic creativity in multilingual situations across cultures.

## Notes

1   For selected case studies and detailed bibliographies, see e.g. Bailey and Görlach, eds., 1982; Kachru, ed., 1982c; Kachru, 1983a; Noss, ed., 1983; Platt and Webber, 1980; Pride, ed., 1982; and Smith, ed., 1981.

2   These nations, however, are not exclusively English-speaking: a number of linguistic minorities live in such nations but the primary majority language is English. The population figures used in this paper are taken from *Encyclopaedia Britannica 1984, Book of the Year*, Chicago: Encyclopaedia Britannica, Inc.

3   Detailed sociolinguistic profiles of some of these varieties are now available. For recent research and extensive bibliographies, see, for example, for Indian English, Kachru, 1983a; for African English, Chishimba, 1983; for Southern African English, Magura, 1984; for Southeast Asian English, Noss, ed., 1983; for the Malay Archipelago, Lowenberg, 1984; for Singapore, Platt and Webber, 1980.

4   See e.g. Iyengar, 1962; Kachru, 1983a and 1983b; King, 1974 and 1980; Mukherjee, 1971; Narasimhaiah, 1976 and 1978.

5   For example, consider the changing status of English in the language policies of Kenya, Malaysia, Bangladesh, and so on. For a discussion of the changing status of English in Indonesia and Malaysia, see Lowenberg, 1984.

6   In this table, I have given the total populations of the USA, the UK, Canada, and Australia. For the other six countries, i.e., India, Bangladesh, Nigeria, Pakistan, Tanzania, and Kenya, I have given four per cent of the total populations as a conservative estimate of the English-using populations.

7   For a detailed discussion, see Kachru, 1984a.

8   One might include here, for example, Chishimba, 1983; Kachru, 1983b; Lowenberg, 1984; Pride, 1981; and Platt and Webber, 1980.

9   See e.g. Bokamba, 1982, and Kachru, 1982b.

10  In recent years, this idea has been presented in several conferences, including the Conference on English as an International Language, 'Discourse Patterns Across Cultures', June 1–7, 1983, East–West Culture Learning Institute, East–West Center, Honolulu, Hawaii. See also Kachru, 'World Englishes and TESOL: Contexts, Attitudes, and Concerns', an invited position paper presented at the Eighteenth Annual TESOL Convention, Houston, 7 March 1984.

# Commentator 1

## Sidney Greenbaum

Professor Kachru has touched on a large number of important issues in his paper. I wish to focus on the question of standardization, which is central to the theme of global English. Professor Kachru has pointed approvingly to the developing of norms in the 'outer circle' of English speech fellowships: in some ESL countries local educated varieties are becoming increasingly recognized and accepted locally as standard varieties in their own right, despite some local ambivalence. He seems to be arguing that recognition and acceptance for these varieties should be extended internationally, particularly by those in the 'inner circle' of English speech fellowships, the native English speakers. He further implies a parallel with the struggle for linguistic independence waged on behalf of the transplanted national varieties such as American English and Australian English. But it is arguable that the situations are different in important respects.

There is no doubt that non-native speakers can acquire native-like proficiency in English as an additional language, whether they belong to the 'outer circle' (ESL) or the 'expanding circle' (EFL) – a distinction in status, as Braj Kachru rightly says, that anyway depends for some countries on the national language policy at a particular period. Among the criteria for educated speakers with native-like proficiency I include two in particular: that they can exhibit the range of language functions available to native speakers and that they can be easily understood, not only by speakers of their own country, but also by English speakers from other countries, to whichever circle they may belong.

Intelligibility is the central issue. Professor Kachru cites an observation by Ida Ward earlier this century to show that, even in the British Isles, speakers cannot understand each other's English. It is true that a Cockney speaker might not be understood by a dialect speaker of Edinburgh or Leeds or Truro. But educated speakers from different parts of the British Isles are capable of understanding each other, despite differences in pronunciation. The standard national variety is fostered by governmental and educational institutions precisely because it facilitates national communication.

At the international level, the differences between the national standards of the 'inner circle' are relatively few, except for pronunciation. And even the pronunciation differences are not a major impediment, once speakers have tuned into each other's system of pronunciation. Because of the essential identity of the national standards, especially for the written language, it is reasonable to refer to an international standard English

31

with some national variation. Here arises the potential problem. If the educated varieties of the 'outer circle' assume the status of national standards without reference to the international norms of the 'inner circle', will they diverge too far to remain part of the international standard English? Cultural and environmental differences are to be expected, and so is interference from indigenous languages. But far more worrying are the effects that derive from the situation in which English is acquired: it is learned in school. Will there be sufficient time devoted to the learning of English? Will the *teachers* have an adequate command of the language? If the emerging national standards are to remain intelligible internationally, then the countries of the 'outer circle' will have to invest heavily in the teaching of English. They may also need to establish language planning agencies to control the development of the national standards, to monitor the printed language, to influence public attitudes, and to promote competence in the English language in public institutions and teacher-training colleges.

I welcome Professor Kachru's ambitious plans for research and teaching programmes. The Department of English at University College London has inaugurated a new MA in Modern English Language. Both the Department and the Survey of English Usage will be happy to collaborate on a project for studying the progress of English as an international language.

# Commentator 2

Jan Svartvik

As a member of the 'expanding circle' I am somewhat hesitant to comment on issues which are chiefly concerned with the 'outer' circle. However, the main point in Professor Kachru's stimulating and informative paper, which I take to be that of standard and codification in global English, does indeed concern members of all circles, not least those of the expanding one. The reason is that the current gigantic investment in the English language in countries such as mine is really defensible only as long as the acquired skill can be put to good use as a means of international communication. In consequence, the role of English in the expanding circle is relevant also to the issue of codification in the outer circle.

There can be no question of an English-speaking community or fellowship among Swedish speakers of English. Their norm is the native-speaker norm, and this is true whether their interests are literary, linguistic or narrowly ESP-oriented. They are not 'norm-producing groups'. Their norm may be that of British or American English, but it is solidly native-speaker based, in spite of the fact that very few EFL users will ever get close to, let alone internalize, the rules of such a norm. I believe that ESL users in the outer circle also benefit more from a native-speaker norm. The main reason for the majority of people wanting to acquire proficiency in English as a second or foreign language is to use it for some general or specific purpose: to do business, administer, read text books or detective stories, attend conferences, travel, and what not. In most cases the use will not be just single but multiple – and, more often than not in a changing world, it is unpredictable. The strong argument in favour of English as an international medium is that it is the most widely used language, but it will remain usefully so only as long as it remains intercomprehensible.

Thus, my defence of the native-speaker norm, or rather *a* native-speaker norm, is based on functional criteria. They are not those of 'correctness' (whatever that may be) or social status (we know what that is) or even admiration of the political systems of the English-speaking nations. Nor is my recommendation based on fear of 'deviations' (which will occur anyway, even when there is a 'home-based' norm, as testified by the popularity of usage-books for native consumption).

In discussing norms, I believe it is helpful to make a distinction between speech and writing. For example, English grammar is strikingly homogeneous in the different standard varieties of written English. As for lexis, there is more variety, of course. Yet, as many of the delightful examples cited by Professor Kachru show, lexical innovations tend to adhere to standard word-formation rules, e.g. *Himalayan blunder* 'grave or serious mistake', *minor wife* 'mistress', or *pin-drop silence*, and they are comprehensible also to outsiders. Furthermore, such lexical innovations do not represent a new feature in the history of English but rather demonstrate the flexibility of the language and add to the richness of its total lexical resources.

I believe that the unique position of English in the world today will work in the direction of greater homogeneity. This is certainly true of spelling under the impact of such forces as the internationalization of printing and the spread of word-processing with international software using electronic spelling-checkers.

The 'fissiparous tendencies' are largely restricted to spoken English. It must be so, since spoken language is at the core of language where any external norm is little heeded. This is an area where native speakers vary as much as non-native speakers. The native Yorkshireman does not *want to* and the Swedish learner *cannot* change in the direction of, say, becoming an RP speaker.

I want to argue that, for non-native speakers, the acquisition of English is an investment worth the effort and the money only as long as the language functions as a means of international communication for a range of purposes. This in no way denies that a certain non-native variety can work well in a particular restricted outer circle context, but – and here I question Professor Kachru – is it really worth having a variety of norms even for institutionalized outer circle fellowships, considering the likely long-term negative consequences for global English?

# Theme I  Summary of discussion

The central issue in these sessions was whether it is feasible or desirable to promote a single standard of English in order to maintain the mutual intelligibility of the language as an international means of communication.

It was pointed out that the emergence of new forms of English is not subject to external control since it is of the very nature of language to adapt itself to the varying sociocultural needs of its users. Different norms of usage will inevitably arise, therefore, as a function of normal social use. Furthermore, language is not only used instrumentally as a means of communication but also as an expression of social identity, as an emblem of group membership. People who use English as a language for communication and self-expression within their own sociocultural environment will naturally develop their own norms of appropriateness.

On the other hand, as was pointed out in particular by participants from countries where English is a foreign rather than a second language, the effectiveness of the language as a means for international communication would be compromised if there were no common norm of reference. The very establishment of different national standards would be a very difficult descriptive task and would also involve policy decisions in education for their maintenance: and unless local standards were clearly established, there would be the obvious danger – especially in ESL countries – of drifting into mutually unintelligible creolized forms. Allowance would always have to be made for some variation of norms, as there is in such ENL countries between British and American standards, but unless there were close correspondence, the mutual intelligibility which was a requirement for the international use of the language for cross-cultural comprehension would be seriously impaired.

On the question of comprehension, it was noted that this was not only a matter of reference to shared norms of the language code as such, but also, just as crucially, a matter of understanding and adjusting to the different discourse strategies which were used for interaction by different groups of speakers. The achievement of mutual intelligibility depends also on an understanding of norms of social behaviour, so that even if there were general conformity to a common standard of English this would not guarantee comprehension across cultures.

Thus, arguments were advanced in favour of three distinct positions: a single standard; the recognition of a multiplicity of standards; a greater concern than hitherto for other aspects of communicative behaviour than linguistic norms in isolation. It was suggested that for English to fulfil its functions as both a local and global medium of communication its users would need to acknowledge and acquire, where appropriate, norms for both domestic intranational and wider international communication and learn to make discriminating reference to them as occasion required. Such a suggestion places the issue of the English language in its global context within the control of educational policy and practice.

# THEME II ENGLISH LITERATURE IN A GLOBAL CONTEXT

## a) **English literature in a global context**

Colin MacCabe

The very title of this paper invites grim amusement. Surely it is impossible for any individual to talk of the whole of English literature? And only a megalomaniac would take the whole world for his topic when asked to produce a forty-five-minute lecture. *Nihil humanum alienum mihi* runs the old saw, but a Latin tag can hardly conceal the embarrassment of a title which commits one to every text and all contexts.

And yet questions about English literature and its place in the world cannot be avoided. They are real and pressing questions which impose themselves, whether we like it or not and independently of the particular occasion of this anniversary. When I first started to think of this paper earlier in the year, I was lecturing for the British Council at the Shanghai Foreign Language Institute. In such a situation it would, in any case, have been impossible to avoid thinking about the conjunction of text and world, of the problems and paradoxes of national cultures. To teach Shakespeare in China poses the paradoxes in some of their more acute forms. What possible justification is there for teaching to members of a nation of a thousand million people, with a culture and a language which dates back over three thousand years, a writer from a small offshore island of Europe whose population when he wrote was little more than five million and whose culture can only be realistically dated from the very time of his writing, for it is then that our language takes on its recognizably modern forms?

But it would be wrong to think that one need go anywhere so distant for these questions to be posed with very considerable force. I teach in a Scottish university which makes me particularly sensitive to the fact that although we are here celebrating the fiftieth anniversary of the British Council, nobody would ever have thought of asking me to talk of British literature. For, of course, there is no such thing. There is, certainly, English literature. But there is also, certainly, Scottish literature, Irish literature, Welsh literature. And yet these 'secondary' certainties pose immediate uncertainties. When we talk of Welsh literature, do we mean Welsh writing in English or the literature of the Welsh language? When we talk of Irish literature, are we talking of a separate tradition within the English language from the establishment of the Protestant Ascendancy

and Swift to its partial overthrow and Beckett? Or is such a separate tradition a chimera, one more giddy fantasy engendered by centuries of
enmity, and should we simply talk of writing by Irish men and women?
Can Scottish literature be understood in terms of a set of national themes
and obsessions? Or is it more important to consider it in relation to the
problems posed by a standard literary language, defined from the seventeenth century onwards by a Southern English dialect? We are perhaps
more honest when we talk of literatures and languages than when we talk
of political institutions. If we are all nominally British, it is instructive to
recall English as a language has been imposed, often by force, throughout
the British Isles. And the peoples of this island find that along with the
imposed language, they have acquired a literature to which their relation
is profoundly ambiguous – one need only think of Joyce or MacDiarmid
in this century to realize exactly how ambiguous.

To grasp the complexity of our relation to our inherited culture, there
is no need even to consider the other nations in the British Isles. For
increasingly, as people learn to value the way they speak and not the way
they are meant to speak, to appreciate fully the cultural forms they enjoy
and not those they are meant to enjoy, English literature can seem a
parochial affair, a minority taste in a minority tongue. But if, from one
point of view, English literature appears to shrink within these islands,
from another it expands ever further. As the British Empire gives way to
the Empire of English, so more and more readers of English literature are
produced. I would hazard an educated guess that more people will pick up
a text of Shakespeare this week than inhabited these islands in 1600.

Why should English literature enjoy this privileged position? Is there
any justification, other than historical accident, for the current state of
affairs? As we teach English literature throughout the world today, are we
simply flotsam and jetsam on tides of history which have swept to
imperial dominance in successive centuries – two powers, Britain and
America, which happen to share a common language?

Such thoughts are not particularly reassuring or comfortable. But some
of the assured answers to these questions are positively frightening. I
know of few more powerful defences of English literature than that produced by the great writer and historian Thomas Babington Macaulay.
Newly arrived in India in 1834, Macaulay was asked to chair a committee
which was considering the educational clause in the India Act in order to
decide between the rival claims of Indian and English culture in the educational system. Macaulay produced a subsequent Minute in which he
left no doubt which claim was superior. He declared that he had not
found one Orientalist 'who could deny that a single shelf of a good European library was worth the whole native literature of India and Arabia'.
Macaulay further held that 'all the historical information which had been
collected from all the books written in the Sanskrit language is less valu-

able than what may be found in the most paltry abridgements used at preparatory schools in England'. The issue could be succinctly summarized:

> The question before us is simply whether when it is in our power to teach
> the [English] language, we shall teach languages in which . . . there are
> no books on any subject which deserve to be compared to our own . . .
> whether, when we can patronize sound philosophy and true history, we
> shall countenance at the public expense medical doctrines which could
> disgrace an English farrier, astronomy which would move laughter in
> girls at an English boarding school, history abounding with kings
> 30 feet high and reigns thirty thousand years long and geography made
> up of seas of treacle and rivers of butter.[1]

One could profitably pass a full hour in analysing the examples in
Macaulay's comments for they weave the very texture of imperialism: the
examples of ignorance within the master-culture are the working classes
(farriers) and women (girls in a boarding school) and yet even these are
infinitely more knowledgeable than those who are outside the master-
culture altogether. One could pass another engaging hour in asking how
convincingly 'sound philosophy and true history' have survived the race
of time. It is doubtful whether Macaulay's Whig conception of history
affords much explanatory power when we consider the thousand-year
Reich proclaimed by Hitler. Indeed it may well be that any conception of
history which could begin to explain the appalling successes of fascism
might have to draw on aspects of that Indian tradition that Macaulay so
derides. And as the very planet seems on the verge of exhausting its huge
resources, the attitude to reality embodied in Indian geography may seem
more useful than the sound philosophy of English empiricism.

All I have said so far falls within what I imagine would be a widely
agreed reaction to Macaulay's remarks. They would be condemned for
their bigotry, and some declaration of the worth of every separate culture
would be voiced. The capacity to value other cultures than our own is a
great human advance and must be encouraged to the utmost. However, it
is not evident on what basis we can value other cultures and it is my
opinion that the most widespread beliefs about the relations between cultures are couched in theoretically untenable forms. Indeed, it is not clear
that we can dismiss Macaulay as simply as we would all wish to dismiss
him; it may be that confronting his views more directly is a necessary preliminary to ridding ourselves of the reflexes of colonialism which are still
so prevalent.

The theoretical justification for valuing very diverse cultures throughout the world is often couched in some version of what is often called the
'incommensurability thesis'. This holds that meanings are language or
theory specific. It is therefore impossible to compare meanings which only
take form within a much larger ensemble of practices and beliefs.

Cultures, on such an account, do not share meanings and therefore it is impossible to compare them. This very powerful idea has a whole range of specific and precise articulations – but many people believe some version of it who have never followed courses in the philosophy of language or the philosophy of science.

It is worth, however, recalling two of the most influential and theoretically articulate versions. Within linguistics we find the Sapir–Whorf hypothesis, largely developed in relation to Whorf's analysis of the tense system of Hopi verbs. The hypothesis holds that the world is, in important senses, language dependent; that the structure of the language may produce very different conceptions of time and space, conceptions which entail that speakers of different languages inhabit different worlds. More recently within the philosophy of science Kuhn and Feyerabend have challenged that notion of scientific progress which holds that the resolution of difficulties within an old theory produces a new theory. Rather, they argue, changes in patterns of education and in technology suddenly produce new groups of scientists asking different and new questions which do not make sense within the old theory at all. The old and new theories cannot confront one another in a crucial experiment because each theory would construe the experiment differently. In Kuhn's terms scientific advance takes place in 'paradigm shifts' in which the practices and meanings within a particular science take on a whole new configuration which does not allow any dialogue between new and old – for they now speak different languages.

Such theories have obvious affinities with a general valorization of different cultures. On this account, each culture inhabits its own world and there can be no question of comparing these worlds, for there is no common ground for such comparison. We are light years from Macaulay. However, it is not clear that we can really make sense of this 'multiverse' of different cultures. The American philosopher, Donald Davidson, in his essay 'On the Very Idea of a Conceptual Scheme', takes strong issue with any doctrine which partakes of conceptual relativism: 'Conceptual relativism is a heady and exotic doctrine, or would be if we could make good sense of it. The trouble is, as so often in philosophy, it is hard to improve intelligibility while retaining the excitement.'[2]

Davidson's extremely sophisticated arguments can be most easily grasped by considering the examples with which he commences his essay. As Whorf explains the tense system of the Hopi verb, we understand perfectly what he is explaining *in English*. As Kuhn explains the incommensurabilities of pre- and post-Newtonian physics, we understand these incommensurabilities perfectly – *from the viewpoint of post-Newtonian physics*. For Davidson these examples prove the impossibility of any consistent defence of the incommensurability thesis. Either we understand a language or we don't even understand it as a language. We may recognize a different point of view, but that point of view must be operating within our visual space for us to grasp it as a point of view at all. Our comprehension of a language depends on linking utterances to attitudes and behaviour. If we cannot do this then we have no grounds for understanding it as a language. It is only if we can provide some interpretation in terms of our own beliefs that any utterance can make sense. The justification of any interpretative scheme is that it makes the behaviour of others minimally reasonable in our eyes. There can be no leap to some 'neutral' vantage point where we can contemplate completely different behaviours and values. For Davidson our understanding can only proceed from our understanding – we are condemned to ethnocentrism. Thus one of our most eminent of contemporary Anglo-Saxon philosophers would lead us back to a position which has much in common with Macaulay. If it is true that there is no blanket condemnation of other cultures, those other cultures can only make sense insofar as they are amenable to our interpretative schemes. There can be no radical confrontation with difference.

In a recent review, Richard Rorty develops in more detail a new defence of ethnocentrism which avoids the pitfalls of both realism and relativism. The article is entitled 'Solidarity or objectivity?' – and it preserves the force of Davidson's argument within a very different and more acceptable framework. Rorty starts by characterizing the philosophic enterprise since the Greeks in terms of the desire to find a basis for judgement of both fact and value independently of the community in which the philosopher finds himself. Rorty analyses this historic enterprise, which endures down to the Enlightenment and beyond, as the quest for objectivity. In opposition to this he places a host of thinkers from the late nineteenth century onwards: Nietzsche, Wittgenstein, Heidegger, Kuhn, Feyerabend and, most importantly, the American pragmatist tradition with which Rorty affiliates himself. The fundamental ethic of this alternative tradition is an identification with the community. The desire to place oneself in a necessary but solitary relation to the world is replaced by the desire to communicate with one's own kind – with the *ethnos*. In this perspective, truth cannot be considered independently of the community in which it operates and it is only in terms of that community and its practices that we can consider questions of fact and value. This refusal of realism does not, however, entail a fall into relativism. Pragmatism holds that truth is what is good for *us* to believe. There can be no question, for a pragmatist, of trying to produce a trans-cultural account of rationality which would yield a universally valid account of the relation between world and language. It is such a universal account, Macaulay's 'sound philosophy', for example, which would enable one from a position of impartiality to praise certain cultures and condemn others. Rorty argues that the gap between truth and justification is not something which the pragmatist, unlike the realist, feels obliged to fill. For the pragmatist such a gap can only be understood as one between an existing good state of affairs and a potentially better one. There may always be better truths, someone may always come up with a better idea.

But such a conception does not entail a simple relativism. Rorty does not accept that any belief is as good as any other; he admits that David-son's arguments show such a relativist position to be self-contradictory. But the pragmatist does accept that 'nothing can be said about truth or rationality outside the familiar justifications that a given society – *our own* – uses in some domain of research'.[3] Rorty goes on to argue, how-ever, that this ethnocentric position is not a relativist one. To adopt a relativist position is to maintain a theory of truth. The pragmatist, how-ever, holds to no such theory. The basis of his beliefs are not an epis-temological theory of truth but an ethical primacy accorded to the solidarity of 'cooperative human research'.[4]

Rorty is thus happy to reject all relativist arguments which hold that rationality is defined by local cultural norms (what I claimed earlier in the paper would be the unstated theory supporting most of our beliefs about diverse cultures). All such attempts are finally attempts to define ration-ality in terms of criteria (however varied from culture to culture), whereas the pragmatist understands rationality not as a quality but a process: the incessant reweaving of our own beliefs. Ethnocentrism thus amounts, according to Rorty, to the incontestable fact that we can only make sense of another culture by weaving its beliefs into our own. He would regard my early brief remarks about the possible values of traditional Indian his-tory and geography in this light. To take these accounts seriously one must weave them into a set of questions and answers (a problematic) pro-vided within my own culture.

Rorty concludes his paper by considering why so many in the West hold to objectivity as the 'Western virtue'. Why is it that efforts of philosophers as diverse as Marx, Sartre, Oakeshott, Gadamer and Foucault to demonstrate that objectivity is fundamentally an effect of certain forms of solidarity is greeted with fear and loathing? Rorty glosses this fear and loathing as a desire to find an ultimate justification for dearly held truths. But however dear the truths they can only be justified within the kind of ironic and circular terms of Winston Churchill's remark that democracy was the worst form of government imaginable except for all the other forms that have been tried to date. Circularity is inevitable in the defence of any particular set of values but those who privilege the virtues of solidarity expect nothing else. The objectivist, however, will see the world in ruins: either we must grant a particular privilege to our own com-munity or an impossible tolerance towards all others.

Rorty does not shrink before this choice: the pragmatist willingly embraces 'the ethnocentric horn of this dilemma'[5] and the rest of his very brilliant article deals with some of the consequences that follow from this. We must resign ourselves to the loss of a belief in human nature, in human rights and, most bitterly of all, draw the consequence that nothing in nature or law guarantees the triumph of the virtues we prize. What we gain is a strengthened belief in the necessity of struggling for the kind of humanity and the particular rights that we value now and which, if we perish, may perish with us. The details of this further argument do not presently concern me. What I wish to do is to consider the very serious weaknesses in both Davidson's and Rorty's arguments.

Davidson assumes that within our own culture there is a transparent series of links between utterance, behaviour and attitude. Such a position ignores the extent to which in the interior of any given culture there is always a series of struggles about the articulation of these three aspects, most crucially around questions of sexuality and work. The ways we define ourselves in relation to these areas of experience are often self-contradictory. The individual is not even transparent to him or herself. When we recognize that no individual can articulate a coherent and consistent system of beliefs, it becomes nonsense to assume that a language can confer such coherence and consistency on all its speakers. But if we give up the belief that our own language makes perfect sense then it is no longer quite so easy to dismiss the language of others. I am sure we have all had the experience, particularly with the young, of hearing languages which defied all our expectations about the relations between utterances, behaviour and attitudes. While one reaction is to abandon them to their incomprehensibility, another is to try to learn these new languages. But if we succeed in learning them then our own language will have changed. There are perhaps no more obvious examples of such a process than the reading of Anthony Burgess's *A Clockwork Orange* or William Golding's *The Inheritors*, but the very form of the novel, and much drama, is based on such a process of learning. In reading a novel we are not simply mapping utterances onto an already understood world of attitudes and behaviour, or if we are then we are reading an indifferent novel. At its best a novel forces us to re-examine our normal forms of inference, to allow fresh connections in what becomes a new world.

Rorty avoids the problems of Davidson's very static view of language and emphasizes the process by which a new culture is woven into the old. But he retains Davidson's belief that the old culture is homogenous – composed of the *ethnos*, of our kind of people. But who are these people? Are they the West? A particular nation? Or a particular grouping? The problem with pragmatism has been the same from Royce onward – how do you define a community?

Questions of community immediately introduce questions of power. If we are condemned to ethnocentrism then we must seriously consider the unequal power relations which obtain between different cultures. It is

43

true that Rorty makes passing reference to power when he talks of Foucault, but he never seriously considers the question outside of the limit cases where beliefs are enforced by threat of imprisonment and death. I think that it is easier to understand what is at stake if we now return to Macaulay. It seems to me that what is offensive about Macaulay is not the simple statement of arrogance or prejudice. It may be that one important thing that we must learn to do is to state our objections to other cultures, remembering as we do, how sensitive we are to objections about our own. What is terrible about Macaulay's remarks is that they are colonial remarks – not in any imprecise ideological sense but in the precise exercise of political power. An Englishman is deciding an educational system for Indians, after consulting the leading Orientalists – other Englishmen. It would be a mistake to think that the gaining of political independence immediately entails the gaining of power. Even an organization such as the British Council wields considerable patronage and power in other countries, particularly Third World ones, and any decisions about policy must acknowledge that position of power. It is not a question of abdication – to have a voice increasingly requires a transmitter but the forms of transmission may determine a single voice or a dialogic polyphony.

So far I have deliberately talked almost exclusively in what are the most abstract terms about the teaching of literature. I have considered a series of arguments which suggest that there is no escape from the ethnocentric position – that we must teach the values of our kind. But to ask who our kind is, is not, at least for me, a rhetorical question. Rorty, himself, becomes very confused when dealing with Western secular intellectuals, whom he defines as his kind, when he has to consider the very widespread influence of Nietzschean antinomianism amongst such intellectuals. His response is to divide Nietzsche into two component parts: an acceptable attack on forms of objectivist epistemology and an unacceptable, and for Rorty unrelated, attack on bourgeois civility, Christian Love and ideologies of progress. It may be that Rorty's reading of Nietzsche is justified but it ignores the fact that the vast majority of those influenced by Nietzsche have not made such a division. In the middle of Rorty's *us* he finds a *them*, a process which I would argue reaches right down to the individual riven by contradictions, a member of competing and incompatible collectivities. In teaching about *our* kind, in speaking for *our* values, there is always a greater or lesser degree of contradiction. Given my own racial background, one of the most persistent contradictions for me is that the greatest poet, novelist and dramatist of this century of English literature have been Irish – Yeats, Joyce and Beckett. In their writings one can read all the strains and contradictions of working within a tradition which is both alien and their own. If Beckett's retreat into French marks the absolute limit of this engagement, Joyce's writing addresses forcefully the questions that we are considering here today. One problem that runs through Joyce's writing is the dilemma posed by the Gaelic revival enjoining Irish writers to write in their native tongue. For Joyce such a choice is to avoid the reality of his contemporary Ireland – English-speaking and urban – and to substitute for it a mythical Gaelic-speaking peasantry. At the same time Joyce is aware of the inadequacies of the standard English literary language for the forging of the consciousness of *his* race. The solution he adopted was heavily dependent on the ten years that he had spent as a teacher of English as a foreign language. Into his writing he incorporated borrowings from the vast number of European languages that he had encountered. It seems to me that in his desire to use other cultures and other languages to break open and reveal the contradictions in his own, Joyce is very much the prototype of the post-colonial artist. If we look to *Finnegans Wake* it is no longer appropriate to talk of English language in a world context but of a world literature in an English context. It is at this point that we must remember that English literature is not simply a past, that astonishing body of writing which is the first to record imaginatively those two terrible adventures of capitalism and industrialism, it is also a contemporary body of writing which is above all a literature of decolonization from Joyce and Yeats to Rushdie and Lessing. Whereas for two centuries we exported our language and our customs in hot pursuit of the acquisition of raw materials and fresh markets, we now find that our language and our customs are returned to us but altered so that they can be used by others. And alteration alteration finds so that our own language and culture discover new possibilities, fresh contradictions.

If we understand the current dominance of the English language throughout the world as an opportunity to evangelize English literature, to impose an already existing canon and state, then we shall undertake a task which is both contemptible and futile. If, however, we understand that for the language to live it must begin to find new voices, to articulate different experiences, then we will have a genuine justification for the teaching of literature – the teaching, that is, of imaginative writing. It is when we seriously commit our efforts to encouraging our students to write imaginatively in the English language that they will engage with our literature, seeking in it both models to imitate and repressions to be destroyed. And from the viewpoint of this multicultural, multilectal present, the canon will itself be transformed.

If ethnocentric we must be, it is an ethnocentrism ruined by a dual contradiction: on the one hand, the contradictions historically present within the culture and, on the other, the contradictions produced by the act of teaching in and to another culture, another *ethnos*. It is here that we can locate Rorty's most important insight – that the meeting between cultures is a process of interweaving radically different sets of beliefs. For as cultures truly meet it becomes impossible to tell the teacher from the taught. But no – that is an old lie: the Utopian formulation of a literary intellectual who would forget questions of power. For power there is in the teaching situation and it is not symmetrical. We can always tell the teacher from the taught but in the best of cases they should all be learning.

## Notes

1  Quoted in Geoffrey Moorhouse, *India Britannica*, London: Paladin, 1984, pp. 77–8.

2  Donald Davidson, 'On the Very Idea of a Conceptual Scheme' in *Inquiries into Truth and Interpretation*, Clarendon Press: Oxford, 1984, p. 183.

3  Richard Rorty, 'Solidarité ou objectivité?', *Critique*, December 1983, p. 926.

4  ibid., p. 927.

5  ibid., p. 934.

# Commentator 1

## Nils Erik Enkvist

My task is to fly around the globe in the slipstream of Professor MacCabe, but in five minutes. I should therefore say at once that I found his paper highly stimulating. It mentions certain challenges that English literature, and literature in English, may have to meet. Such challenges have been met before: like many other languages, English too has shown a tremendous potential for responding to new social, scientific and literary requirements on a global scale. And such challenges will no doubt be met in the future.

Of course there is no such thing as a global setting. There are countless non-global settings, many of them very different from one another. And in each setting, the position of English literature may be different. One operationally concrete approach to the study of such positions goes through school and university curricula and syllabuses: they may reveal something of the goals of their designers, and thus about the position, both actual and ideal, of English literature in their particular setting.

The goals can be different, reflecting their settings. I once hosted the Leavises during their British Council tour of Finland and heard Dr Leavis on the goals of English teaching. He had no doubts about what they should be: surely the reason why Finnish students should learn English was to read the classics of the Great Tradition. There are others who have shared the view that the noblest reason for learning a language is to read its literature, which has its own peculiar cultural, ethical and moral values.

But there are curriculum-builders who see things the other way round. To them, literature is part of the language. To caricature this position: if you are to 'know' a language you must cope not only with menus, laundry lists and telephone books, but also with novels, plays and sonnets. Literature is part of language, in more senses than one. And unless you know something of the literature of a language, you do not really 'know' the language.

There are other goals motivating the literary sections of the language curriculum. For instance, English literature can provide a highway to major currents in British and Western history and thought, which our students ought to be familiar with. Yet another approach could be called 'rhetorical' in a wide sense of the term. If you see what others have done with, and to, a language, you can get ideas as to what you yourself could do with, and to, a language. I am here speaking about the ideal kind of rhetoric which inspires people to do new things and not merely to imitate. English literature has inspired new approaches and styles in literatures other than English: it can be a source of innovation in various ethnic and literary contexts. Given the dynamism of today's world, I doubt that the old canons of traditional literary history can retard or stifle aspiring writers in England or anywhere else. English has already proved its importance as a vehicle of literary innovation on a global scale, not least in Africa and Asia.

Such goals are not mutually exclusive. But they may be differently combined and differently weighted in each setting. All the same they all build on one presupposition. They assume that the receptor can interpret a text. Behind the goals problem I have discussed so far, there lies an even more basic problem – the access problem or the problem of interpretability. Interpretability becomes a crucial concept when we look at English literature in a global context.

And what is interpretability? Linguists speak about grammaticality, acceptability and appropriateness, but not, so far as I know, about interpretability (though they have discussed discourse comprehension at great length). Where in fact does the border run between interpretability and non-interpretability?

The best I can do on my own, without once again citing Sapir and Whorf and a host of linguists and philosophers and psychologists, is this: a text is interpretable to those who can build around it a possible world, a universe of discourse in which that text makes sense, a universe in which that text might be true. I say 'might' to include fiction, and suggest you test this definition on potential borderline cases such as modern, syntactically 'deviant' poetry, or science fiction. To repeat: if I am right, you have succeeded in interpreting a text once you have evoked or constructed a world in which that text might be true.

Note that interpretability does not reside in the text as such. The text serves to trigger off a process of interpretation, and this process depends crucially on what the receptor brings to the text. The same text may be interpretable to some people and uninterpretable to others, even if they 'know' the language. And people with different backgrounds and different individual talents and experiences may interpret the same text differently. Sometimes we can specify what prerequisites people will need for certain types of interpretation: to understand technical articles on physics we should know some physics, to respond to styles we must have previous experiences of comparable texts, and so forth. Obviously a text can only be valued if it is interpretable, and interpretation will therefore inevitably affect evaluation.

In a global context we should pay special attention to the influence of different cultural and social and linguistic backgrounds on interpretability and on actual interpretation. Very often, interpretability results from a transfer of concepts from a different cultural or social or linguistic background, which in turn affect the interpretation, sometimes with undesirable and weird results.

If my argument holds good so far, it also suggests some concrete, empirical measures. We should study more systematically the interpretative equipment people from different cultural and social groups bring to their interpretation of certain definite types of discourse. How do their schemata, frames, scripts and scenarios differ? Should we try to develop a new type of study – call it 'contrastive literary semantics' if you like – to answer such questions? And would answering them help us to understand the problems in discussions of the global position of English literature, including those of exposing it to speakers of other languages?

# Commentator 2

## Keith Jones

The main feature of the global context of English literature seems to me to be a healthy pluralism – a plurality of literatures in Englishes, a plurality of critical and interpretative procedures, a plurality of connections perceived and propagated between literature and society and literature and language, a plurality of teaching purposes and procedures, a plurality of readerships and audiences. This is partly a function of ethnocentricity, partly a function of the global *inter*cultural uses of Englishes and partly a consequence of the nature of literary texts. Literary texts are unfinished. They are more like musical scores than legal documents. Their meanings have to be co-produced by readers or auditors. Attempts at tight control of their meaning and use are misplaced. It is all to the good that our British literatures are used as social documents, as cultures or sub-cultures speaking through authors who are only partly aware of the meanings they are making possible, as ways of deepening language mastery, as a means of cultivating sensibilities, as examples or exemplars of moral quests or rhetorical constructs, as raw material for scholarship or performance or translation or the personal history and political persuasion of the reader to transmute. Pluralism is not chaos: it is untidy but it is to be cherished.

But the existence and appreciation of pluralism does not mean one subscribes to a supine relativism. One contributes to pluralism by voting for some of its elements. One I would want to vote for is Professor MacCabe's belief in the centrality of the role of imaginative writing by the student in the teaching of literature. One best learns to read poetry by trying to write it, to appreciate drama by trying to perform it, to enjoy fiction by exploring the narrative mix of revealing and concealing what is going on in a proposed world. English *Studies* as a covering phrase for our concerns worries me a little by its connotations. It can too easily be construed as implying *only* the study of someone else's meanings. Knowing *that* can only be deepened by knowing *how*, and knowing how is a legitimate aim in itself.

In drama the argument for knowing how is fairly obvious. It should embrace however not only stage but also educational radio and TV productions, and where facilities allow, video production. The commitment to perform is a long-term social commitment often requiring three or more months but it can create an English-speaking fellowship for whom a printed text becomes a subtle inward possession, a lived-in crafted world so that foreign word incarnates in local flesh. Beyond performance however is co-operative creation. In Nigeria we worked with local playwrights who wrote, not plays, but improvisation outlines treating a number of contemporary and mythic themes. Students then discussed, improvised, rehearsed and created their own co-operative texts and performed them on stage, radio and TV.

Poetry is perhaps a less obviously social activity but, as initial exercises, chain poems and 'exquisite corpses' provide a non-threatening environment in which group-created initial drafts can appear and the craft of redrafting can be tackled, by a group, with perhaps a single technical constraint – line length, an internal rhyme, the grammatical parallelism of a litany. And spoken performance can follow. Once such processes are under way the use of models with simple rhetorical frames – many of Adrian Henri's poems for example – can be imitated individually. The point is: it is possible, as recent work in Germany at upper secondary school level has shown, to devise a pedagogy that liberates the imagination and increases the constraints of the poetic craft and so increases the appreciation of a poem as a linguistic artefact that calls for imaginative completion.

Fiction presents special problems, length being the most obvious, and time does not allow me to enter into discussion now, but the work that Professor Piepho, other German colleagues and I have been collaborating on, a project called *Story's Way*, indicates one approach to overcoming them.

Knowing how in the poetry, drama and fiction of a foreign or second language is an undervalued activity. I have seen it make very useful contributions at school level. A question I would like to address to Professor MacCabe is – how can its status and practice at university level be increased?

# b)  English literature in a global context

Edwin Thumboo

Approaches to this large, complicated topic are varied, even contradictory. There is a colonial history to contend with, especially in areas where
the force of that history is still valid. There is disquiet about the adoption
of 'western' values and styles and how the tendency is best balanced by a
return to traditional roots. Yet the language is promoted for practical
reasons. We see the genuine desire to comprehend the issues co-existing
with residual prejudices which at times are pre-emptive, patronizing or
dismissive. Consequently, there are ambiguities to resolve and points of
view to reconcile. Nor should the mixed reactions surprise us for the
literature is the most widely read and taught of any, and in sharply dissimilar circumstances and settings. For example, despite strong cultural
and linguistic bonds, students in Britain and America do not relate to it in
precisely the same way. All the more so for those in Zambia, India, Fiji,
the Philippines, Singapore or elsewhere who use English as one of two or
three languages. Cultural-linguistic pluralities make it impossible for
their needs and expectations to be identical, though visiting specialists
have rather surprisingly on occasion thought otherwise.

The study of English literature in its many global settings is beset by
these and other considerations. On the one side are political, educational,
cultural, economic and social policies impinging in a manner some regard
as crucial, others dismiss as irrelevant; on the other, debates about what
organizing principles, scope, methodology and critical stances best
sustain its study. Departments teach and research, presumably according
to how they conceive either is best advanced. But what they offer must in
some sense accord with the requirements and demands of society. Two
sets of questions arise, the first connected with the external, non-
academic assessment of the value of English literature, the second with
what we do, given our societal contexts. Has it any value? Should we not
concentrate on language? What should we teach and how? Would
'English literature' include 'American literature'? Where do we put Pound
and Eliot, Patrick White and V. S. Naipaul? What of Anglo-Scottish,
Anglo-Welsh, Anglo-Irish and Commonwealth literatures? Should we
instead settle for 'literatures in English' which for some time to come
would consist mainly of English literature?

Given the present occasion, it seems best to touch on why we teach English literature, sketch a working background, outline a framework that would cover the study of English literature, then conclude with some reference to pedagogical issues.

The background — seen as such by the outsider, but as foreground by the insider — composed of social, cultural, economic, political, religious, linguistic and aesthetic histories, which include instances and phases of calculated neglect and active suppression, explains why our societies are what they are and why we take a particular tack. However discomforting, our past is precisely that: the past. The present and the future dominate our thoughts and energies. All societies wish for a better age. The Third World which forms a significant part of the global context in which English literature is studied, is compulsive about 'development'. The nations within its broad categories feel deprived by history, observe large gaps between them and the advanced, First World nations. Comprehensive five-year plans are drawn up for the developments necessary to bridge that gap, plans in which integrated educational policies play a key role. The enormity of the concurrent tasks can be gauged from what they often have to take into account: multilingualism, low literacy, chauvinism, tribalism, the growth of national (not regional) loyalty, economic and industrial restructuring and sociocultural development, creating a pool of trained manpower, better transport, housing and health facilities. It is within this scenario that academic disciplines, including ours, are located. They cannot function detached from the processes of nation-building, from a consciousness of what political leaders call 'the basics'. A grasp of the context is vital to an appreciation of why synchronic preoccupations arise out of diachronic awarenesses.

We constantly examine the *raison d'être* of our subject. Unlike the scientist, our answers are ultimately provisional, open to controversy. The burden to come up with justifiable and justifying answers becomes all the greater in this age of the pocket calculator, quick to demand quick results from quick investments of time and money.

The question why we teach English literature lies within a larger one to which I shall return. It is a great literature, with remarkable variety, depth and scope, though obviously it is not the only literature that justifies these large claims. Nor is it the only literature worthy of serious study. But the case is strong, especially as it is in *the* global language in which many countries have a growing stake. It carries almost endless permutations of human experience, offers commentaries on them. We study it but it simultaneously studies us, invigorating and stretching our capacities for analysis and synthesis. Those who enter find a capacious world which maturity will test but not exhaust and which challenges and instructs the imagination and sensibility, augments the power of judgement and discrimination. It is the most contemporary of literatures. No other draws on as extensive and varied a body of twentieth-century experience, a claim put well beyond dispute if we include American, Commonwealth and other new literatures in English. But these reasons may not be enough. A major one remains. We construct our own links between *langue* and *parole*, *competence* and *performance*, *structure* and *event*, thus multiplying ways of discovering, releasing 'meaning potential'. That challenge is unremitting, as we seek to extend our imagination and intellectual reach, rise to the level of our own dreams and those of others.

Let us remind those who need reminding that life and contacts are denotative and connotative. A white butterfly is not a white butterfly and Blake's tiger will always prowl in the imagination, grow as it grows. Literature is concerned with both meanings, in a manner and to a degree that accounts for its special powers of instruction. No other subject encourages the student to proceed in quite the same way. The few who push 'language as communication', important as it is, on to the tertiary level which affects to provide the final, formal training and education to those likely to shape opinion and policy, teach and generally be among the custodians of their society, do serious disservice because by implication they discourage the more subtle, inward possession and use of language. These processes do not end with the three or four years spent with us. If our students successfully develop lively perspectives and analytical tools, ask fruitful questions, are able to marshal their responses and convert them into insights and judgements and have a genuine interest in both texts and the broader literary issues, they have the foundation and the momentum to continue developing and adapting. Such sensibilities have acquired ways of looking at and receiving experience. They do not need to discover parallels between literature and life, or that either should or should not be neater than the other, before coping with the new, the unexpected. We know that has happened when former students say they have made sense of a tutorial remark which seemed obscure at the time, a sense that is now there because *they* have made the connections.

The intrinsic reasons for studying English literature remain but there are new implicit and explicit factors which qualify the contexts for its study. These factors gain sharper focus when discussion is linked to the spread, present global status and role of English. Three broad groupings suggest themselves:

(i)   Native Language (Great Britain, Ireland, the USA, Canada, Australia, New Zealand, South Africa);

(ii)  Second Language (India, Pakistan, Africa, Philippines, Malaysia, Singapore);

(iii) Foreign Language (Japan, China, Russia, West Germany, Saudi Arabia).

The West Indies is a special case: English language continuum but culturally, socially and economically closer to countries in group (ii). Nor have I fully listed the countries that could fall in each of these categories.

Countries in (i) are the bases for English. In the case of Britain and America, they have a certain linguistic standing, authority if you wish, and so provide models for countries in (ii) and (iii), with the latter almost certain of relying perpetually on these models for their English. The linguistic destinies of groups (i) and (iii) promise stability because their native languages are *de facto*, dominant, official or national languages. Perceiving themselves to be officially monolingual, their languages develop in a manner and at a pace broadly evolutionary, reflecting normal tendencies, with perhaps an intensification of British and American influences, the latter especially.

On the other hand, countries in group (ii) which in the past relied on the British model – a major exception being the Philippines – particularly during the colonial period, when the King's English was taught and used, are in a radically different position. With political independence English emerged as *the* second language. Certain changes occurred. From norm-dependent countries they became both norm-dependent and – for themselves at least – norm-creating. We therefore have a range of attitudes as to which English should be the norm and, on the ground, a growing number of varieties. The pressure to indigenize is great, arising from actual practice and, in many instances, despite official disapproval. The desire in some quarters to attain an internationally acceptable standard form is part and parcel of the energies that bring into English local idioms, special usages, etc. At the formal level, the phenomenon is reflected in and extended by the new literatures in English. As a foreign language, English remains an instrument whose function is external. It might cause nightmares. You only dream in it when it has been internalized, turned into a deeply possessed means of expression, a powerful genuinely 'second language' which, in practice, is the first language of many acrolectal users. There comes the nerve to create, to write poetry, drama and fiction. Naturally, the language of the new literatures is often shaped to portray particular communities and societies. The writer has to negotiate between the pressures exerted by the sense of a standard English and those pressures working to localize it. We think of Amos Tutuola's *The Palm-Wine Drinkard* or Gabriel Okara's *The Voice*. These are manifestly extreme examples, but they embody that impulse to re-tool English to give it a local habitation through local roots.

Differences between varieties affect the study of literature, including English literature. Countries in (i) have only the one literature in the one language central to national life. Whatever the combination of texts, English literature is dominant and complemented in varying degrees mainly by American literature (in English) and works by Australian, South African or New Zealand writers. We find a substantial homogeneity, a setting down of boundaries, an insistence on firm divisions. Even when there are links provided by common origins, shared political, philosophical, religious and other systems as in the case with, say, French, German and Italian literature, they are nonetheless studied as foreign literatures, important and influential, but at a definite remove from the national life. They are brought together in Comparative Literature programmes which, unfortunately, seldom cover non-European languages.

Protected from the pressures arising elsewhere in the global context, English literary studies in category (i) countries flourish despite the lament of colleagues in the UK, America and Australia about students lacking seriousness, ignorant of the Bible and Greek mythology, writing poorly, etc. They teach in native language domains, relatively secure in their continuity, free of competition from national or official languages such as Swahili, Tamil, Hindu, Sinhala, Bahasa Malaysia, Tagalog or Mandarin, all requiring substantial, if not equal, time. There is room for ethnic literatures, but these at the moment get attention on principle, not because of their literary weight. Changes in how and what of English literature to study may be thought radical in a category (i) context, but are nowhere near the re-orientations that can occur as when a Department of English Literature becomes a Department of Literature. The philosophical underpinnings are generated from within the discipline; syllabus revisions generally a matter of fine tuning, shifts in emphasis catering for new thematic foci (women's studies would be an example) or specialized courses or new critical theory and practice.

By the same token English literature in group (iii) countries would be seen as a foreign literature, doubtless important, but distinct from the national literature in the native language. Paradoxically, because the literature is in a Foreign, not a Second Language, higher standards and greater sophistication are increasingly achieved through improved English language teaching materials and methods, and academic contact with the native bases.

Although our primary interest is the literature, we cannot overlook the importance of English language as a discipline, particularly if it emphasizes both a knowledge of the language and the development of active linguistic skills. Levels of response to the literature correlate fairly accurately with levels of competence in the language. Apart from failing to serve any purpose, it damages the enterprise if we try teaching Shakespeare or Donne, Joyce or Dylan Thomas, to a student without the necessary command of English. Whether the study of English literature thrives or declines is directly related to the size of the English language base. It has to be broad enough to sustain a significant proportion of *acrolectal* users among the population. Countries in category (ii) had enough acrolectal users under a colonial government which, for practical reasons, created an English-speaking middle class. Many became graduate teachers after following a 'traditional' English literature syllabus. Whether this was suitable is another question, but it did mean that at the time of political independence a sizeable English language capital had accumulated, the currency being the King's English, kept tidy by Nesfield's *Grammar* and *Chambers Dictionary*. Daniel Jones was less successful, but then we were not expected to 'speak *pukka*'. There were no written or spoken varieties, only good or bad English. This stability, ensured by carefully selecting pupils and drilling them hard in grammar, vocabulary, comprehension, etc., virtually guaranteed a steady stream of English literature students.

The position in almost all category (ii) countries changed with political independence. The role of English extended in scope, in function. The vision of a better life made education generally available in most countries, compulsory in some. The rapid expansion in the teaching and use of English, promoted by expediency and rushed rather than planned, caused a decline in standards. The band of *mesolectal* and *basilectal* users grew, gained confidence by using English when they would previously have used a native language. *Acrolectal* users felt compelled to switch registers/codes. Other languages interfered. 'Indigenous' languages (some supported by their own network of schools) that had been hitherto neglected were given official status, pushed hard under a policy of bilingualism. In a situation of linguistic and cultural pluralism, standards invariably declined, with fairly obvious consequences for the study of a literature in a variety that is a standard, metropolitan. The actual situation in each country would require detailed, individual treatment, but these brief statements give some idea of what could and did happen.

Globally then, English literature is studied in three basic contexts closely allied to the three categories thus identified. In the first – native language – it has no direct competition to face; in the third – foreign language – it does not compete directly. In the second, it has competition, and is competing, to a degree that depends on circumstances. English itself rubs verbs and adjectives with the national or official languages. There are the new literatures in English and the literatures in the other official/national languages, some with literary traditions going back four thousand years. The point here is that the study of their literatures, in what are native languages, need not take English literature into account, as the general principles for group (i) apply. However, the group (ii) student of English literature cannot ignore the literatures in his native language, which means a minimum of three in a multilingual society. They are an essential part of his inheritance. The result is a tripartite syllabus comprising English literature (including American literature), new literatures in English (mainly Commonwealth literature) and literatures in native languages. They ought not to compete, and the challenge is how to transmute any sense of competition into complementarity. I have no confident answers. Perhaps there are none and we are left with the constant necessity to refine the syllabuses, searching for a combination more satisfactory than the last, adopting in part a comparative approach. We learn from others engaged in similar tasks but remain fully aware that no one else can do our work. We must work out our own salvation; it will not come from over the hills.

But whatever the calculus we adopt, I am convinced that choosing texts is generally less arduous than has been made out. Whatever the notion of an appropriate literature to suit this or that part of the globe, it seems possible to manoeuvre, to select texts to match interests, to stake out ground without feeling besieged. After all, English literature has an embarrassment of riches, a great tradition augmented in the last hundred years or so, by strong offshoots in the United States, Canada, Australia, South Africa and New Zealand. Moreover, there are the literatures from the West Indies, India, Africa, the Pacific nations – including the Philippines – and, let us not forget, the minorities who write in English in predominantly Anglo-Saxon countries, of whom the blacks in America, the Blacks and Coloureds in South Africa, would be examples. They collectively provide a body of critically acceptable texts whose particular interest is how themes and issues closer to our experience are taken up, how the language gets domesticated. The literature and the literati of the metropolitan centres have moved beyond issues of nation-building, national consciousness, the conflict between 'traditional' and 'modern' ways of life, deracination, the destructiveness of political and moral corruption, the re-interpreting the history and folkways of a people and so forth. Almost all the ex-colonies are facing these issues, which have entered their literature with imagination. Lists would include texts such as Mulk Raj Anand's *Coolie*, Raja Rao's *The Serpent and the Rope*, Wilson Harris's *The Far Journey of Oudin*, V. S. Naipaul's *The Mimic Men*, Wole Soyinka's *The Interpreters*, Nick Joachim's *The Woman with Two Navels*, Lloyd Fernando's *The Scorpion Orchid*, Kamala Markandaya's *The Golden Honeycomb*, Chinua Achebe's *Arrow of God*, Albert Wendt's *The Sons of the Return Home*, Peter Nazareth's *In a Brown Mantle*, Ngugi's *Devil on the Cross*, Vincent Eri's *The Crocodile*, Michael Anthony's *Green Days by the River*, Narayan's *The Guide* and Bessie Head's *A Question of Power*. The list can obviously be extended to include more fiction, and then taken across poetry and drama.

There is an equally impressive list of literary works in the native languages. You can start anywhere, with texts such as the *Upanishads*, the *Bhagavad-gita*, *Romance of the Three Kingdoms*, *The Dream of the Red Chamber*, Lu Shun's short stories, African or Filipino oral epics and praise-songs or Wu Ch'eng-en's *Monkey*. The literary range is tremendous. Arthur Waley, who translated an abridged version of *Monkey* (1942), was of the opinion that it

> is unique in its combination of beauty with absurdity, of profundity with nonsense. Folk-lore, allegory, religion, history, anti-bureaucratic satire, and pure poetry – such are the singularly diverse elements out of which the book is compounded. The bureaucrats of the story are saints in Heaven, and it might be supposed that the satire was directed against religion rather than against bureaucracy. But the idea that the hierarchy in Heaven is a replica of government on earth is an accepted one in China. Here as so often the Chinese let the cat out of the bag, where other countries leave us guessing. It has often enough been put forward as a theory that a people's gods are the replica of its earthly rulers. In most cases the derivation is obscure. But in Chinese popular belief there is no ambiguity. Heaven is simply the whole bureaucratic system transferred bodily to the empyrean.

There are other intriguing possibilities, surely.

A syllabus based on English literature, mainstream texts, with selections from the new literatures in English and translations from appropriate native languages combines the necessary academic challenge and the basis for a strong, rooted, lasting interest. This assumes that we have sufficient time set aside for their proper study, that students are not overloaded, that connections between the work in the three broad areas are made for the student. Only connect. The emphasis on mainstream English literature must remain because we go to it for the best the language has to offer and we will have to for a long time to come. This is one view. You could choose to start with or emphasize literature in native languages, then proceed outwards.

There remains a vexed and complex question of which critical approach or approaches to adopt. Ours is an age with a wealth of critical theory and critical practice, including a quantity of meta-criticism. Teachers feel obliged to keep up. They have to decide how to feed their understanding and perceptions into teaching, within the consensus of a broad approach. This is vital as there is little more damaging than the havoc wrought by fundamental disagreements which turn acrimonious, splitting departments into camps, and worse, confusing the students. There is room for disagreements, but only if the critical positions they represent are discussed in the more advanced courses, where they should have the wherewithal to judge for themselves. There should be disagreement in order to provide the dialectics without which the subject stagnates. One way of resolving matters is to bring each approach to bear on a text or a series of texts, to test the degree of its usefulness and therefore its ultimate validity. A play, a poem or a novel could be examined and interpreted from a formalist, structuralist, deconstructionist, sociological or other point of view, and the procedures and conclusions compared with those deriving from a pluralist approach, to which the whole undertaking could lead. For it is through our engagement with a specific text that we discover the usefulness and limitations of a particular critical procedure and its underlying assumptions. This is time-consuming and possibly unwieldy but, if undertaken judiciously, the exercise can prove invaluable.

To assert that literature is language is to state only the obvious. But it does stress, and keeps in view, the importance of language in the study of literature. The application of linguistic concepts can only be useful. But as in the case of critical concepts they have to be applied with discrimination and sensitivity. They ought to add substantially to our understanding of literature by throwing light on how language works, on how it behaves and misbehaves. All this ought not to, but does occasionally, prove disagreeable to the more orthodox advocates of 'practical criticism'. Linguistic concepts have added certain kinds of precision to the analysis of texts, a precision that consists in part of how certain effects are explained more specifically, of identifying specific features of the language and how these features work. Literature cannot be considered comprehensively unless we seek to examine the language it uses, any more than the advanced study of that language can be undertaken away from its literature.

Recent major developments in criticism apply insights garnered from disciplines such as anthropology, sociology, politics, linguistics and linguistic philosophy. New literary ideologies, each with their own insistent assumptions and procedures, have emerged. Whereas literature grows slowly, new critical approaches assume a retrospective force, move back in literary time to reassess what proves congenial to them. Shakespeare has been visited by at least one structuralist with real benefit to the understanding of his plays. To the degree that it is innovative and detailed, work at the frontiers of a subject is never easy to relate to the centre, to the core activity. Moreover, the energies of new theories, new lines of enquiry are generally missionary. They are assertive and rejecting of others that held the stage before them. Their reception is not always comfortable. There is the possibility of mistaking the transient for the permanent. Theories come, make their contribution, then go. But it is the literature that remains. This is why it is the understanding of the individual text or a group of texts, taken to the highest possible point, which remains paramount. That is the primary activity, the one certainty in the midst of conflict, doubts and so forth, caused by differences and disagreements between proponents of particular theories and doctrines. State-of-the-art criticism may prove attractive as a serious intellectual undertaking but it must, in a very basic sense, return to the fundamentals of literary studies, whether in English or the national languages.

# Commentator 1

Alan Davies

I enjoyed reading Professor Thumboo's wide ranging and non-limiting view of literature and of approaches to literature, incorporating new literary theories as well as linguistic concepts, extending English literature on the one hand into English as a Second Language/Literature, and on the other hand into the literatures of indigenous languages. I also appreciated the importance he gives to literary value, the way in which literature can provide denotative as well as connotative meanings. Professor Thumboo argues that 'the writer has to negotiate between the processes exerted by the sense of a standard English and those pressures working to localize it'. What has always been interesting about the anglophone writers is that they have appeared to find less interest in their own cultural/linguistic alienation, little trace of the *négritude* of Césaire and Senghor, that insistence on the despair of black writers forced to write in French because the French language had alienated them from their own culture. Soyinka's caustic 'does a tiger proclaim its own tigritude?' was sufficient put-down of that possibility.

Professor Thumboo raises the interesting question, not for the first time, of the status of Amos Tutuola's *The Palm Wine Drinkard*, which is either a brilliant (though not followed up) example of profound literary meaning being conveyed in non-standard English or a spoof of some kind which we value because James Kirkup worked on it, a confidence trick full of linguistic error which we would certainly identify if it had not been published by Faber & Faber. *The Palm Wine Drinkard* reminds us that in normative contexts such as publishing and education we need clarity about standards, we cannot leave them to the individual. The standards issue thus becomes which standards to require – ENL, ESL, EFL. This then changes into the pragmatic question of definition.

An example of Professor Thumboo's group (ii), ESL countries, is Tanzania. In group (ii) countries, he tells us, 'standards [have] invariably declined, with fairly obvious consequences for the study of a literature in a variety that is a standard, metropolitan'. The results of a survey in ELT in Tanzania indicate that very few first-year university students are able to read even the simplest of texts required by their academic studies. The great majority of students need simplified texts. It may be that English literature students are all among the few skilled readers but even they will find difficulty with authentic literary texts, especially contemporary texts. It should be noted that in the case of Tanzania the decline in English is no doubt related to the national policy of Swahilization over the last twenty years. Professor Thumboo's view of literature students is over-optimistic:

'If our students successfully develop lively perspectives and analytical tools, ask fruitful questions, are able to marshal their responses and convert them into insights and judgements and have a genuine interest in both texts and the broader literary issues, they have the foundation and the momentum to continue developing and adapting.' It is doubtful whether even ENL literature students can achieve that foundation and momentum.

And so I pose a question: throughout Professor Thumboo's paper one detects a kind of lip service to language, which is certainly regarded as necessary but always as a handmaiden to literature:

> 'the language is promoted for practical reasons'
> 'The few who push language as communication . . .do serious disservice'
> 'we go to it [literature] for the best the language has to offer'
> 'literature cannot be considered comprehensively unless we seek to examine the language it uses, any more than the advanced study of that language can be undertaken away from its literature'

I agree with the first verse of that last quote but for the second, as Falstaff said to Prince Hal: 'I deny your major'. The argument Professor Thumboo adduces is that we are in a remedial situation; that is why we must pay so much attention to language. We are plugging the linguistic holes; we are not seriously interested in the language. My question then is: is it necessarily the case in group (ii) ESL countries that the advanced study of the English language cannot be undertaken away from its literature? I recognize that in the absence of the remedial problems of the group (ii) kind (avoiding the issue of to what extent L1 remedial problems are the same as those of group (ii), thereby opening up the question of the status of the L1), we are near or into an L1 situation. But my question is not addressed to that situation; it is a question for the ESL and the EFL situations in which, of course, English literature can be one of the few communicative inputs. Is it the only one and is it the best? In other words, can the advanced study of the English language in ESL countries be carried out away from English literature?

Professor Thumboo does seem to be denying that even descriptive linguistic studies of English can stand alone: they need literature as well in order to study English properly (' . . . any more than the advanced study of the language can be undertaken away from its literature'). That seems to me an untenable position. But there is the further issue of content versus skills. It is language skills studies, not literature and not descriptive linguistics, that fail to achieve high academic status. This is just as much the case in French, German, or Spanish university studies as it is in English. It is as though language needs to have content, if not literature then linguistics or life, culture or institutions. University English as generally taught is thought to need definition as a content-based rather than a skills-based subject. So I repeat my question: can the advanced study of the English in ESL and EFL countries be carried out away from English literature?

# Commentator 2

## Ramón López-Ortega

Underlying Professor Thumboo's presentation is the idea of the multi-cultural character of the new literatures written in English, and this gives one the opportunity of adding a marginal note on the complex relationship between language and culture, and the way it might affect their future development.

It is evident that these literatures spring from different cultural settings, having in common the important fact that they are written in English, in one or another of its social or geographical varieties. It is also obvious that sharing the same language facilitates cross-cultural dialogue when the culture of the writer and that of his or her reading public are not too distant from one another. But when the distance is greater, the communication barriers are not so easily overcome, because culture and meaning, and hence language, are intrinsically related – in fact, in some way, they presuppose each other. Indeed, each meaning system is *originally* one interpretation of the universe, one analysis of experience and, as such, the basis of a culture.

Each meaning system segments and organizes the world in a distinct way, and therefore such concepts as 'world view', 'way of life', or even 'ideology' are not ultimately alien to the nature of language. This property of meaning makes one wonder whether the varieties of English in some of the literatures referred to are not in danger of deviating from the commonly intelligible norms so markedly as to become unrecognizable. One can already detect symptoms of this deep deviation in, for example, the literary discourse of some African and Asian writers, in which metaphor, image and symbol are so deeply rooted in the autochthonous culture that English often seems to be reduced to a surface structure bereft of meaning, or rather, to something barely intelligible without an awareness on the part of the reader of the semantic clues of the author's culture. In the last analysis, the content or substance of the linguistic sign – namely, the signified – tends to be conditioned by a specific mode of social organization, by the economic needs, values and preferences of a speech community. These values and preferences, in turn, often determine the choice of the assembly of metaphors which constitute a language. In other words, no natural language – and English is no exception, in spite of its special status – is ever a *completely* transparent or passive vehicle; and, of course, this is also true of literary registers.

The above considerations raise an important question concerning the new status of English as international literary currency: will English assimilate the enormous cultural flux of these new literatures, and so increase its metaphoric and expressive potential? Or, on the contrary, will it be overwhelmed by this powerful stream, and prove unable to integrate the new literary voices from these distant and distinct cultures?

# Theme II   Summary of discussion

Whereas there were reservations in the previous sessions about encouraging the emergence of local forms of English language, there seemed to be few comparable misgivings about the emergence of local works of English literature. These were broadly accorded recognition. It was indeed generally accepted that the Conference must take as its legitimate concern not only the traditional canon of English literature but literatures in English whatever their provenance. There was a widespread assumption in the discussion that literature had a special status as the expression of the sociocultural values, attitudes and aspirations of individual societies and had particular importance therefore in establishing a sense of national identity especially in the ex-colonial countries of the Third World. It was pointed out, however, that such a function was not confined to literature but was realized also through the conventional use of language in everyday social interaction. There was some doubt about whether, therefore, it was possible or desirable to distinguish literature sharply from these other uses of language in this respect.

There were doubts expressed also on thinking of literature too exclusively as the vehicle for particular sociocultural values, on the grounds that this could lead to a neglect, or even a denial, of the essentially aesthetic character of literature, and tend to reduce it to data for pragmatic analysis or to a source of cultural information. It could be argued that it is this aesthetic quality of literature which provides for the expression of universal significance beyond the confines of particular literatures or cultures, so that if literary works were so closely associated with particular cultural values that they depended on special background knowledge for their interpretation, then their significance would be only locally accessible and their aesthetic values accordingly diminished.

The relationship between literature and culture was, therefore, seen to be problematic. So was the relationship between literature and language. A lack of linguistic knowledge would also, of course, impede access to literary meaning, so the question arose as to how much language proficiency was needed as a pre-condition for literary interpretation. It was argued that literary interpretation operates at different levels and that it was possible to derive benefit from a literary work and grasp something of its significance without a comprehensive understanding of its language. There was no necessary direct correspondence between literary appreciation and language proficiency. Furthermore, language proficiency could be developed as a function of literary interpretation. Consistent with this line of argument was the view that literature might best be regarded not as a set of artistic products, of linguistic or cultural artefacts, but as the means for encouraging a range of responses and for stimulating a process of variable interpretation.

As with the preceding sessions on the English language, the issues that were debated in these discussions seem to arise from the need to reconcile the apparently conflicting claims of universality and particularity, of intranational and international values. If the aesthetic nature of literature is to be respected then it must free itself of absolute linguistic or cultural dependency and be capable of cross-cultural appeal, but this must somehow be achieved by representing a particular perspective of reality which would otherwise be of only limited local relevance and interest.

# THEME III INFORMATION AND EDUCATIONAL TECHNOLOGY

## a) Making IT available

Peter Roe

## I Introduction

In the beginning there was teacher voice, the perfect synthesizer. This is still the original and greatest of all the language teacher's media – it can demonstrate, inform, motivate, amuse . . . it is (normally) totally under teacher control, and responds sensitively to the use of creativity and imagination. It even responds directly to the teacher's thoughts. And how effective is it in language teaching? The answer, alas, depends not so much on the voice itself as on the teacher's teaching strategy and the learning opportunities provided. In my view, teacher voice remains the greatest single medium available in the whole field of Foreign Language Teaching (FLT), but all too often the most despised, the most rejected, and the most abused. It is a miracle of information technology which is sadly under-exploited, and possibly in danger of even greater eclipse by the bright lights of the new media.

After 'talk' came 'talk and chalk', with all its ramifications – text editors (stick on sand, stylus on wax, chalk on board, print on paper), graphics displays (coloured chalk drawings, felt-boards, wall charts) all accompanied by the same teacher voice. But if IT could be seen as in some way enhancing good teaching, could it alone turn a bad lesson into a good one? Or does IT fundamentally alter the very nature of the learning process?

Next came two major developments: potted voice and animated chalk – sound, cine and video recording. This was truly a great leap forward in the development of IT, allowing a vast range of new referents for person, time and place. It provided the opportunity to do all that had been done before, only better, and made it possible to break down the barrier between the classroom and the outside world. But in the case of the tape-recorder something went wrong. Like the giraffe (or the white elephant) its genetic development produced a species too dependent on a transitory ecological niche (theory and methodology of the 1960s?). If only we could put the clock back and design a use for the tape-recorder, knowing what we know now, we would surely not invent the language laboratory or today's common denominator of audio-visual dogma. But perhaps each new development which IT produces genetically fixes some current orthodoxy from which it can henceforth neither retreat nor progress.

Today we are faced with the chance either to get things right this time, or to make a more pernicious blunder than ever before. Computer-Assisted Language Learning is still in its infancy. In spite of an impressive bibliography on the subject, it is still very much an embryonic science, or perhaps rather an armchair philosophy, since what we think we know about it has not been subjected to long-term trial in the classroom at any level of pedagogic sophistication, although such projects as PLATO are clearly technically sophisticated. Even conventional video cannot be said to have been truly put to the test and will soon be eclipsed by computer-controlled video disc while video cassettes are still in their infancy.

In one sense IT has never changed. It is still basically all about talk and chalk. It mediates voice, text and graphics. The quality and speed have improved enormously, but the essential nature of this mediation has remained the same. Yet two powerful changes are currently taking place, one technological, one methodological, and these could combine to 'fix' language learning for a long time to come and in a restrictive, ineffectual mould, if we are not careful. Both concern pupil power. Technologically, it is no longer the teacher who holds the chalk; it is the learner who henceforth will have his fingers on the keyboard of power. And methodologically the emphasis is passing rapidly from teacher to learner. True the teacher *can* still retain keyboard control, and use the computer as just another teacher-dominated resource, or as a self-access supplement to grammar/translation drills. But that would be to miss the whole point of the new dimension in IT, i.e. the fact that a machine can act as a negotiation partner. Moves and speech acts formerly the prerogative of the teacher can now be initiated mechanically in such a way that given sufficiently sophisticated software, learners can be made to forget that their interlocutors are not made of flesh and blood. The machine becomes a surrogate interactive teacher (a 'knower' who can set tasks, act as a work of reference, correct factual or morphosyntactic error, or spelling, in a non-threatening way, monitor progress, avoid unplanned repetition, respond to student initiatives during the solution of a convergent problem, etc.), freeing the real teacher for higher level tasks (see below). Perhaps the genetic freak of the future in foreign language teaching will be the take-home, computer-controlled hi-fi laser-disc total language learning package.

These developments are threatening the very foundations of our assumptions about the nature of language learning. The notion of 'classroom' could, at least in theory, become irrelevant. If the learner can have regular access to a teacher by videophone (cf. the use already made of the telephone) may not the conventional classroom come to be regarded as a stone-age monstrosity? But that raises the question 'Who is my teacher?'

If the learner has the option of calling up an officially assigned 'teacher', or the au-pair down the road, or a 'video friend' in a neighbouring country, he or she may well opt for the choice that proved most rewarding last time.

Objection: 'But the au-pair and the video pal are untrained. They don't know how to teach. No learning will take place.' However, the force of this objection depends very much on what it is the learner wishes to learn, or is required to learn. It is possible so to formulate the learning objectives that the place of the institutional teacher is assured (e.g. by building in a requirement for arcane theoretical information or by establishing criteria of evaluation which the learner is unable to apply). But it is also perfectly possible to establish performance objectives which require neither theoretical statements nor any criteria of evaluation other than a successful outcome, transparent to any learner.

Objection: 'But the learners will flounder in a sea of the unknown. They will not be able to establish a learning curve or to place themselves on it.' Well then, someone must do it for them. Unfortunately, however, the kind of programme necessary for this purpose would have to be radically different from those underlying current classroom textbooks. They, after all, are mainly produced with an institutional teacher in mind. And almost all self-study books of which I am aware take conventional courses as their underlying model.[1] Provided the series of learning tasks is sufficiently palatable and finely graded, preferably with a considerable element of choice of task for the learners, it should be possible to equip them with a guided programme designed for computer-controlled video disc and naïve native-speaker informant, and perhaps supplementary reading material.

This paper is not the appropriate place for me to attempt to specify a new alternative strategy for language teaching/learning;[2] I would only stress that over the next decade or so we risk seeing all the power and glory of space-age technology being harnessed to an antediluvian approach to language teaching[3] unless there are fundamental changes on three related fronts.

1  The stated goals of language teaching will have to be formulated in much more pragmatic, performance-related terms than the platitudes and lists so common today outside a modest number of centres of excellence.
2  Our systems for evaluation and certification will have to adapt themselves accordingly.
3  Our notion of appropriate methodology will likewise have to undergo radical transformation.[4]

Otherwise the effect of space-age technology will be to 'fix' archaic methodological assumptions and procedures, a more glorious packing for the same old talk and chalk.

Nor do I propose here to explore further the technical innovations which are already in the pipeline. This has been ably done by my colleague, Martin Phillips.[5] I would only:

1 stress that we are merely on the threshold of the IT revolution. We need to be ready to respond rapidly and meaningfully to each innovation. What will happen to books, paper, handwriting, classrooms, teachers . . . ?
2 add a sober note of caution. What about the poorer countries of the world? It may be that international political muscle will in future be linked to a lead in VLSI (very large scale integration) and fifth-generation computers. It may be that second-tier nations will be dominated by those who have mastered software applications for other people's hardware. But those who can afford neither the hardware nor the software that others are producing are faced with the prospect of seeing the gap (information, trade, wealth) between them and the rest widen at an alarming rate. I have seen sad cases of expensive advanced hardware unusable for lack of spares, maintenance or expertise. Can educationists keep its cost down without sacrificing increased efficiency?

Instead I should like to sketch what I consider to be the minimal set of methodological foundations which should underpin *any* elaborated methodology, a set of questions which the methodologist should always be able to answer. The criteria I offer could be applied, with suitable emendation, to very basic or very sophisticated learning environments. But for present purposes I shall assume the existence of a class, a class-room, a teacher and a network of interconnected screens and computer keyboards all able to access the same set of files and programs and to create new files as necessary. The hardware may be enhanced by audio and/or video cassette or laser disc, but this enhancement is not assumed. No assumptions about classroom procedures are made other than that the learners use both keyboard and screen during the learning process.

## II  Methodological foundations

The five questions I raise in this section all relate to what I call a 'pedagogic segment'. This may be a lesson, or part of a lesson, or a series of linked lessons – e.g. a project. It might, in a conventional lesson, be a dictation, a spelling test, a 'mingle', a simulation, putting on a one-act play, etc. It is intended as a coherent unit in both pedagogic and discourse terms.

I can now turn to the first of the questions we can use to test the methodological foundations of any language learning programme. For any given pedagogic segment ask: 'For what level of learner ambition is it intended to cater?' By level of learner ambition I mean the outcome of the language learning programme (or lesson or lesson segment) to which the learner aspires. Varying degrees of delicacy are possible, but I find the following six sufficient for most cases:

1 *Knowledge objectives*: the learner wishes to acquire information about the L2, and a greater understanding (whether conscious or unconscious) of its underlying system.
2 *Citation objectives*: the learner wishes to acquire skill in manipulating segments of the language to produce larger stretches of discourse. (Criteria of evaluation: syntax, morphology, lexis, spelling, pronunciation.)
3 *Comprehension objectives*: the learner wishes to be able to extract data (explicit or implicit) from spoken or written text. (Criterion: has he/she got the facts right?)[6]
4 *Performance objectives 1–1*: the learner wishes to be able to negotiate successful outcomes with another person. (Criterion: successful outcome.)
5 *Performance objectives 1–many*: the learner wishes to work efficiently as a member of an L2 group of more than two members. (Criterion: acceptance/tolerance, contribution to group performance?)
6 *Performance objectives many–many*: the learner wishes to function constructively as a member of a group which in turn negotiates with other groups. (Criterion: effective contribution to the success of the group?)


Some observations on the above set of levels:

1 Successful performance at level 6 presupposes success at level 5, which in turn presupposes success at level 4, and so on.
2 Failure at any one level may be related to the criteria of evaluation at that level or at any lower level.
3 It may be that the best road to success at level n may be to attempt level n + 1 or higher.[7] Learning can take place at any or all of levels n and below. The teaching programme can (and perhaps should) be planned for skill enhancement at all operative levels, although it may be wise to restrict new learning barriers to one or at most two levels.
4 The function of the teacher and the geometry and social structure of the learning environment are necessarily different at different levels.
5 Discourse structure will naturally differ, often radically, from one level to another.

6 The function of the computer or any other IT in the learning environment must *ipso facto* differ from level to level.

7 By far the majority of teachers I have spoken to seldom operate beyond level 2.[8]

8 The level at which a class is working is determined not by the teacher's methodological persuasion, but by the level of the criteria of teacher 'correction', irrespective of how delicately this may be handled.

9 Functions can be practised only at levels 4 and above, although they can be discussed at level 1, illustrated at level 2 and appreciated in context at level 3. Much 'functional' teaching, in my experience, does not rise above level 3.

Now one cannot *prescribe* an answer to the question about the level of learner ambition for which the pedagogic segment is appropriate. But one may be able to infer something from the response, e.g.:

1 The matter was not considered when the segment was constructed.

2 The segment turns out to be wasteful in that it focuses on one level without any spin-off at lower levels.

3 The anticipated level of learner ambition does not match that of the actual learner to whom it is being administered.

The second question concerns the communication network and man/machine interface in the learning environment. There is no limit in practice to the possible layouts, but most of them can be reduced to one of a limited set of basic options involving the learner (L), a hardware unit consisting of at least a keyboard and screen (S), and a linking communication channel $\longleftrightarrow$ .[9] I distinguish the following:

1 *One-to-one*: each learner interacts with his/her own private screen and keyboard;

viz. $\boxed{\text{S}} \longleftrightarrow \text{L}$

2 *Competitive pairs*: two learners, acting as competitors, interact with one screen and keyboard;

viz. $\text{L} \longleftrightarrow \boxed{\text{S}} \longleftrightarrow \text{L}$

3  *Collaborative pairs*: two learners, acting in collaboration, interact with one screen and keyboard, and with one another;

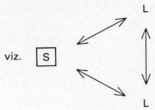

4  *Single group*: where a group of three (or more) learners collaborate to interact with one screen and keyboard, and with one another;

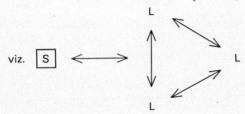

5  *Multiple groups*: as for network 4, but group further communicates with group, in competition or in collaboration, through the computer network;

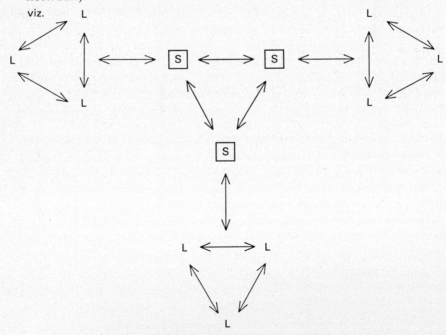

or with direct group/group contact.

The question to be asked is this: 'To what extent does the communication network match the level of learner ambition envisaged by the pedagogic segment?' Clearly, network 5 is appropriate only for level 6, network 4 for level 5 and network 3 for level 4. But either network 1 or 2 can be chosen for any of levels 1, 2 or 3.

The third question concerns the extent to which what the learner is asked to do (the activity, task etc.) is appropriate to the chosen level and network.

For level 6, one might choose a simulation based on e.g. *Telemark*,[10] where factories are established to build and market television sets. Real roles or functions can be allocated to the members of each team, who together constitute a company. One of their functions would be to negotiate trade agreements (à la *Diplomacy*) with competitors, as well as discharging duties allocated within the company. Primary focuses could include negotiating the holding of a meeting with competitors, plus any of the lower focuses listed below.

At level 5, one might use the same set-up without the inter-group negotiation. One primary focus might be holding a trade agreement meeting.

At level 4, each group of students could work in collaboration to agree decisions calculated to outwit competitors. There might be a specific focus on e.g.:

1 negotiating agreement on company decisions;
2 rapid reading and skimming skills (background information on changing market trends, only some of which is relevant).

For the lower levels of ambition, simulation exercises are obviously less appropriate, although one could easily include target lexical or structural items for introduction during an audio or written (screen or paper) input stage and exploitation during subsequent interaction stages. But for levels 2 and 3 one might choose something like *Storyboard* or *Storyline*.[11] Here, at level 2, a text could be chosen for its frequent inclusion of a specific structural item, or, at a level 3 focus, for its wealth of opportunities for inferential reasoning. *Storyboard* is essentially a level 3 task with abundant spin-off for levels 1 and 2, but *Storyline* is designed to operate at higher levels, e.g. level 5, where one might arrange for each group to work to produce its own story, which then forms the input text for a *Storyboard* exercise by another group. So the third question is: 'To what extent is there a match between what the learners are asked to do during the pedagogic segment in question, on the one hand, and the communication network at their disposal on the other?'

My fourth question is concerned with whether the part of the learning package which we are looking at is flexible and adaptable to learner wants and needs. To what extent can the teacher or programme organizer change the variables, e.g.:

1  make the text handled by the machine easier or more advanced?
2  eliminate culturally unacceptable references in the software?
3  vary the morphosyntactics of a text in the computer in order to introduce or reinforce a certain item?
4  vary a task to enable learners to collaborate rather than compete?
5  change a game where a factory makes television sets to a workshop which assembles bicycles?
6  allow the learners to alter the variables for themselves?

I see little future (at least as a teaching aid) for programs which are not subject to editing by the teacher. Even the most exciting game of bridge would pall if played again and again with identical hands of cards.

My fifth question (and the last I propose to ask here) is: 'Does it work?' That is, after the learners have done what is asked of them are they any better for it? Was the improvement the one intended? This is an empirical matter to which I shall return briefly in the next section. But until this question is answered, one cannot know for sure whether an IT learning package is worthwhile.

To sum up: we need to get our methodology on a sound footing before we rush into Computer-Assisted Language Learning (or any other programme based on advanced technology). Yet already research students are appearing, claiming that they are evaluating CALL. But CALL does not exist! It is at best embryonic. Evaluating CALL at this stage is like evaluating the flying ability of an unhatched, unidentified egg. Evaluating an item of current software is like evaluating a single lesson torn from an unknown book. Instead of accepting current software as established CALL, so that it becomes 'fixed' as an unchallenging benchmark whereby the mediocre appears good, we must first specify what we want CALL, or any other IT facility, to do, and then see whether we can design software appropriate to our needs. We must make a crucial distinction between:

1  the underlying pedagogy of what is being evaluated (i.e. irrespective of the media used), and
2  the effectiveness of the media used to mediate all or part of the learning package.

Otherwise we run the risk of CALL being seen as synonymous with trivial software, and we lose the baby with the bathwater.

We would do better to exercise caution (not reluctance) in making IT too readily available in the language classroom. If we act too precipitately, we run the risk of alienating both teachers and learners. Already the positive motivating power of the computer is waning in some areas, and could become a negative force. Students used to high quality video in their homes are becoming more and more critical of the imperfect products often seen in the classroom. Soon computers will be equally commonplace, the novelty effect will wear off, and unimpressive hardware and software may some day, if we are not careful, make us wish we had never hung the electronic millstone round our necks. But in some sense at least, electronic aids are clearly useful. For example, the teacher cannot possibly:

1  handle all the data feedback points required for level 6;
2  match the computer for speed and accuracy of response on factual matters or in keeping track of developments in a simulation;
3  provide accurate instantaneous feedback in response to a student input at whatever level is required, and simultaneously for all available keyboard positions.

IT will undoubtedly prove a powerful force for change in the language classroom. It remains to be seen whether we, the teachers, will be its unhappy slaves or its benevolent masters.

I now turn to a consideration of what the British Council is doing to help make IT available.

## III  IT and the British Council

By its Royal Charter, the British Council is called upon to promote cultural, educational and technical co-operation between Britain and other countries. This involves, among other things, making Britain, its culture, its language and its literature better known overseas. One of the ways in which it seeks to do this is through its direct teaching operations,[12] which are arranged through Headquarters to enhance the image of Britain and the British Council overseas by setting high standards of excellence. This 'shop window' function means that the Council cannot afford to be out of date; it must remain well up in the forefront of beneficial innovations in methodology and IT.

The driving force for such innovation comes of course from the large body of teachers working in the DTEOs. But being so thinly spread out across the world,[13] they cannot afford to maintain a satisfactory research and development unit in each centre. They must look to a central unit to carry the necessary R & D overhead, a task currently allocated to the English Language Services Department (ELSD) in London.

But even in its London headquarters the Council is not geared to supplying all the services demanded by a significant R & D programme. It is not in a position to maintain a full professional cadre of hardware developers, software programmers, pioneering applied linguists or publishing and distribution specialists – nor indeed would it wish to. For such services the Council looks to other organizations in the public and private sectors, e.g.:

1  to Acorn International, for generous hardware support for the CALL project;
2  to the Universities (e.g. of Edinburgh and Lancaster) for developments in testing and evaluation;
3  to the Universities (e.g. of Birmingham and Lancaster) for advances in the construction and exploitation of linguistic databases;
4  to the BBC for many collaborative ventures, notably the current archives project;
5  to British ELT publishing houses (e.g. Macmillan in the case of the Video English project, Pergamon for publishing our *ELT Documents*, etc.);
6  to schools in the private sector (like Bell and Eurocentre) for assistance in the fields of CALL and materials accessioning systems.

The staff of ELSD, with their modest resources, are faced with the task of acting as orchestrators and co-ordinators, linking the creative drive of the teachers overseas and the impressive resources of the ELT and education industries in Britain. They are facilitators, necessary links in the collaborative chain which serves to make IT available to our schools overseas, and to the ELT profession as a whole. Current work includes:

1  the ambitious Video English project mentioned above, developed principally by Mike Potter and Chris Bury;
2  the BBC Archives Project. The pilot stage, managed mainly by Clive Holes and Tony O'Brien and tried out by numerous colleges overseas, is now complete. Development work on the main project is increasingly being undertaken overseas, particularly by Jane Willis in Singapore;
3  the Teacher Training Video Project, developed mainly by Bob Neilson and Tony O'Brien, now complete;
4  the Computer-Assisted Language Learning (CALL) project, developed and managed by Martin Phillips. Of this I shall say more below;
5  a video project being developed by Elizabeth Moloney and Sarah Barry, designed to link literary texts and language teaching. This follows the pioneering work of Keith Jones in Germany with his *Story's Way* materials;
6  a Computer-Based English Language Testing (CBELT) project currently in its early stages of development by Peter Hargreaves, Terry Toney and Martin Phillips in ELSD and Mike Milanovic in Hong Kong;
7  the Video on the Oral Testing of English (VOTES) produced by Clive Bruton.

All of these projects have involved collaboration on a wide scale, particularly with colleagues overseas. The CALL project, for example, was set up following consultations with the Council's English Teaching Advisory Committee, overseas representations, the Department of Trade and Industry and many bodies already engaged in work involving computers in education. With generous assistance from Acorn International a network of six work-stations was set up in the DTEO, in Abu Dhabi, Barcelona, Hong Kong, Madrid, Munich and Singapore. The number of other centres participating in the project or actively following developments grows by the month, and interest is widespread. We are now at a stage where we can point to an up-and-running project investigating the potential of CALL in the classroom in a wide variety of environments, with a set of programs already produced and many more on the drawing board, all developed in the context of a well-thought-out methodological framework. Even at the present modest level of development, we would claim to have at least some coverage of all the levels of ambition and all the networks mentioned earlier, to have developed tasks appropriate to most levels of network pairings that provide simultaneous training at more than one level or focus, with the possibility of the language used, and other task parameters, being easily varied by the teacher. We have not yet answered by fifth question, but at least we are in the process of asking it.

The next phase of development is to make IT (in the form of the fruits of the CALL project) available to a wider public (both within the Council and outside). To do this, however, we shall once again turn to the private sector, possibly a publishing house with world-wide access to the foreign language teaching profession. And I need hardly point out that where one can 'author' the materials by substituting one English sentence, phrase or caption for another, one can just as easily substitute a foreign language with a roman script and even, though less easily, other languages.[14]

To sum up: IT must be our slave. We must summon it whenever there is a job for it to do, never because of our fascination for it. Its tasks must be generated by our methodology, although (caution!) we must allow our methodological imaginations to be stimulated by it. We need to realize that IT is still in its (Herculean) infancy, and that we may have to discard many a cherished preconception before it has finished growing.

## Notes

1  H. H. von Hofe, *Im Wandel der Jahre: ein deutsches Lesebuch für Anfänger*, Holt, Rinehart & Winston, 1955, is one of a number of interesting exceptions, which could form the basis for an (albeit unsophisticated) teacher-free, task-based, limited-objective computer program.

2  There are already plenty of seekers after alternative strategies. See, e.g. 'Humanistic Approaches: an Empirical View', *ELT Documents*, 113, The British Council, 1982, and 'Approaches, Methodik, Enseignement', Triangle 2, Goethe Institut, British Council, AUPELF, 1982.

3  In spite of so much excellent theory and practice in modern ELT, it leaves a large proportion of classrooms, particularly in national education systems, relatively untouched. And much of the software available for computer-assisted foreign language teaching reflects a conventional grammar/translation approach.

4  Unfortunately, encouraging developments such as the British Council's 'banding system' (see *English Language Testing Service: An Introduction*, British Council, and the related test report form) as far as testing and evaluation are concerned, or the Graded Objectives Movement (see A. Harding *et al.*, *Graded Objectives in Modern Languages*, CILT, 1980; revised reprint, 1982) for pedagogic innovation in the classroom, do not seem to have shaken the foundations of conventional classroom practice. Some of the possible lines along which such transformation might take place are discussed in the second part of this paper.

5  See Martin Phillips, 'Educational Technology in the Next Decade: An ELT Perspective', British Council, 1984, to be published in *ELT Documents*.

6  This level encompasses the traditional four skills: reading and listening followed by regurgitation in speech or writing.

7  cf. S. Krashen *passim*, e.g. from *Second Language Acquisition and Second Language Learning*, Pergamon, 1981: 'the major function of the second language classroom is to provide intake for acquisition' (p. 101). His i + n (p. 127), however, refers to structures. My n + i refers to levels of focus or learner ambition.

8  This applies more to state schools than to private language schools, but most teachers will admit to creating in the minds of their pupils the expectation of being corrected for one or more of: morphology, syntax, pronunciation, spelling or choice of vocabulary, and a consequent mental set to avoid errors of these types. Any communicative goal can, for them, fade into insignificance. The learner's ambition is reduced to that of getting his grammar etc. right. The student's current level of ambition is in reality determined not by his 'world picture', or the use he/she may wish to make of the language, if any, but by the level of the teacher's (or computer's) correction, no matter how subtly or humanely that correction may be administered.

9  In what follows, the interesting question arises as to whether we should not in each case replace (S) by (T) for Teacher. There are two kinds of justification for not doing so: (a) because one would need several teachers in the classroom, and (b) because the activity is pedagogically desirable, but no teacher is capable of doing what the computer is required to do.

10  Published in A. J. Reeve's, *Business Games*, Acornsoft, 1982, *Stokmark* and *Telemark* are simulations not designed for the foreign language market, but adaptable for that purpose. *Stokmark* (one to eight players buy and sell shares in competition) is less easy to adapt for higher levels than *Telemark*, in which four teams (or individuals) make and sell television sets, controlling a number of critical variables on which decisions must be reached.

11  Or other derivatives of the original *Storyboard* idea. For further details, see J. Higgins and T. Johns, *Computers in Language Learning*, Collins ELT, 1984.

12  There are currently forty-three such operations operating in thirty-two countries and employing a total of 994 members of staff.

13  Only a few centres, notably Hong Kong, exceed a staffing complement of fifty.

14  But see Yang Huizhong's paper on the problems of Chinese.

# Commentator 1

Kari Sajavaara

Technological innovations are today being introduced at a rate that is unsurpassed in human history. Many of the things for which we are now considering applications will be technologically outmoded by the time we are able to develop suitable software. The advances in learning theory, and more specifically the theories about how people learn second or foreign languages, are by no means comparable with what goes on in technology. This means that in many respects we have to cope with language learning problems using up-to-date educational technology but applying outmoded thinking, or no thinking at all, to language learning – often disguised under a veil of eclecticism.

The tone of modest enthusiasm mixed with caution in Peter Roe's paper deserves positive comment. After outlining the parameters which should come up in computer-based programmes, he asks a highly relevant question: 'Does it work?' We can go on along the same lines. Is the investment in educational technology for language teaching necessary, and does it pay? Will the final product of computer-assisted language learning be any different from that of the language laboratory? Today it is easy to visualize very sophisticated hardware which integrates video discs and microcomputers into interactive systems. The technology is already there. But do we have the necessary knowledge to solve the problems involved in processing the details of the *language teaching programme* which must be fed into the machine? The weak point is not the technology; the weak point is the language teaching programme designer and the applied linguist on whom it falls to prepare the ground for soundly based programmes.

It is easy to agree with Peter Roe that technology should not dictate methodology. Yet if it were really the case that technology can change the learning process, we would have no cause for complaint – provided that we knew that the change is in the right direction. But we know no such thing. One of the problems with sophisticated technology is that it is only too easy for the teacher to hide behind it – this happened in the heyday of the language laboratory (many teachers do it even today). If the teacher runs into problems, he or she can always find fault with the technology, the lack of suitable materials to go with the machines, etc. The problem is that it is always easy to keep the students seemingly busy doing *something*, but unfortunately just doing *anything* is not necessarily helpful in language learning.

Today there is still a long way to go before we can conceptualize language learning in terms of a model in which due attention is paid to all relevant factors, psychological, sociological, and linguistic. So far, we have had tentative partial models only, mostly concentrating on one of the three major areas. Moreover, the development of the language code as reflected in learner products has been confused with various social or socio-psychological processes or intervening variables. Neither have various communicative processes and strategies at work in interpersonal communicative interaction been distinguished from those leading to the ability to communicate in the second language. The grid through which learner language has been observed has been unnecessarily static – even where the very nature of language is dynamic. We lack even the methodology to describe language in precise socio- and psycholinguistic terms.

Since we have not progressed very far in our inquiry concerning the ways in which people go about learning second languages, the most profitable way in which computers can be used is perhaps not for straight language teaching. Using a microcomputer is an excellent way of increasing the amount of the learner's contact with the language to be learned, i.e. to provide input through making the learner do things with the computer and perhaps learn the language as a side effect, which is exactly the way we learn languages in natural situations. This means fact-finding, fact-analysing, problem-solving, which are all activities found in all human endeavours to learn. This actually brings forth the old problem of the integration of language studies with other subjects. So, perhaps instead of spending too much time on talking about the merits and demerits of technologically assisted language teaching, we should combine our efforts to find out what uses of the microcomputer and other media really do pay.

Producing good materials for the computer is very time-consuming. Even without broaching the problem of the scarcity of research results available, or their highly contradictory nature, it is a fact that, out of the total time needed for producing sophisticated computer-based language teaching programmes, the time needed for working out the technical aspects of the programme takes the lion's share. If we consider this against some of the more traditional ways of handling the teaching situation, it is easy to see that the time needed for materials production as against the time the learner needs to work with it has been multiplied enormously. It must also be remembered that the computer does not make the teacher obsolete; his role only changes. All this is taking place at a time when, in most countries, investment in education is on the decrease. Computerization of language teaching may mean, under present circumstances, that despite the fact that the very nature of the computer favours the introduction of more flexibility into teaching, we may have to rely, even more than before, on materials produced for use all over the world, on English for everybody.

An important part of human interactional behaviour and learning is creativity, the ability to rewrite the 'rules' for each individual communicative situation through the interaction with the interlocutors. The existence of this sort of variability seems to be, implicitly at least, written into the description presented in Peter Roe's paper but – and this is a question I wish to put: Is it possible to envisage developing teaching materials to go with new information technology that introduce a sufficient amount of creativity into man–machine interaction?

# Commentator 2

## Keith Morrow

One of the many reasons why I like Peter Roe's paper is its clear commitment to a cause. There is a fervour behind the academic prose which I applaud. In its implications for the methodology of language teaching it is radical and, to a degree, revolutionary.

But, like all revolutionaries, Peter Roe lays himself open to the charge that he distorts the present and the past in order to maximize the evil which the revolution is to expunge. This does seem to me to be the case in some of his comments on the influence of technology on methodology (surely the language laboratory was a symptom, and not a cause, of audiovisual dogma) and in his blanket characterization of present language teaching as 'antediluvian' and (caught) 'in a restrictive, ineffectual mould'.

These are, however, minor quibbles. Where I must take more serious issue with him is over his claim that 'using the computer as just another teacher-dominated resource would be to miss the whole point of the new dimension in IT'. Well, would it?

Certainly this new dimension offers exciting possibilities, and exploring them promises to be fruitful. But it does seem to me that on a more mundane level there are already practical applications for microcomputers in language teaching of a 'teacher-dominated' type which more than justify the new technology. I am referring, of course, to programs of a 'drill-and-practice' type which are, in my view, too often and too easily disparaged. What they offer is an unrivalled medium for the individualization of work on the mechanics of the language. My view is that, for certain students, at certain times in their learning, such work is essential. It is precisely because this view does not extend to *all* students at *all* times that the necessity for individualization arises. This, of course, is not a new insight; it derives directly from current methodological practice in many areas, but computers give us the opportunity to do it better.

So I must ask this: on the level of tactics, wouldn't we do better to use IT to develop existing methodologies rather than claiming that IT has no value unless we formulate and subscribe to a radical change of methodological direction?

# b) The use of computers in English teaching and research in China

Yang Huizhong

## 1 The background

Foreign language teaching has long occupied an important place in education in China. In the thirty-five years since the founding of new China a great number of English language translators, interpreters, and teachers have graduated from universities and colleges. They have filled various posts, rendering services to our socialist construction and to international communications.

However, foreign language teaching has followed a zigzag path in China. In the early years after liberation the only foreign language taught in China was Russian. In the period from 1954 to 1959 the teaching of foreign languages was dropped from the curriculum of junior secondary schools. Later, during the turmoil of the cultural revolution, the whole educational system, let alone English language teaching, was suspended. After the cultural revolution was over, schools very soon returned to normal and education underwent a period of rapid development. In order to select the best of the secondary school-leavers for higher education, the National College Entrance Examination was restored, with a remarkable improvement in the standards of education as a result.

Foreign language teaching, however, showed a slower than average pace of development, despite being restored even in secondary schools. This time the emphasis was placed on English, but because of the absence of foreign language teaching in the curriculum for many years, standards were initially low. The scores on foreign languages in the National College Entrance Examination had initially to be either wholly disregarded or allocated only 30 per cent of the total scores. This had a very bad backwash effect on English language teaching in the secondary schools because many students chose to give up English in the hope of gaining higher scores in other courses. Corrective measures, however, were very soon adopted, so that now English is a major course in secondary schools and a compulsory course in universities and colleges.

In recent years the Government has adopted an open-to-the-outside policy and as a result international exchanges in the scientific and technological, economic and cultural fields have been greatly increased. The

Government has every year been sending a large number of students and scholars abroad for further study. Since English is now the main language for international communication, scientists and technologists have shown great eagerness to have a better command of the English language. There has appeared an enthusiasm for learning English all over the country. Apart from formal English language teaching, there are all kinds of extramural English classes, including English courses on radio and TV such as the extremely popular series based on *Follow Me*. Every year millions of people take part in all kinds of English courses.

At the tertiary level English is mainly taught for two different purposes: English as a major course and English as a service course (EST/ESP). Service English courses in universities and colleges involve hundreds of thousands of students every year. The students are usually highly motivated and EST/ESP has been receiving special attention in recent years.

Nevertheless there are many difficulties to overcome in this field, the main problem being a shortage of adequately trained English language teachers. There are over ten thousand teachers in the EST/ESP area, about 60 per cent of them formerly specializing in Russian. Such being the case, the English courses that are now offered are far from satisfactory. The Ministry of Education is determined to change this situation as soon as possible and has taken a series of measures. Two ESP/EST Information Centres have been set up, one in Shanghai Jiao Tong University, the other in Qin Hua University. The English syllabus for EST courses at tertiary level is now under revision. The British Council is currently running three teacher training centres in China. Other measures include materials development, research into English language and teaching methodology, etc. Educational technology, including the use of computers, is yet another measure, and the present paper deals with the applications of computers in ELT in China.

## 1.1 Educational technology

Looking back over the long history of English language teaching in general, we find that educational technology has always occupied a place. To cope with the ever increasing demand on English language teaching the teacher is always looking for aids to increase the efficiency and effectiveness of his/her teaching. And the dramatic growth of science and technology has always been able to provide such aids. In the last fifty years, all kinds of technical devices have been introduced into the English language teaching practice. Nowadays English language teachers have at their disposal a whole series of aids, ranging from slide and film projectors to sound and video tape recorders; many are far better equipped than anyone could have imagined in the past (Brumfit and Roberts, 1983). Such devices are used to provide vivid and authentic audio-visual images, transcending the limitations of time and space imposed by the classroom environment. This helps to enhance the students' motivation and increase their interest in learning. In language teaching these machines are also used to create the situation and environment of language activities, providing topics and content for speech activity. Audio tape recorders are of special value in language learning because they provide authentic language material for self-study. In China we always try to make full use of the limited technology available; dozens of students listening through headphones to a single tape recorder is a commonplace in language classrooms.

In the 1960s the audio-lingual method was developed, supported by the use of audio-visual equipment. Then language laboratories were introduced, based on the heavy use of tape recorders to provide the possibility of individualization, self-pacing, instant feedback and self-evaluation (Dakin, 1973). This created the possibility of self-access-learning and seemed to bring much hope to the language teacher, who took language laboratories to be a panacea for all the difficult problems in English language teaching. Teachers in China tried to follow suit. In a few years after the cultural revolution was over many leading universities were equipped with language laboratories.

## 1.2   The language laboratory

The language laboratory, however, has failed to bring about the desired effect. This is because the theoretical basis of language laboratory practice is, psychologically, behaviourism and, linguistically, structuralism (Higgins and Johns, 1984). The famous three-phase or four-phase drill, which was prevalent in the 1960s, was based on this theory. This kind of practice, based on the S–R theory, however, was originally designed to exclude meanings and covered only morphological and syntactic structures. In other words, this kind of practice was aimed at acquiring the formal system of the language. Isolated sentence pattern drills were often separated from context and situation. A command of the formal system of a language does not necessarily entail an appropriate use of the language in communicative situations. The use of the language laboratory is therefore highly limited.

In the last twenty years or so, linguistics has thrown a new light on the teaching of languages. Traditionally, foreign language teaching has been governed by the grammatical model of language. The present trend is to shift away from this grammatical model towards a communicative approach, from structural accuracy towards communicative competence. The command of a language involves two types of competence, the grammatical/linguistic competence and the communicative competence. The former refers to knowledge of a set of abstract linguistic rules emphasizing accuracy, the latter to the ability to use this set of linguistic rules for effective communication, emphasizing appropriacy. Since language use is a social process, it involves such factors as settings and situations of speech, social relationships of interlocuters, intention of the speakers, etc. The same language form may have different functions. Language use is therefore also a process of interpretation, carried out at discourse level as well as at sentence level. Language teaching should deal with above-sentence level structures, including discourse development, devices of cohesion and coherence, etc. Language communication is also an interaction, heavily depending on feedback, eye contact, facial expressions, etc., a process which has a non-predictive nature. Common understanding is often achieved through negotiation. If language is viewed as a means of communication, isolated work in the booths of the language laboratory obviously cannot meet all these requirements. Pattern drills, which are based on isolated sentences, can only develop a knowledge of the language as a coding system, but cannot guarantee a transfer of this knowledge to actual ability of language communication. The basic weakness of the language laboratory is the lack of genuinely interactive facilities. Developments in language laboratory hardware to include pair work and group work mode reflected an effort to improve the situation, but the success has been limited. Many language teachers have become sceptical about the role of language laboratories and even think of language laboratories as a failure (Farrington, 1982; Sanders and Kenner, 1983). Language laboratories are declining in use. Nowadays they are mainly used as listening facilities.

## 1.3 Computers

The language teacher, however, has not stopped looking for new aids in his/her teaching. The use of computers in language teaching and research started under such circumstances. The computer as a machine for storing, retrieving and monitoring data, is a powerful means of manipulating symbolic (including linguistic) codes. It is thus ideal for processing texts. Its advent naturally attracted the attention of the language teacher. The computer was thus introduced into teaching (Davies and Higgins, 1982; Higgins and Johns, 1984). Early practice in computer-assisted instruction (CAI) started in the early sixties, and, limited by the developments in linguistics, was confined within the realm of structuralism. At that time CAI was little more than an automatically paging teaching machine (Beinashowitz *et al.*, 1981), based on a theory of learning similar to that underlying pattern drill. Technically, early CAI depended on main frames. Because of the high cost of main frames and computer time, it was very expensive either to develop courseware or to have on-line computer-assisted instructions. Not all universities and colleges, even in the highly-developed countries could afford this. CAI was totally out of reach of most language teachers and learners. Early CAI failed to produce much effect on the practice of English language teaching.

Computer-assisted language learning (CALL) in its true sense started with the advent of microcomputers and the microcomputer revolution in the seventies. Nowadays computer science and technology is developing at such a speed that every four to five years there appears a new generation of machines. The trend is to have more memory capacity, faster speed and lower prices. Many of the microcomputers are already within reach of individuals. Free-standing desk-top personal microcomputers have entered into people's daily lives. They do not look as fearsome as the main frames (Higgins, 1981). At the same time software technology has also developed, making the computer more accessible to non-professionals and more intelligent and powerful in data processing. We have to explore how far this now accessible and powerful technology can be put to the service of the language learner and the language teacher.

## 1.4   Summary

Interestingly, China is the country where both paper and printing were first invented. They were essential ingredients of early educational technology, which made the supply of course books in large quantities possible and produced a profound change in education. Later, tape recorders brought the spoken language to the language teacher's classroom. The advent of the computer, as another technological development, will change the context of learning, and possibly change the relationships of the teacher and the learner. Its potential influence cannot be overestimated (Johns, 1984). It is against this general background that China has started work in the use of computers in English language teaching and research.

## 2   Computing in China

The development of computer science and technology has been given priority in China since the 1950s. As early as 1958 China had already begun to design and manufacture her own computer systems and formed the DJS series, which at the time met the general computing requirements of scientific research and the national economy. At that time the gap in computer hardware production and software development between China and other advanced countries was no more than five years. However in the years of the cultural revolution the development of computer science and technology was totally suspended. As computer science and technology outside China has witnessed remarkable progress during those years, this gap became all the more marked. After the cultural revolution was over computer science and technology regained its impetus for growth. Nearly all the leading universities and colleges have set up departments of computer science and technology. China has restarted the production of computers of her own design and at the same time imported computer systems from outside to equip leading universities and research institutions. Optional computer courses are available to liberal arts students. Many of the foreign language institutes are considering acquiring their own computers.

## 2.1 Chinese character processing

One specific problem must be solved before computers can become an integrated part of Chinese life; that is the problem of Chinese character processing for the purpose of man–machine interaction. Different from Indo-European languages, Chinese is an isolating language. There are more than eight thousand common characters in everyday use. Nearly all the high-level programming languages in present-day use are quasi-English languages. This means that before a Chinese can make true use of computers he/she must first have some command of the English language. This will certainly limit the use of computers in China. Chinese character processing has thus attracted the attention of many scientists. More than one hundred different projects have been put forward, which fall into three main categories.

### 2.1.1 Large keyboard design

This has the form of a Chinese character typewriter, with all the eight thousand common characters put on the keyboard. It is apparent that this is the easiest way of implementation, yet it is the least efficient. Moreover it is operator-oriented. A sophisticated operator can input no more than twenty characters a minute.

### 2.1.2 Medium-size keyboard design

Most of the Chinese characters are composed of radicals, which may occupy the left, right, top, bottom or middle of the character. About 270 radicals will be enough to form most of the common Chinese characters. The keyboard also contains some function keys for assembling the character from radicals. This design is also operator-oriented. It needs about half a year of special training.

## 2.1.3   Small keyboard design

This means the use of standard keyboards or keyboards with no more keys than the standard European ones. With such keyboards, schemes for encoding the characters are indispensable. There are again three basic types under this category.

a) *Encoding schemes based on phonetic sounds.* As early as the 1950s the Chinese Government approved the Pinying System for the spelling of the Chinese language. The System is based on Latin alphabets. The Pinying System allows the use of standard keyboards. The readability of the encoded text is quite high. The main problem is the high rate of code-repetition. The Chinese language is a syllabic language. The number of available syllables is far less than that of the characters. Character forms naturally become the most important distinguishing parameters. If they are left out the rate of code-repetition will inevitably be high, some syllables standing for more than one hundred homonymous characters. Another major difficulty is that there are numerous dialects in China. The same character may have totally different pronunciations in different dialects. Moreover, if the user does not know the character how can he/she encode it by its phonetic sound?

b) *Encoding schemes based on character forms.* The easiest way to implement this system is to provide ten special keys on the keyboard, representing the ten basic character strokes. The user may then input the character just as he/she writes the character. This is very straightforward and needs no training at all. It is truly user-oriented. The problem is again the high rate of code-repetition, because the same set of strokes may comprise different characters with just slight differences in the forms. Low efficiency is also a problem as some of the Chinese characters consist of more than thirty strokes. Other schemes under this category are based on the corner forms of the character, hence the four-corner coding scheme or the three-corner coding scheme. Some Chinese word processors of this type are already available on the computer market. They make use of standard keyboards, but require much training. Other problems are high rate of code-repetition, high rate of key strokes and low readability of encoded texts.

c) *Encoding scheme based on the combination of character forms and phonetic sounds.* The aim is to eliminate the shortcomings of the above-mentioned schemes.

## 2.1.4   Summary

Chinese character processing is one of the major problems in computer science and technology in China. At the present moment many of the schemes have already been or are being implemented. Experience will identify the best. However, the character library, i.e. the codes for the characters as stored in the machine, are standardized. The best scheme should pass all the major criteria of evaluation, which include the average number of key strokes per character, the length of training period, the rate of code-repetition, efficiency, the type of keyboard, the readability of encoded texts, etc.

It seems that the best scheme should base itself on words rather than characters. In contemporary Chinese most words are disyllabic. There are certain rules for forming characters into words. By making full use of the data-processing facility of the computer it would be possible to have a far more efficient implementation of Chinese character processing, provided the computer can afford the high overhead.

At the same time work has also started in the fields of optical Chinese character readers, Chinese speech recognition, and Chinese computers and Chinese programming languages.

# 3   Linguistic computing in China

Linguistic computing in China mainly serves the purpose of improving English language teaching, covering the fields of corpus linguistics, language testing, computer-assisted language learning (CALL), and machine translation.

## 3.1   Corpus linguistics

Corpus linguistics is a new development in language study, which has been made possible only by the advent of the computer. Corpus linguistics is able to provide a better model for the description of the English language, which because of the very large amount of data involved cannot be studied directly by human observations (Sinclair, 1980, 1970). In language study the sampling of linguistic data is indispensable. The study of language as a system, on any of its levels such as the lexicon, syntax, or semantics, requires large-scale collection, manipulation, and analysis of linguistic data. Language as used in everyday speech and writing, however, is as vast as an ocean, and, moreover, language as a complicated structural system is in a continuous state of change. Therefore it is impracticable to collect all the linguistic facts. Language study must be based on sampling. The mass storage system of the computer provides the facility for storing the bulk linguistic data collected on the basis of principled sampling. Such a collection of linguistic data is called a computer corpus. To meet the different needs of language study, linguistic data sampling must be carried out on a random basis, the capacity of sampling should be large enough both in terms of individual sample size and of the corpus as a whole, and the sampled texts in a corpus should be systematically organized. These are the three basic requirements for a computer corpus of texts.

There are at the moment several well-known computer corpora for linguistic study available in the world, which are of two basic types – computer corpora for reference use and large computer corpora for 'monitoring' the language in current use (Sinclair, 1982). The first standardized, edited computer corpus ever built in the world is the Brown University Corpus of Present-day Edited American English (Svartvik *et al.*, 1982), which is of the reference type. The largest general computer corpus now in the world is the Birmingham University Collection of English Texts, comprising over twenty million English words, which is moving towards the 'monitor' type (Renouf, 1983).

### 3.1.1 The JDEST Corpus

At Shanghai Jiao Tong University we have also built up a computer corpus of English texts (The JDEST Corpus), with a total capacity of one million English words. The JDEST Corpus is parallel to the Brown/LOB Corpora, but it is a special purpose corpus, of texts of English for science and technology. The Corpus covers ten specialized fields, such as mechanical engineering, metallurgy, computer science and technology, physics and chemistry, etc. The two thousand running texts, of at least five hundred words each, contained in the Corpus are selected on a random basis. In selecting texts, genres and language varieties have also been taken into consideration and are represented by a coding system. Texts are taken from textbooks, periodicals, abstracts, etc., and both American and British English are included. The Corpus is designed to meet different needs in the study of EST. The texts, having been sampled, are keyboarded into the machine. The Corpus, completed by the end of 1982, was first used for word frequency study. Based on the statistical results, mainly on frequency, distribution and coverage, a 5,000-word service list of EST has been worked out. Then with reference to Thorndike's Teachers' Wordbook of 10,000 Words, M. West's General Service List of English Words and the practical needs of English language teaching in China, 1,000 more words have been added to yield a 6,000-word service list of EST. This list is included as one of the four appendices to the English syllabus for EST courses at tertiary level. This is the first use made of the

Corpus. In the future it is hoped that the Corpus may be used for syntactic and discourse study of EST.

### 3.1.2 Chinese computer corpora

Work in Chinese corpus linguistics has also started. At Wu Han University in Central China, a group of teachers have built up a computer corpus of Chinese texts, at the moment comprising two novels by Lao She. They plan to expand the corpus to include more works by contemporary Chinese writers.

## 3.2 Language testing

Another important area of the use of computers in English language teaching and study is language testing. There are two possibilities. One is the direct use of computers for testing, another is for the administration of testing. Computer-assisted language testing or computer-managed language testing has a series of advantages. Efficiency of testing procedures is the first to mention. The computer can also help to make scoring automatic, thus ensuring identical standards of assessment. Computer-assisted item analysis will help to build an item bank by standardizing the items, making it easier to produce alternative forms of a particular text. Finally, test security can be much improved. In the future when a computerized test item bank is available, there will exist the possibility of selecting test items by the computer in real-time in response to the testee's input, thus making the test sensitive to the testee's competence. At the same time the feedback from the testee can be automatically collected by the computer to improve the test items.

In China, since 1980, a nation-wide standardized test, the English Proficiency Test (EPT), has been in practical use. This is the first standardized test of its kind, developed by a group of test-setters under the Ministry of Education. The test is designed to provide valid test scores for English proficiency assessment. At present EPT is mainly used for selecting applicants for further study abroad. EPT is a norm-referenced standardized test. In its development the computer is mainly used for item analysis to improve the item performance. A computerized item bank is now under consideration. EPT is the first attempt at a standardized test in China and has already had its positive impact on English language teaching practice.

## 3.3 Computer-assisted language learning

Computer-assisted language learning (CALL) is another new development in English language teaching. As a result of Tim Johns's fruitful visit and a course in CALL in Shanghai in January 1984, a nation-wide CALLNET has been set up in China. Some universities like Shanghai Jiao Tong University are establishing CALL laboratories using the university produced microcomputer MIC-80, which has been developed on the basis of TRS-80. A modest team of teachers are devoting their time to developing CALL courseware.

CALL has a series of advantages over the traditional media (Davies and Higgins, 1982; Higgins and Johns, 1984; Jones, 1982). First of all, computers are patient, consistent, tolerant of repeated mistakes and can provide remedial material for slow students. Secondly, computers are flexible, capable of catering for different needs and pace of learning. With a rich hierarchy of choices available to the learner it makes individualized, autonomous study more feasible and more rewarding. Even in drills of the mechanical type, it can provide step by step help and guide the students towards the correct answer, thus increasing their learning efficiency. With the possibility of random selection CALL can avoid repetition of the same material. Because of its flexibility CALL can easily be adapted to individualized study, pair work, group or class activities. But the major advantage of CALL probably lies in its interactiveness (Phillips, 1983; Schneider, 1983). Language learning should ideally be based on interaction in the real environment, and the computer can be used to help create such an environment for both man–machine and man–man interaction, stimulating the learner to use the language. Computers can receive the students' responses and make decisions on them. Every piece of CALL activity is carried out by the students and the computer in co-operation. Language use is a negotiation between all the participating parties. CALL therefore provides a language use model, far better and far more flexible than that provided by any other traditional model, making above sentence-level communication possible, shifting the emphasis from language form to information and information structures carried by the language, which is important to developing the interpretative strategies and communicative competence (Johns, 1981a, 1981b, 1983). In a country like China where English is not a native language, most of the learners of English have no access to native speakers. Intelligent, expert CALL systems, which provide the learner with far more flexible resources, will then become all the more important.

Computers, however, are not faultless and are far from being omnipotent. Although computer technology has been developing rapidly in the last few years, man–machine communication through keyboards is very inefficient; the amount of information that a screen can provide is far less than a printed page provides; the computer-generated graphics available on microcomputers are still not comparable to colour pictures either in terms of resolution or in terms of information they can convey. Artificial intelligence, which is the future direction of CALL, is still at an early stage. Language activity is a highly complex intelligent process; it will take many years before the computer can simulate such a process. Speech recognition and speech production still have a long way to go before they can meet the language teacher's requirements of the speech sound quality. Therefore, the role of the computer in ELT practice is not limitless. However, CALL has already had its impact on English language teaching. CALL is not yet the mainstream of ELT methodology, but more and more ELT teachers have come to see its potential and become involved in it. Though we have just started our efforts in CALL, we probably already need to consider some of the relationships in CALL.

### 3.3.1   CALL as an integral part of the whole teaching process

CALL does not need to be a simple replica of classroom teaching, nor should it be used merely for the purpose of demonstration. It should not be forgotten that the ultimate purpose of language teaching is to develop communicative competence. Without communication there is no language. Successful CALL depends on whether it encourages and enables the students to use the language. It seems to be the best practice to make CALL courseware part of a multi-media teaching package, which guides the students through necessary drills and provides a great variety of language activities.

### 3.3.2   Teacher and computer

In CALL, teacher–computer–student form a total system, in which the teacher plays the leading role. The computer will complement but not replace the teacher. Especially in the teaching of languages where interpersonal communication is emphasized, the 'live' teacher can never be replaced. However, the computer can replace part of the teacher's repetitious work so that he/she can concentrate on developing the students' communicative competence. The teacher should therefore cast away any feeling of mystery about the computer and willingly introduce it into the teaching process. Moreover, the teacher should take an active involvement in the practice of CALL. The computer is merely a technical aid. It will play its part only when there is suitable courseware, and the active involvement of the teacher is the only guarantee for the quality of the courseware.

### 3.3.3   Software and hardware

In CALL, hardware is the body, software the life. In CALL practice, the present situation is that software development lags far behind that of hardware. In CALL software takes the form of courseware, which is a program or a set of programs developed for carrying out certain teaching objectives. Courseware is used for instructing, practising, and providing topics for language activities. The availability of a large variety of high quality courseware is the key to successful CALL. CALL courseware may have different forms, ranging from drills of the mechanical type to games and intelligent simulations; it may aim at developing certain language skills such as writing or reading. Whatever form and purpose courseware may have, it seems that it should be generative, intelligent and communicative (Johns and Higgins, 1983; Beinashowitz *et al.*, 1981; Sanders and Kenner, 1983). By 'generative' we mean that CALL courseware should be able to generate teaching materials on the spot to suit the needs of different teaching situations; by 'intelligent' we mean that CALL courseware should incorporate into it the research results of artificial intelligence, and be able to make intelligent evaluation of the student's responses – courseware should also be student-friendly, providing necessary help as well as catering for different learning strategies; by 'communicative', we mean that CALL courseware should replicate the authentic use of language and involve sociolinguistic factors of language communication.

### 3.3.4   CALL development and the teacher

The development of CALL requires the teacher's active involvement, which may take three forms. First, the teacher may make use of the ready-made courseware available on the market, and integrate it into the teaching process. This is the easiest and most convenient way but the disadvantage is its inflexibility. The teacher has no way to adapt the courseware to suit his/her particular teaching situation and it is very rare that teaching materials can be made use of without any adaptation by the practising teacher. However, if the teaching process is well organized, the ready-made courseware can provide a great variety of language activities, greatly enriching classroom teaching. Secondly, the teacher may make use of the authoring systems (or authoring languages) to develop his/her own courseware by inserting teaching materials into the preset format provided. This is relatively convenient and does not require special programming techniques on the part of the language teacher. Its disadvantage is low flexibility because the format is usually preset and cannot be easily adapted to suit the different needs of teaching. Besides, it is usually limited to drills and practice of the mechanical type, though some authoring systems allow the teacher to develop creative and imaginary games. Finally, the teacher may try to learn programming, and this will give him/her much more freedom to exercise his/her imagination and creativity in the fascinating field of CALL. The disadvantage is that most current programming languages are relatively difficult to learn. For most language teachers, the first two forms of involvement are probably their main experience of CALL. Programming, however, is within the reach of language teachers. Many language teachers with a liberal arts background have now become professionals or semi-professionals in the field of CALL and have developed a variety of courseware, which is elegant even judged by the standards of computer scientists. Whatever the form of the teacher's involvement, the development of a great variety of high quality and imaginative courseware is the key to successful CALL.

### 3.3.5   *The eclectic approach*

In foreign language teaching one need not go from one extreme to another. It is not easy to learn a foreign language. The mere command of a certain number of vocabulary items and a set of grammatical rules does not mean a command of that language. It is therefore quite natural and necessary that the present trend should shift from linguistic competence to communicative competence; from accuracy towards fluency. However, practice of the type associated with drills is still very important, because it builds up the necessary habits through repetition, positive feedback and monitoring. In this area the computer can be found extremely useful. The flexibility of the computer makes it possible to bring meaning into drills and avoid the monotony of purely mechanical drills. We should take a similarly balanced attitude towards the whole of CALL. On the one hand, we should not shut out CALL; on the other hand, we should not be so carried away by the fascination of CALL as to forget the strength of conventional classroom teaching or the ultimate aims of language teaching. A good teacher is usually eclectic, making use of the merits of every school of thought in EFL methodology to improve the efficiency and effectiveness of teaching. In CALL practice, the teacher should always keep this in mind when he/she comes to use and develop courseware.

## 4   Machine translation

Research in the field of machine translation in China started early in 1958. It was stopped in the years of the cultural revolution and then restarted in 1978. The Research Institute of Linguistics of the Chinese Social Science Academy is the main body for machine translation research. The Scientific and Technical Information Research Institute of China and two or three universities are also involved in this field. The main projects are English–Chinese machine translation. There is also one project in Russian–Chinese and one in German–Chinese. Two national conferences on the subject have been held. All the projects consist of two parts: the machine dictionary and the rule system. The machine dictionary provides information on word class, word meaning, grammatical clues, and the Chinese equivalents. The rule system is mainly based on the traditional grammar model, which, with the information provided by the machine dictionary, tries in several scans to analyse the syntactic relationships between parts of the sentence, and then reorder them in the Chinese version. Recent efforts have been to introduce logico-semantic analysis into the rule system, giving a certain degree of intelligence to the automatic translation system. All the projects at the moment are aimed at sublanguage texts or abstracts (i.e. of certain specialized fields). Some of the projects have already been able to produce a readable translated version without the need of post-editing. However, most of the work is still of an experimental nature. There is a long way to go before such automatic translation systems could be put to practical use. Research in machine translation is not directly relevant to language teaching, but in the long run it will throw some light on the nature of language, from which the language teaching practice may eventually benefit.

## 5    Conclusion

The use of computers in English language teaching and research is still in its infancy in China. But it has made a sound start and has already shown great potential. In the future it seems that there exists a possibility of building up a powerful linguistic data base, integrating teaching materials, audio/visual resources, and language data taken from the actual use of language, to provide direct service to language teaching and testing.

In the last fifty years the British Council has made substantial contributions to English language teaching and research. British academics are always among the leaders in English linguistics and have contributed many new ideas in English language teaching methodology. In the field of computer use in English language teaching and research they have once again secured a leading position. We will, as we did before, learn from them. The British Council has encouraged and helped co-operation between institutions and individuals in our two countries. We will further this relationship of co-operation between China and Britain.

### Note

I am indebted to Professor J. McH. Sinclair, Tim Johns and Antoinette Renouf for their help in preparing this paper.

# Commentator 1

Tim Johns

I wish to suggest a link between my own concern with computer-assisted language learning and ESP on the one hand, and on the other Mr Yang's recent work at Birmingham on the automatic recovery of technical terms from text. Discussion of computer-assisted language learning has in the past tended to assume that the computer has – or should have – a single, identifiable, and assessable role in language learning. That view is, I believe, mistaken. The computer is flexible – it is also neutral, waiting for us to impose on it whatever metaphor we wish. It can be exploited in the service of any of the many current methodologies.

Work within the traditions of computer as tutor or as trainer has been around for over twenty years. Recently we have begun to consider and develop uses which assume instead an autonomous learner, the machine being used as a tool under the learner's control in exploring and developing a command of the target language. The argument for the computer in this role depends on its ability to respond immediately to the user's input. This gives the learner a wider range of non-trivial decisions about how he should learn, and the opportunity to experiment with different modes of learning, than any other medium. The computer offers *inter alia* to be a teacher, an informant, a demonstrator, a partner or a source of information. It is from this point of view that I find Mr Yang's recent research most interesting.

There are two ways in which corpus-based research may be of use to the learner. The first is indirect. The researcher discovers patterns of regularity in the data: his results can then inform the decisions made by syllabus constructors, by textbook writers and by dictionary compilers. The specification of lexical content for a syllabus is nowadays a somewhat unfashionable procedure, and the use of information as to frequency and coverage even more so; nevertheless, reference to objective corpus-derived information will I believe have at the least a useful steadying effect on the materials that are prepared to implement the new EST syllabus for China: certainly the lexical appendix to the syllabus has a much stronger feeling of authenticity and practicality than the subjectively-decided syntactic syllabus.

Looking at the data for two- and three-word terms recovered from scientific text by the programs developed by Mr Yang, one is struck that this is evidence too valuable to be restricted to researchers and teachers: it should be directly accessible to learners also. If words can best be learned by the company they keep, the automatic recovery of technical terms joins the computer-created concordance as a powerful potential tool for the learner of English for science and technology. It is exactly the terms identified by Mr Yang that do most of the work in articulating the conceptual structure of the text – to use Martin Phillips's term, they provide powerful evidence for the 'aboutness' of text. This implies that Mr Yang's program could be used by a learner to investigate which technical terms he can expect to find in text, and it could further provide a program which highlighted their actual occurrence in a text or texts. In addition the learner could use the program as an indexing system to recover texts on a particular theme or topic. At present such facilities can be offered only on a mainframe computer; however, the spread of network facilities linking mainframes to microcomputers could make it possible for the learner to explore and analyse a text data base from a classroom or from the home.

A question arises in connection with the possible applications of Mr Yang's research about the typology of texts. His program, when applied to texts extracted from science textbooks, produces a large number of two-word combinations which turn out to be technical terms of the subject. The same program, when applied to a novel by Graham Greene, produces very few combinations. There would appear to be important implications here for the way we classify different texts and one would like to know whether the program could be developed to produce automatic text classification.

# Commentator 2

Roger Bowers

My comments relate to both of the preceding papers on information technology and educational technology which I take to be distinct areas of operation and enquiry.

May we first examine the relation between learning devices and learning theories. For it seems to me that in the present, as in the past, it may be of value to separate technological advances in education from philosophical or procedural developments, and to decide which is the master. We may take two examples.

The first is the tape recorder. It is difficult to imagine the mid-century 'pattern practice' revolution without the pedagogic function of intensive modelling performed by the tape recorder. It is equally difficult to imagine the development of empirical descriptive linguistics without the tape recorder's informational function – the storage and retrieval of oral data. In both cases, it should be noted, the technology was put to the service of substantive approaches – in language learning, where it was closely identified with the behaviourist school and in descriptive linguistics applied to the contemporary spoken language. I would argue that in the case of the tape recorder the pedagogic and linguistic approaches preceded, but were facilitated by, the device: the approach retained the mastery.

Our second example is the video recorder, which again performs both a pedagogic and an informational function. In pedagogic terms, this device makes authentic communicative behaviour available in the classroom, in such a way that the teacher has quick control and can freeze, repeat, omit etc. In informational terms, the video recorder facilitates the storage and retrieval of behavioural episodes, and in thus expanding the data base makes possible the sociological and linguistic analysis of both verbal and non-verbal communication. Exploitation of this function in discourse studies has barely commenced. In the case of the video, it is less easy to see the distinct pedagogic and linguistic approaches which the device serves: but one might refer to contemporary interest in authentic input for language acquisition, and to total behaviour as the proper material of communication studies, as the respective pedagogic and linguistic correlates of the technological advance.

But what of the computer? What are the theoretical correlates of this technological development? Are there any?

In pedagogic terms, CALL is often promoted for its power to individualize learning – a ready theme in the 'programmed instruction' debates of the early 1960s. But CALL seems to have little to offer regarding the *nature* of the learning process thus individualized, while it seems in its present form to run counter to the prevailing tendency towards authentic input and authentic learner response. If teachers have in general failed to individualize instruction in non-technological ways, and I believe they have so failed, will hardware make any substantial difference?

In terms of linguistic theory and description the computer has made possible the rapid and efficient processing of statistical data. But this capacity has become widely available through the personal/educational microcomputer only at a time when the profession had appeared to be turning towards the observational study and qualitative assessment of data in reaction to quantitative analysis, however accurate and comprehensive.

So, what are the educational and informational approaches which current technology serves? Or are we enthralled by the technology?

I would approach the second point I wish to make by referring back to the useful distinction made by Professor Kachru: the 'inner circle' of speech fellowships – the norm-providers; 'the outer circle' – the norm-developers; and 'the expanding circle' – the norm-dependers. Those terms were developed with reference to general language use. How would they apply to the use of English to teach English? Without any statistics to back my claim, I would suggest that the largest category of those teaching English in the world today are of the 'expanding circle', and certainly the minority are of the 'inner circle'.

In applying the three circles to language *teachers* rather than language users, we need to re-examine their differential dependence on the norms – by which I mean now not the norms of linguistic usage but the norms of classroom behaviour. The further a teacher is from the centre of the inner circle, the greater his linguistic insecurity, and the more he will, generally speaking, seek security in the norms of teacher-dependent text-based, linguistically and communicatively circumscribed teaching. Innovative methodologies and educational technology are developed primarily by the norm-providers and are best suited – for linguistic, cultural and economic reasons – to 'inner circle' contexts. If this is indeed the case, and taking the global view, are we putting our technology to its best use?

A second question, then, is this: How can information and educational technology be applied to the needs of the common context – of teachers and learners in (to use the old term) 'difficult circumstances' – rather than reserved for the entertainment of the inner circle?

# Theme III  Summary of discussion

The general attitude to technological innovation in the description and teaching of language was one of interest tempered with caution and some distrust.

The caution was particularly evident in the discussion of the pedagogic potential of computer-assisted language learning (CALL) and parallels were drawn with the over-enthusiastic reception of the language laboratory. There was the worry, very generally evident, that approaches to methodology might be modified, or even expressly devised, to exploit the capabilities of the machine without regard to pedagogic desirability. We should of course resist the exercise of ingenuity for its own sake and concentrate on whether, and to what extent, the activities of learners stimulated by computer programs were actually beneficial to learning. In language testing it was suggested that the computer would always tend to test what could be tested rather than what needed to be tested and so to confuse the criteria for validity.

Questions were particularly raised about the very limited capacity of the computer to simulate the conditions of communicative interaction and the interpersonal negotiation of meaning which figured so prominently in recent pedagogic thinking. Such conditions cannot be incorporated into computer programs at present, nor was it likely that they would be in the foreseeable future. Premature moves in that direction would run the risk of distortion and the imposition of techniques which deny the learners the exercise of the independent initiative so necessary for learning. In this view, the function of computers was to provide language data and not to mediate methodological procedures.

It was acknowledged that the capacity of the computer could be exploited to beneficial effect both for the description and learning of language. No one questioned its contribution to descriptive linguistics, its value for the analysis of text and the discovery of facts about language usage. Nor was there any doubt about the possibilities within CALL for the rapid manipulation of data, immediate feedback and self-management of learning activities, all of which could enhance motivation by a sense of achievement. The point at issue was whether programs which were devised to take advantage of such capabilities were to be considered a useful means for servicing developments in methodology independently conceived, or as discovery procedures for new developments which, presumably, could in principle be applied in places where computers were not available, but which might actually be determined by the capacity and limitation of the machine itself rather than by informed pedagogic decision.

There was agreement that explorations into the use of computers in language learning should be strenuously pursued but that they should be at the same time monitored by reference to other developments in the theory and practice of language teaching pedagogy so that computers are seen as a useful service and not as themselves the agents for change.

# THEME IV   TEACHER PREPARATION

## a)   **Teacher-centred training: costing the process**

Christopher N. Candlin

## Preliminaries

In attempting to honour the call of the British Council to chart past and present developments, to take a bold stand on future possibilities, and to evaluate fruitful avenues of exploration, I wish in this paper to draw on research studies, experience with teachers in INSET (In-service Teacher Education and Training) programmes, and cautious speculation. The paper has one overriding theme, that of assessing the costs and benefits attendant on INSET choices in the area of English Studies, in its global and not narrowly European or Anglo-American context. This theme will be addressed via two interdependent areas of choice, that of teacher need and that of trainer action. In the former, I focus on the issues and costs of what my title calls 'Teacher-centred training', in the latter to the identification of INSET principles for growth and development, mindful here of the need to locate responsibilities and to evaluate modes of action.

I would be happy if the paper itself were to incorporate the three purposes of any INSET activity: to inform, to demonstrate and to develop. To achieve these purposes, even in part, will, as we shall see, involve us in a mix of modes of presentation in this paper: to summarize research, to portray issues and to outline strategies. In sum, I hope that the paper will give us one means of rendering an account of the balance-sheet of INSET, so that we can determine priorities among those futures that seem possible.

## I   Teacher need

### I.1   *What are the issues?*

Innovation in INSET, for English language teaching as for any other discipline, depends on the balance struck between two forces, that of 'product' and that of 'process'. In this equation, however, lurks a problem in semantics. 'Process' can be both the means by which a 'product' is transmitted and the object of its own 'process'. In can be both means and goal. In essence, this paper has this tension as its focus, and it is one which imbues both INSET in general and the nature of our discipline in particular.

We are at an exciting time in the development of programmes for language teaching and learning and for the consequent training and education of teachers. For the first time, ideas which were speculative in the late 1960s and 1970s have the increasing support of philosophical investigation, laboratory experiment, and classroom experience. Our view of language as both form and function, as an interdependent system of text, ideation and interpersonality with a focus on the negotiation of value receives current support from studies in both linguistic pragmatics (cf. Leech, 1983; Levinson, 1983, *inter alia*), and pedagogic grammar (cf. Rutherford, 1982, *inter alia*); our view of second language learning as a process of psychological and social psychological negotiation with a focus on the enhancement of cognitive capacity receives support from both experimental studies in classroom language learning (cf. Krashen, 1982; Long, 1983; Porter, 1983, *inter alia*) and from ethnographic accounts of language learners' behaviour (cf. Long and Sato, 1984; Faerch and Kasper, 1983; Selinker and Gass, 1983, *inter alia*); while our view of classroom practice and management, with its focus on the social context of teaching and learning, acts to create the conditions whereby both the prerequisites of this view of language and this view of learning can be met in practice (cf. Allwright, 1982; Breen, Candlin and Waters, 1979; Breen, 1983; Prabhu, 1984). This powerful confluence of interest among the three indispensable participants in the process of language teaching and learning imposes inescapable demands on all those involved in the development and implementation of curricula, not least upon the teacher-in-training.

In terms of the document reproduced below from an INSET workshop at TESOL 1981 (Breen and Candlin, 1981) it constitutes a demanding argument:

Basic principles of communicative language teaching and learning

1 IF      the purpose and content of the teaching and learning of English is *communication*,

   THEN  we are working upon a process which is:
         a) a unity of three knowledge systems (text/ideation/inter-personality)
         b) variable in the ways in which these knowledge systems interrelate within any language data
         c) a negotiative system in itself
         d) not transmissible directly to the learner in terms of pre-selected categories of form or function, with assigned co-selection
         e) influenced by:
            (i)  socio-psychological factors of attitude

        (ii)   sociolinguistic factors of role, status and social
              knowledge
        (iii)  psychological factors of learning capacity

2  IF      learning a language involves different types of learning and different preferred styles of learning,

    THEN  the teaching-learning process in the classroom will need to allow for and accommodate these differences.

3  IF      learning a language involves different learning strategies – depending on the particular task or the particular learner,

    THEN  the teaching-learning process – and the materials used for that process – will need to activate and uncover these strategies.

4  IF      learning is a negotiative process – between the learner's prior knowledge and experiences and the new knowledge and experiences,

    THEN  our teaching-learning methodology needs to be negotiative.

5  IF      the purpose of language learning is the development of the learner's communicative competence,

    THEN  how can we activate and involve the initial communicative competence which the learner brings to the learning?

6  IF      the social context in which the learning takes place influences both the learning process itself and what is learned as content,

    THEN  the classroom will need to be an arena where joint interpretation, shared expression and cooperative negotiation take place and where the content can be both authentic to the target and authentic to the classroom and to the participants within it – although unpredictable in terms of what precisely that content might be.

      (M. P. Breen and C. N Candlin, TESOL 1981, INSET Workshop)

Moreover, it is an argument which for INSET targets two points of pressure, innovation and change, viz.

i)   the curriculum guidelines and their associated syllabuses;
ii)  the classroom and its procedures.

For the former it foregrounds firstly the need for a curriculum approach, one which seeks interdependence and mutual influence between purposes, method and evaluation much in the manner suggested by Breen and Candlin (1981) and Candlin (1984), rather than one which views each component separately; secondly, it suggests that any curriculum concerned with communication as an objective and as a means is bound up with ideological issues of the exploration of value systems; thirdly, it implies that learner variability will impose pressures upon our capacity to pre-plan learning, and thus argues for greater classroom freedom for determining syllabus direction; and, lastly, it sets a premium upon task-based learning guided by two principles of differentiation and problemposingness. As is made clear in Candlin (1983) and Breen (1983), these implications have a powerful re-orienting effect on the nature and procedures of the classroom, compelling us to reassess the relationships between language content, enabling information and processes of access; to regard learners as contributors of personal and interpersonal knowledge, expectations, styles and strategies of learning as well as takers and absorbers; to regard teachers as informants, resourcers, guides and coordinators, curriculum designers, classroom researchers, and above all, as sharers of responsibility; to view, lastly, the classroom as a resource where language can be observed and worked with, where language learning can be investigated, and where issues of social responsibility can be debated.

The teacher stands in the centre of a complex system of demanding worlds, each of which interacts with the other, and each of which contains elements which are themselves interdependent, much in the manner illustrated in the following 'flower' produced by Danish teachers in an INSET workshop (Breen, Candlin and Dam, 1981). In the view of at least one INSET group, therefore, these worlds and their interrelationships constitute the issues for INSET. They offer a partial perspective on training needs. They need, however, to be augmented by teacher contribution from teaching experience and by research into curriculum innovation before they can become an agenda for INSET action.

## I.2  What are the costs?

In this section, I propose to offer some answers to this question by drawing on two sources: firstly, from the teacher's viewpoint, to illustrate a range of costs associated in teachers' minds with the curriculum and classroom demands posed by the issues above; secondly, from the viewpoint of INSET research, to identify common problems (costs in another sense) associated with curriculum innovation.

### i)   Teaching costs

*Group 1 (for teacher background, see Appendix, p. 120)    Costs*

Need for greater resources (human and material), time.
Unwieldy process, requiring greater teacher competence.
Creativity is difficult to implement across a system.
Unavailability of tools for determining process needs.
Lack of objectivity in teacher/learner evaluation.
Practical problems of syllabus sequencing.
Danger of public disapproval and colleague disenchantment.

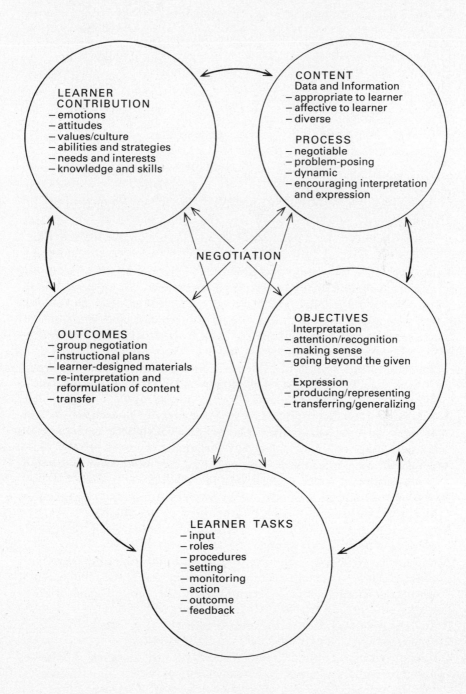

*Group 2 (for teacher background, see Appendix)   Costs*

Non-native teachers expend much time and energy.
Poorly-trained teachers have difficulty in classroom management.
Difficulty in curriculum and learner evaluation.
Not easy to find appropriate tasks and texts.
Requires high level of language proficiency.
May disadvantage some learners who are less autonomous.
May set up disorienting cultural blocks to learning.
Danger of confusion among teachers and learners.
Difficult to reconcile flexibility with need for systematicity.
Difficult to cater for mixed ability learners with different learning styles.
Hard to realize an integrated curriculum when only partly in charge of the
　　process.

*Group 3 (for teacher background, see Appendix)   Costs*

Difficulty of facilitating social demands of learners, their desire for
　　qualifications and their interests, experiences and learning possibilities.
As a source of knowledge and authority over content, teachers face two
　　ways: towards understanding of the subject and of education, and
　　towards the particular personalities of learners and the performance of
　　learning groups within the class.
Teachers transmit systems of value and belief, yet need to enable learners
　　both to understand their own ideologies and to critique them and those
　　of others.
Teachers are required to withstand the demands of the school, its con-
　　straints, and yet direct their pedagogic and subject knowledge to
　　learners, co-operatively with their colleagues.
Teachers are co-participants in processes of communication, yet retain
　　co-responsibility for their enactment and evaluation.
Problems with initiating opportunities for expression and interpretation
　　and establishing conditions for authenticity in the classroom.
Frequent difficulty in making the interests and experiences of learners the
　　point of departure in teaching.
Many teachers lose sight of human and educational goals under pressures
　　of large classes, student selection, anonymity within the school, actual
　　or supposed demands of society and consumers, and too high a work-
　　load.
Many teachers find their profession dissatisfying, or refuse to critique
　　their own work.
Co-operativeness is difficult to achieve because teachers feel themselves
　　under personal pressure to achieve; moreover co-operativeness is
　　burdensome, difficult and often creates fears of discussing plans with
　　learners and colleagues.

Many teachers are afraid to use the foreign language and consequently cleave to their textbook models.

Many teachers know little more about the foreign countries whose language they are teaching than they themselves learned from their own books when at school or at work.

Many teachers cannot see beyond the syllabus demands for 'language-learning units', and as a consequence learners suffer personal stress which works against communication and encourages avoidance strategies.

Many teachers have difficulty in understanding young people, and compensate by adopting authoritarian and teacher-centred forms of instruction.

### Group 4 (for teacher background, see Appendix)    Costs

Difficulty of finding an easy way of keeping a record of pupil progress (strategies being used/needing development).

Difficulty of helping pupils to realize what they have achieved and conveying that to them, to parents and to others.

Possibility of pupils only choosing material they want rather than materials which will increase/develop their knowledge.

Hard to evaluate so that pupils all have a feeling of working towards the same goal.

Exacerbates the likelihood of personal social conflict affecting learning.

Difficult to create situations which provoke students to explore their own language and learning.

Lays great stress on provision of new content.

Requires teachers to discover appropriate tasks to develop learner strategy.

No ready means of cataloguing and accounting for classroom behaviour.

Hard to accommodate to external modes of assessment.

Difficult for teachers to learn to direct without manipulating.

Requires teachers to focus on language, learning and social management at the same time.

Creates considerable fear of failure.

## ii)    Costs in curriculum implementation

Although the preceding sets out, sometimes in personal detail, the costs involved in meeting the curriculum changes implied by the account of issues in section I.1 above, it would be wrong to see these teacher statements in isolation from general costs of effecting curriculum change. In her paper on curriculum reform and in-service teacher training, Knab (1981) identifies three intermeshed problem areas, each of which carries INSET implications:

a) Prescribed curriculum decisions, even if accepted, cannot simply be carried out. The premise implicit in our issues is that instruction (and *a fortiori*, the curriculum) is to be interpreted, and not, in Knab's words, 'pre-formed'.

b) If the curriculum is to be interpreted, against which and whose criteria is this to be accomplished? As Knab makes clear

> society is increasingly interested in rigorously restricting the possible range of interpretation. The more difficult agreement on goals and contents of school becomes in society, the more rigorously it is demanded that they be observed. The more important comparable achievement standards become, the more important it is that they be guaranteed by the curriculum. The proclaimed 'educational freedom' of the teacher is regarded with utter mistrust under such conditions. The teacher is suspected of misusing it for certain socio-political aims.
>
> (Knab op. cit. p. 187)

c) If there is a tension between curriculum form and curriculum function such that no curriculum can be 'teacher-proof', how can INSET bring teachers into fruitful interaction with curriculum guidelines?

These three general areas of cost serve to identify some common threads running through the teacher statements. In particular, they emphasize that although costs to curriculum change are most immediately seen in terms of classroom demands, such demands cannot be identified independently of the language and learning content and the learning process to which classrooms are directed, nor can that interrelationship of form, function and action be seen as independent of the need to take a curricular view of the language teaching and learning enterprise. Much as in the following diagram, then, we can discern two interrelated worlds lying behind the statement of teacher costs; worlds, moreover, where different teachers will locate differently their personal weight of cost.

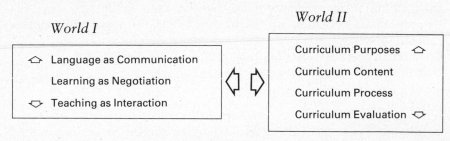

*World I*

- ⇔ Language as Communication
- Learning as Negotiation
- ⇔ Teaching as Interaction

*World II*

- Curriculum Purposes ⇔
- Curriculum Content
- Curriculum Process
- Curriculum Evaluation ⇔

Furthermore, the costs within each of these worlds, and between them, cannot be identified independently of the ideologies which lie behind them; specifically, the terms in which the purposes, content, method and evaluation of language teaching and learning are couched, and the sociocultural and institutional frameworks in which these curriculum components are to be realized in action. It is these which I propose in the second part of this paper to regard as the key foci for an INSET concerned with the accomplishment of the philosophy of language learning and teaching set out in section I.1 above.

## II Trainer action

### II.1 What are the INSET principles?

Anyone who has been involved in the development of curricula in public educational systems, and in particular concerned with the place of INSET in such development, will be only too painfully aware that the objectives of such curricula (and of the INSET that forms a crucial motivating part) can only be attained when there is a realization by all parties that the attainment of such objectives requires on the one hand a principled basis, and, on the other, action based on a sense of participation and collective responsibility. I have written recently elsewhere (Candlin 1983, 1984) on the latter, stressing the need to reach agreement on the curriculum objectives, their manner of attainment, and the procedures for evaluation of that attainment, by *all* parties involved in the curriculum process. Here I propose to identify those principles which, in my view, ought to guide the INSET process in the attempt to meet its costs. As elsewhere, one hopes that the principles will inform the practice.

### 1 The ideological principle

By this we mean that INSET programmes are not timeless constructs. They are designed in a context and under the influence of a variety of social, cultural, educational and subject-specific ideologies. They can either sustain these or critique them. In that INSET is not teaching, but the embodiment of intentions *about* teaching, it is, in the last analysis, political, and its intentions can only be understood against societal factors. *A fortiori* this is true of the participants and agents of INSET. In that INSET, in Wallin's (1981) phrase, 'does not aim to change teaching but to change the prerequisites for changing teaching, i.e. the teacher's conception of what he is doing and why', the recognition of this ideological principle is of first importance.

### 2 The curricular principle

By this we mean that as INSET directs itself upon the curriculum, it is itself subject to the curricular principle, specifically, that the purposes, method, content and evaluation of INSET programmes should not be conceived of independently of each other, but be mutually supportive and in harmony. One ought not to devise INSET purposes without considering how these purposes are to be carried out, what appropriate methodology they suggest, and what content they imply. Most important of all, given the absence of much relevant study in this area, they should not be devised without thought for modes of evaluation, themselves targeted not only on INSET participants but on the INSET curriculum itself.

## 3    The practical principle

By this we mean that INSET derives its curriculum from practical action. Its purposes arise from the products of an enhanced awareness by teachers of their classroom realities and their personal needs, its content and methodology reflect the heterogeneity against all relevant variables of its participants, a sensitivity to local situation, and an empathy with the learner, and its evaluation addresses participant knowledge, skill and attitude. Its essential quality is that it is differentiated, and that it poses problems.

## 4    The competence principle

By this we mean that the INSET curriculum focuses on content, process and management, and seeks to reflect, guide and evaluate participant competences in all three areas, both in terms of the participants' personal competence and their competence in developing that of their learners. It is, however, directed at improving capacity not only in respect for teaching solely, but also for curriculum action.

## 5    The participatory principle

By this we mean that if INSET is concerned with imparting 'curriculum products' (in Knab's (1981) phrase), then the process of transmitting these products is crucial. Furthermore, this will be more effective if those directly concerned participate in, and take partial responsibility for, the process itself. Ideally, of course, this principle implies that participation is not only a means for transmission, but a necessary prerequisite for curriculum creation.

## 6    The accountability principle

By this we mean that INSET be responsible for its curriculum. It should be so in respect of various sponsors (educational authorities, course organizers, agencies, participants, researchers), at various times (precourse, in-course, end-of-course, post-course), for a variety of reasons (to justify expenditure, raise funds, improve present/future courses, offer participant/sponsor feedback, give research insights/data), in a range of settings (in-course, at school, at home, in INSET centres), and by various means (critique of the curriculum, evaluation of teacher attitudes/ rewards, case studies, interviews, questionnaires, observations, simulations, diary studies, follow-up reports), via a range of agents (INSET trainers, participants, outside evaluators).

## 7 The reflexivity principle

By this we mean that INSET is enjoined to critique its own ideology, to denaturalize the frameworks, goals, rules, content and action of which it is constructed, and to do so within the process of INSET itself. Moreover, that the INSET organizer seek to mirror in training the action for classrooms, working interdependently with participants, sharing work experiences and conditions, seeing potential in INSET tasks, resourcing participants, researching into the effectiveness of INSET programmes, and, above all, making explicit their products and their processes.

## 8 The experimental principle

By this we mean that INSET is not a transmissive process but an experimental one, where the participants are active in research. Specifically, that INSET programmes ought to follow the cycle of data observation – hypothesis formation – hypothesis (dis)confirmation – principle, not only as this concerns language teaching and learning but also the procedures and principles of INSET itself.

These principles govern INSET, but for them to be adequate to the task of meeting the costs of the issues we have identified, they require the presence of three enabling conditions.

## 1 The resource condition

This holds that the effectiveness of INSET requires extensive commitment of human and material resources extending over lengthy periods of time, and argues against sudden and short-term investment.

## 2 The consistency condition

This holds that the effectiveness of INSET requires consistency of purpose, direction and action, and argues against momentary reactions to prevailing fashion.

## 3 The patience condition

This holds that the effectiveness of INSET is long-term, whether in product, curriculum change or participant attitude and behaviour, and argues against too premature closing of accounts.

117

## II.2    What directions for INSET action?

The issues and costs in the first part of this paper, when taken together, and when set against the principles and the conditions above, constitute a range of possible directions for INSET action and research. In this final section, I wish to highlight two directions only, and to see them as a means of leading this paper, more oriented to macro-issues, into the paper that will follow, one which concerns itself with the realization of INSET in practice.

### i)    Developing INSET tasks

In what follows, I propose a series of questions, objects for the research implicit in the definition of INSET captured in this paper.

### 1    What is an INSET task?

'One of a set of sequenceable, differentiable and problem-posing activities which involve teachers in some self-reliant selection among a range of variably available cognitive and communicative strategies applied to existing or acquired knowledge in the exploration and achievement of a variety of pre-specified or emergent goals via a range of INSET procedures, desirably interdependently with other teachers in some social milieu.'

   In other words, INSET tasks require us to specify:

– input
– roles
– procedures
– setting
– monitoring
– action
– outcomes
– feedback

### 2    Why tasks?

Because our principles require us to explore the relationship between product and process, and this in turn involves us in creating the conditions for the following characteristics of tasks:

– exploration
– challenge and critique
– negotiation of content and process
– interaction and interdependence
– differentiation
– problematization

## 3 What criteria for the sequencing of tasks?

In other words, on what basis do we determine which tasks to select and how to order them within an INSET programme? We might offer the following criteria:

- cognitive load (i.e. how intellectually demanding?)
- communicative stress (i.e. how much demand on communicative capacity?)
- particularity and generalizability (i.e. how idiosyncratic, how transferable?)
- input complexity (i.e. how complex the input upon which the task is to work?)
- process continuity (i.e. a 'skill oriented task' presupposing some other enabling 'skill oriented task')
- content continuity (i.e. the content worked upon a task presupposing some other enabling content)
- target continuity (i.e. tasks sequenced in relation to classroom events and their sequencing)

## 4 What criteria for the evaluation of INSET tasks?

Here we refer to formative criteria, designed to guide the INSET within a course. We might offer the following:

- problematicity (i.e. how problematic for the participants?)
- differentiatability (i.e. how differentiated among the participants?)
- implementability (i.e. how easy/difficult to enact by the participants?)
- combinability (i.e. how linkable as a task to other tasks?)
- ratability (i.e. how assessable against other tasks according to criteria?)
- generalizability (i.e. how extendable to post-INSET classroom experience?)

## ii) Developing an INSET typology

I propose this second direction as an urgent need in English studies, one which I hope that we can be encouraged to satisfy. Experience with the development of Exercise and Task Typologies for language learning (Edelhoff, 1978b; Candlin, 1981a) has shown how productive teachers can become if they are provided with a model for task design and an ordered collection of sample types which they can use to create their own materials. I would like to advocate a similar development for INSET. We might begin by collecting (much as our Federal Working Party for English in Comprehensive Schools in Germany did in the early 1970s) examples of INSET organizational and methodological types, from a wide variety of countries, educational systems and sociocultural conditions. For each

119

we might apply some of the criteria suggested above for the design, sequencing and evaluation of INSET tasks themselves. From such a collection we could derive some basic types, which could then be ordered in an accessible fashion and offered, not as some finite set, but as a treasure chest for trainers. This would make an admirable project for the next period of active development of English studies.

## Appendix

1  I should like to acknowledge my debt to my colleagues Michael Breen and Christoph Edelhoff, from whom I have not only learned a great deal about communicative curricula but also experienced the delights and despairs of many INSET workshops and courses.

2  Teacher groups (see p. 110ff.)

*Group 1*: Teachers at a TESOL Summer Institute at Ontario Institute for Studies in Education (OISE, Toronto), Summer 1983, mainly Canadian teachers of English to Francophone Secondary School pupils, but including some Language Advisers and teachers from the USA.
*Group 2*: Teachers at an East–West Center INSET course on English as an International Language in Summer 1984 in Honolulu, from Australia, Japan, Truk, Palau, New Zealand, Malaysia, USA, Qatar, UK.
*Group 3*: Teachers, Teacher-Trainers and Curriculum Designers from some twenty European countries, attending the 3rd International Workshop on Communicative Curricula in Modern Languages, Giessen, FRG, 1982.
*Group 4*: Teachers in Bilingual Education attending an INSET program in Second Language Learning, Honolulu, 1984.

# Commentator 1

Patrick Early

In his paper on INSET (In-service Teacher Education and Training) Professor Candlin begins at the beginning. His first concern is to establish that process/product in which we are setting out to educate/train teachers. It is necessary to analyse teacher need in order to specify trainer action. The subject of our concern turns out to be a communicative approach to language teaching and learning, characterized by ambiguity of process and product in this professional context. Thus language itself, just as teaching and learning a language, is both process and product. The suggestion is that in-service teacher-training shares in this ambiguity.

Central to language use, and hence to the communicative classroom, is the notion of negotiation. This notion of negotiation not only characterizes what learners do as they struggle to make sense or be made sense of in the second or foreign language semantic negotiation but also the kind of relationship which will prevail in the classroom. It seems that everything, from the content of learning to the choice of learning activities and tasks will be open to negotiation. The traditional *a priori* language teaching syllabus has little place in this view of language teaching/language learning; instead a flexible inventory of communicative procedures and tasks will emerge to replace it. These may well be drawn from a typology, but essentially teachers and learners will hammer out syllabus and content of learning in a participatory, negotiative process. There are no 'preselected categories of form or function'. Individual learning styles will be taken into account in a differentiated approach to teaching/learning. Individual learning strategies will be uncovered and activated in relation to specific tasks. The sole type of syllabus which can emerge from such an approach is what we might term '*a posteriori*'. At the outset, all is unpredictable. Then negotiation takes place. By close of play, everything has fallen into place, and it all makes sense.

Richard Allwright has spoken of 'weak' and 'strong' formulations of communicative language teaching (personal communication). If I have understood Candlin and Breen's proposals correctly, their formulation would fall into the 'strong' category.

It is in short a fairly revolutionary programme. But we are not here to consider its merits or disadvantages, however tempting it may be to do so. We are here to consider the implications of setting out to educate or train teachers in such an approach, and in his next section Professor Candlin draws our attention to the human costs of doing this. But before we go into this question it does seem legitimate to pose a preliminary question. Why should we take on such a daunting INSET task? Isn't it all rather a tall order? Professor Candlin is quite clear on this point: the confluence of recent research, philosophical speculation, and classroom experience leaves us little option but to take up the challenge – imposing 'inescapable demands' on curriculum developers and teachers-in-training. We are, it would seem, in the grip of history, and there is little choice but to march forward into the future.

We shall do this with our eyes open. A communicative approach of the type outlined means a major reassessment of the roles of teachers, and learners. Teachers become 'informants, resourcers, guides, co-ordinators, curriculum designers, classroom researchers', and so on, while learners become human beings. Changing the metaphor, it is at this point that our good ship encounters the sharp rocks of reality. These are the 'costs' already referred to, and Professor Candlin has sampled these with teachers in a variety of overseas settings – Canadian teachers attending a TESOL Summer Institute at the Ontario Institute for Studies in Education (OISE); a mixed bag of overseas teachers at an INSET course in Honolulu; a mixed European group of senior professionals at Giessen in West Germany; a different group, this time of teachers in Bilingual Education, again in Honolulu. It seems a good idea to find out what teachers think or feel about these revolutionary proposals. In a negotiative approach it is, in fact, mandatory. (I take it that curriculum planners would submit gracefully to being overridden if the teachers, upon being consulted, pronounced the whole programme of curriculum innovation unworkable and refused to implement it?) What is interesting about the samples of reaction presented here is how much more articulate the views of the group of Senior European professionals – all leaders in their forty European countries – are than those of the ordinary teachers. The comments of the latter seem relatively ill-formulated. No attempt has been made to sift through these basketfuls of teacher misgivings (as I did in a paper written on similar lines with Rod Bolitho, identifying, for example, those which relate to objectively discernible constraints in the school system and distinguishing these from more subjective or psychological factors), nor to discuss their relative importance as obstacles to a programme of curriculum innovation. This seems a pity, since it is precisely when teachers and planners engage in a dialogue about ultimate purposes, and ways and means, that plans become reality, the ideal the real. INSET can only gain from more systematic analysis of constraints as they affect teachers in classrooms. We should not accept all such 'costs' as inevitable, any more than we should fool ourselves that every obstacle can be overcome. But Professor Candlin, and perhaps even more a teacher-trainer like Christoph Edelhoff knows this – we all know it – but do we put it into practice?

This brings me to a major issue arising from Professor Candlin's paper. This is the extent to which the present state of theory and practice in our field justifies our confidently espousing a particular model of language teaching and learning – the communicative approach in one of its stronger embodiments – with a view to disseminating it through INSET throughout the world, even in those areas of outer darkness described by Professor Kachru? If so, how would he propose to accommodate his radical vision to the wide variety of teaching and conditions that exists in the education systems of the second and third world countries? At what point do the 'costs' of curriculum innovation become too high for us – and more important, for teachers – to pay?

# Commentator 2

Raymond Janssens

I should like to thank the speaker for a stimulating and even allegoric talk and also for his bold stand in favour of communicative language teaching. In his paper there are so many ideas, problem issues, principles for in-service education and training that one can easily speak of a *treasure chest*, a term he uses himself when referring to that collection of INSET tasks that could be offered and ordered by a cultural agency like the British Council world-wide. An admirable suggestion indeed.

As a commentator I want to limit myself to making one main point and it is about individualization or differentiation, i.e. the different learning styles of individual learners and how a teacher can cope with these. This point is geared to the speaker's second basic principle of communicative language teaching and learning (p. 109).

In my experience as a classroom teacher this is a serious challenge which teachers everywhere have to take up, and which, in my country, Belgium, caused renewed interest and concern, even worry, along with the introduction of so-called Renewed Secondary Education (i.e. the Belgian version of the comprehensive school) and the proliferation of mixed-ability classes. This educational reform gave rise to structural differentiation. An example to illustrate this: There are learners in the second year who take English as a third language and others who do not. A year later, in the third form, English is compulsory for all. Result: those who have had English for one year already come together with those who are beginners, thus causing an ability rift. Teachers and learners are not prepared to cope with such a situation, which, in my opinion, was unnecessarily created by administrators and curriculum planners.

Apart from this structural differentiation, there always remains the natural differences between learners as individuals. How can a teacher best cope with this unavoidable phenomenon? Let me mention two possible answers to this question, the first one supported by a minority, and the second one more widely adopted:

a) A minority says that one should individualize completely and offer each individual learner the English s/he needs. This is an admirably bold view, but can it be put into practice by a teacher?
b) Others, especially textbook writers and their followers, try to programme differentiation material in a three-phase standardized way: remedial, consolidation and enrichment. Still others speak of a basis-extra approach by which they mean that all learners should master to

a sufficient degree a common core of subject matter and that extras are needed for both the more gifted and the slower learners.

It seems to me that this rational approach does not sufficiently take into account that there are other types of learners, more intuitive, associative, i.e. less cognitive types than those for which this three-stage (or two-stage) approach seems to be designed. The latter will not profit from this kind of pre-packed, all too rigorous individualization.

# b) A view from teacher in-service education and training

Christoph Edelhoff

## 1 Teaching for communication

We have come to regard modern language teaching as a communicative task. Language as communication is not confined to face-to-face interaction situations. Indeed, it would be misunderstanding the Council of Europe approach to language teaching if this were to be taken as a purely functional or job-oriented curriculum. Communication in its broader sense embraces all types and modes of communication, person to person, text and media-based, symbolic and fictional. Teaching for communication is aimed at enabling learners to understand – even though they fear that they cannot understand and will be drowned in the vast sea of unknown sounds, signals, signs, words and meanings. They must use the foreign language in order to establish and maintain contacts, seek and give information, make reference to and transmit what they have heard or read, and to convey meaning and opinion both in their freetime activities and for professional purposes.

It is the willingness and capacity for international encounters (*internationale Begegnung*) which covers all areas of communicative involvement.

It must be assumed, however, that a good part of the foreign language classroom mirrors these purposes in only a rather distorted way. Many classes are still governed by the dominant input of the teacher and the more or less patient intake of the learner who listens, imitates, repeats, memorizes, reproduces and learns items and rules rather than strategies for understanding and creatively using the foreign language.

For all language learners the proof of the pudding is in the eating – for many an indigestible meal when they are confronted with real people, real texts and real tasks inside or outside their own country.

International encounter cannot wait until the learners, in real life situations outside the school, finally experience it. Indeed, it must be prepared and trained for from the very first foreign language lesson. This requires the teacher to use his language classes to introduce the learners to the attitudes and skills of negotiation.

Negotiation is the term used by Candlin and others to describe the complex attitudinal, mental, intellectual, intercultural, pragmatic and linguistic domains which must be developed and controlled by the learner when he prepares for encounter (Candlin, 1979).

This comprises

> – learning about himself, his beliefs, motivations, background, history, social environment, culture and intentions. It is experience-based learning which primarily deals with his *own* experience, what is there and what can be gained.
>
> (Dewey, 1916)

and

> – learning about others, their beliefs, motivations, backgrounds, history, social environment, culture and intentions. It is *other* people's experiences which the learner has got to come to grips with, so that the process of perceiving other people's experiences opens up a new level of experience making.
>
> (Edelhoff, 1980)

This process, however, is not self-evident or easy. It is difficult to understand people, the way they speak or write, what they say or write, why they are saying or writing things the way they are saying or writing them. In the first place, activities of understanding on the part of the learner are mental and pragmatic activities concerning his own knowledge, feelings, associations, predictions and the analogies which he draws, including ones about language. It is trying to make sense (*Sinn entwerfen*) which in fact is *negotiating meaning*.

There are two sides, as always. They have got to be brought together, yet they are distinctly different, firstly in a purely linguistic sense, but more important, in a cultural, aesthetic and moral sense. This is why the notion of international encounter through negotiation is an educational concept of intercultural learning (Robert-Bosch-Stiftung, 1982).

We have got to revise traditional concepts of *Landeskunde*, a term which I am using here only for lack of a better English word. The basic need then for teacher training for communication is that of education for negotiation.

It is obvious, of course, that this conflicts with the generally accepted role of the teacher, as depicted, for example, in the passage from an English textbook which I also quoted in the Council of Europe teacher training symposium at Delphi, in May 1983:

> Good morning, everybody. Listen to me, please. I am your teacher. You are my pupils. I teach you every day. Yes, this is what I do. I teach you English. Every day you learn English from me. You come here, you sit

down at your desks, you listen to me, and you speak English to me. You all learn English. You all like the English language. This pupil learns English, that pupil learns English, those pupils learn English, everybody learns English. And everybody likes English. English is a beautiful language.

Please notice:

| I you we they | speak learn teach | English |
|---|---|---|
| he she | speaks learns teaches | Portuguese |

In this example it is the teacher's role to instruct, to quote grammar and make the students listen and speak. The students are seen as the teacher's property. He forms them in his own image.

It seems that a good deal of teacher behaviour all over the world still reflects the teaching and learning philosophies of an earlier age. Many teachers and school authorities seem to believe that the teacher is and must be the centre and focal point of all teaching and learning activities in the classroom. He is expected to know everything, whereas the learners are seen as empty vessels to be filled with what is presented. 'We should like to do group work', teachers keep saying during residential courses which we run at Reinhardwaldschule centre regularly, 'but how can we control what is going on in the groups, language-wise?' It is the teacher who knows all about the target language, the students do not, that is why they are students. The teacher, moreover, is seen as a bearer and ambassador of the other language and culture.

On the other hand, language learners, like all learners, draw on what they have already learnt, not only in language classes and, indeed, not only in school. All second language learning, as is well known, relies on experience and knowledge of the world and on the way learners have acquired their mother tongue (and possibly other languages). They base their foreign language learning on this knowledge and their development or even mastery of communication skills at large, which we have described by the term 'negotiation'.

Language learning for communication requires teachers to be aware of this basic educational framework, which gives learners the opportunity to become experimenters and negotiators rather than input receivers of linguistic and topic inputs.

## 2 Teacher competence and teacher education

Teacher competence in the framework of the Council of Europe Modern Languages Project has been described under the headings *attitudes*, *knowledge* and *skills* (Edelhoff, in Council of Europe, 1981).

The basic *attitude* for the teacher himself to acquire is that of a learner, to be precise a language learner. In principle, he, as a non-native speaker of the target language, is in the same position as his students. Naturally there are differences but they are gradual rather than basic.

The communicative approach to language teaching, moreover, requires him to be a communicator both in his language classes and privately.

> It is in the nature of the communicative approach to foreign language teaching that the teachers should be effective and pedagogically-oriented communicators themselves. It is therefore of the greatest importance that the foreign language teacher should be able to use the target language in a communicative way, i.e. in such a way that he or she is able to initiate communicative situations in the classroom, assist the learners in finding their own learning goals and methods and . . . to encourage understanding and the use of the foreign language – even though comprehension is difficult and uttering/using the language a problem.
>
> (Council of Europe, 1983)

Language competence is one thing, even more important is the teacher's attitude towards international learning, an attitude 'where teachers are ready to accept that communication is free interaction between people of all abilities, opinions, races, and sociocultural backgrounds and that foreign language communication, especially, is there for international understanding, human rights, democratic development and individual enrichment. The very nature of free communication demands an attitude of respect for the learner, his or her needs, and a readiness to regard teaching as enabling learners to develop their talents in a self-directed way both as members of groups and individuals.' (ibid.)

Therefore the teacher's efforts should be directed towards facilitating rather than instructing, and counselling rather than assessing. Indeed, he should regard teaching and learning as the negotiation of meaning both among those present in the classroom and between the classroom and the world outside.

Attitudes are difficult to transmit. Teacher training cannot endeavour

to teach them directly. It should rather provide a framework and opportunities for teachers-to-be and teachers-in-service to experiment,
negotiate, gain experience with people and content matter from target
language communities. The key issue is one of being in touch, ready for
encounters and increasingly equipped to analyse and control one's own
awareness, perceptions and attitudes.

I anticipate the objection here that teacher training should not aim too
high. Indeed, this is not an area of qualification to be tested and labelled.
However, knowledge and skills ought to be firmly rooted in an educational and communicative frame of reference. In German we speak of
*Lehrerbildung* and in English of teacher 'education' rather than mere
training.

Likewise, I find it difficult to accept that communicative teaching can
be developed only in steps, from the less advanced (traditional) method to
the more sophisticated (advanced) set of strategies. Surely communicative
teaching and a system of teacher education serving this principle cannot
be produced by simply repeating other people's historical developments
(and mistakes). With developing countries (in all continents) it appears
rather to be a case of *need-oriented* transfer of know-how, not one of
passing on a graded pack of recipes from a supposedly superior
standpoint.

It is in the same line that the term 'teacher *preparation*' to me seems
quite inappropriate since teacher education should be a lifelong process
of self-determined, autonomous adult learning rather than a temporary
act of instrumental training. This is not only essential for the path initial
teacher training follows but crucial for the organization and format of in-
service teacher education since it is our belief that teachers should do
learning and developing work themselves rather than be given ready-
made results and teaching instructions. If learning through experience is
of primary importance, teachers must be given the opportunity to have
experiences themselves.

In the realm of *knowledge*, many well-informed catalogues of teacher
qualifications have been compiled. There are good reasons for including
findings, insights, facts from educational psychology, pedagogy, learning
theory, sociology, language acquisition, linguistics, applied linguistics,
culture and literature, and the science of communication. However expert
and scientifically well founded university curricula may be, it must be said
that, from an in-service teacher training point of view, all the knowledge
from relevant disciplines will be useless if it cannot be applied in the daily
tasks and routines of a language teacher.

Knowing about things does not do the teaching. This is why *skills* are
so important. One may distinguish between *curricular* and *methodological* skills, as I have done for the Council of Europe project (Council of
Europe, 1983).

130

Curricular skills, the ability to assess syllabuses, courses and textbooks, to decide upon the choice and the editing of texts, to process texts, to evaluate orientation frames or guidelines, to devise and use differentiated exercises which enable the students to experiment, do tasks and solve problems – all of these have got to be matched by the methodological skills, i.e. the ability to use a variety of classroom tactics, grouping practices, methods and different applications of media.

The teaching skills cannot be divorced from the overall communication skills which enable the teacher to 'share meanings, experiences and affects' (Candlin, 1981b) rather than limiting him to the knowledge and handling of the formal systems of the foreign language.

## 3 Learning about oneself, learning about others: *Landeskunde* requirements

It has been a recognized principle for some time now that 'sociocultural' or 'background' or 'area' or simply 'cultural' aspects and studies ought to form an integral part of the foreign language curriculum. The German term *Landeskunde* reflects the traditional attitude, one of factual knowledge. It was the belief that *knowing* about the target language community from one's own point of view was enough to establish 'cultural co-operation'.

To give an example, in a well-known textbook for fourth-year Gymnasium pupils (13–14 years of age) we find a full chapter on 'Local Government in England' in the form of a personal story of one Bob Smith (who 'like many other boys and girls in his town, led a happy and carefree life'), who happened to wonder about a hole in the road and subsequently found out all about local government in his town and in England. It is assumed that students are interested in this and will take in both language and *Landeskunde* content by simply identifying with the figure in their textbook.

We have come to realize in recent years that international learning requires more than just one-sided knowledge about what is different. In the recent *Landeskunde* literature in West Germany increasing attention has been paid to the questions of authenticity, oral history, intercultural learning, international encounter and learner as negotiator (Buttjes, 1980, 1982; Robert-Bosch-Stiftung, 1982; Solmecke, 1982).

The picture is by no means clear, however. There is also talk of a new *Kulturkunde* (Keller, 1983) and a good deal of the new teaching material seems to reflect a rather naïve view of documentary authenticity of language and text without caring much about authenticity of situation and of learner (Edelhoff, 1983b).

This is why the problem is one for teacher training, especially for in-service teacher training. The majority of the teaching force now in schools was trained some ten to fifteen years ago when the encyclopaedic view of *Landeskunde* was still prevalent.

Since the issue is one of immediate interest to a cultural agency like the British Council, I am offering here some points for debate, summarizing a communicative *Landeskunde* curriculum for teacher education:

## I   Attitudes

1 Teachers who are meant to educate learners towards 'international learning' must be 'international learners' themselves.
2 Teachers should be prepared to consider how others see them and be curious about themselves and others.
3 Teachers should be prepared to experiment and negotiate in order to achieve understanding on both sides.
4 Teachers should be prepared to share meanings, experience and affects both with people from other countries and with their own students in the classroom.
5 Teachers should be prepared to take an active part in the search for the modern languages contribution to international understanding and peace-making at home and abroad.
6 Teachers should aim to adopt the role and function of social and inter-cultural interpreter, not ambassador.

## II   Knowledge

1 Teachers should have and seek knowledge about the sociocultural environment and background of the target language community/ies or country/ies.
2 Teachers should have and seek knowledge about their own country and community and how others see them.
3 Teachers' knowledge should be active knowledge which they are able to apply and interpret and to make accessible to the learning situations and styles of their students.
4 Teachers should know how language works in communication and how it is used successfully for understanding. They should know about the shortcomings of language and foreign language users and how misunderstandings can be avoided.

## III   Skills

1 Teachers should have and develop further appropriate communication skills in the foreign language which are suited for negotiation both in the classroom and in international communication situations at home and abroad.

132

2 Teachers should have and develop further text skills, i.e. the ability to deal with authentic data in all media (print, audio, audio-visual) and in face-to-face interaction.
3 Teachers should have and develop further the skills necessary to connect student experience with ideas, things and objects outside their direct reach and to create learning environments which lend themselves to experience learning, negotiation and experiment.

## 4   Teacher training

Since school and education in many countries are the responsibility of the state, the training of the teachers is taken care of by the state, too. Due to tradition and political background there are considerable differences, however.

*Basic* teacher training is mostly organized in universities or university-like institutions, whereas *pre-service* and *in-service* teacher training is often organized under direct state control.

Frequently, academic courses for language teachers tend to have little or no direct connection with school life. It is still true that much academic study is confined to theoretical linguistics and literature, with perhaps a few hours in language and area studies. This seems especially true of West Germany where young teachers coming from non-service teacher training at university (if they can find a job at all) suffer from the 'shock of practice' and are confronted with well-meaning colleagues who advise them to 'forget everything' they have brought with them from their studies.

The merging of theory and practice is expected to be achieved by *pre-service* training institutions like the German *Studienseminar*. Indeed, the language teacher, like all teachers, has to take a second state examination at the end of the *Studienseminar* period to test his practical teaching skills and applied knowledge. Observers from abroad have often envied us for this long and intensive teacher training structure. It is no secret, however, that many teachers feel badly equipped when they assume their first responsible jobs and, indeed, it has been criticized that much of the *Studienseminar* is ritualistic and oriented towards a short-term show effect. It is no wonder that great expectations are placed in the INSET of language teachers.

Other European countries face the same problem even though they may organize the phases of pre-service training in different ways. The training of practical skills, the handling of language and communication and the application of sociocultural knowledge and experimentation are rare. Once formal qualifications have been attained teachers are left to themselves.

In my definition of In-service Teacher Education and Training

(INSET) I should like to stress the fact that while pre-service training deals with the preparation of teachers-to-be, INSET includes all kinds of job-oriented learning activities for teachers on the job. It is regarded as part of the teacher's work and expected to have a direct connection with the practical school situation. It may be organized individually, privately or collectively, making use of a variety of ways and means, e.g. individual study, books, media, correspondence materials, informal and formal groups and courses at local (school), regional and central or national and international levels (Edelhoff, in Council of Europe, 1981).

It seems to be most effective when it takes into consideration the teachers' own fears, preconceptions, role definitions, their perceived situational problems and constraints, their own social and communicative behaviour in groups. Teachers must be actively involved in the search for and proposal of solutions to their perceived problems and constraints in the teaching situation (Candlin, 1981b).

It is because of the direct control of the state over the school system mentioned above that a large number of INSET activities are organized under the auspices of education ministries, inspectorates and institutions under direct state control, especially if and when INSET activities take place during teaching hours.

One of the common features of state INSET is the traditional advisory capacity of the school inspectorate which, in many cases, is seen as a necessary tribute to the authority of the state.

Both state authority-controlled and the university-based INSET organizations have suffered a certain amount of criticism, the one because of its orientation towards current regulations, the other for its lack of practical links with school life.

It is certainly right that a number of socioculturally determined INSET targets can be achieved while remaining within the confines of the local institution. This is the case with media and authentic texts courses, even language and communication training on a simulated basis. Working for international learning, however, by definition, includes travel and exchange, project and experiment abroad. It also requires teacher time and money.

This is why a large number of international learning INSET activities are left to the initiative of the individual teacher who uses her/his holidays, finds a course and the funds, and spends a kind of professional busman's holiday abroad.

There are a great many language schools, universities and other agencies in the United Kingdom which have begun to offer courses for teachers which can undoubtedly be very useful, yet have no direct connection with the sociocultural and teaching situation of the participants. There is a danger of one-sidedness, this time the other way round.

This is where the cultural agency, the British Council, can do a special job by advising and liaising and, through its representations in the various countries, making sure that courses and visits are actually geared to the needs and styles of the teacher participants.

## 5 The role of the British Council as a cultural agency in teacher education and training

Fifty years is indeed a long time to look back on. The British Council has been very active in many fields, always contributing a great deal to teacher education as one of the key areas of concern.

Looking back to my own education in West Germany where the British Council started work twenty-five years ago, I remember doing the Cambridge Proficiency Examination at the affiliated Münster University British Cultural Centre, Die Brücke, for which I worked as a young student, and later, from Tübingen University, using the Cologne central office library because our university library could not cope with the demand.

I remember the lively conversation groups, theatre and reading clubs, readings and recitals, presentations, films and exhibitions, and I will never forget the sadness of a large anglophile community in Frankfurt, most of them teachers, somewhere in the middle of the Federal Republic, when the thriving regional office there was closed ten years ago.

I am also grateful for the friendly professional atmosphere and substantial assistance we are receiving these days for our bi-national teacher workshops which we are organizing with the Danes, from the Hamburg regional office, where we hold our preparatory seminars, and the Cologne and Copenhagen central English language offices.

To me the first task of the British Council is simply to be present in the countries of the world, irrespective of their attainment in the English language, representing English language and culture in an authentic way and making its living context accessible.

A second task, of course, in teacher education is preparing and offering information, both literary and non-fictional, live, print and multi-media. In an age of information explosions and undreamt-of technological advances this task demands new attitudes and efforts on both sides – the givers and the recipients.

Another task is that of opening doors and making contacts for teachers through guidance and counselling and staging encounters: a fourth that of advising and participating in local projects, using the British Council premises as meeting centres and service stations where people can get assistance of different kinds – personal advice, media help, print and duplication, and simply meeting and working facilities for groups and individuals; in fact, using the premises wherever this is possible as regional educational, cultural and teachers' centres.

Ideally one might describe a cultural agency such as the British Council as being:

– competent
– resourceful
– altruistic
– supportive
– participatory
– consistent
– patient.

Certainly, it must be difficult to live up to such an image and, under the demands of intercultural negotiation, the tasks are by no means easy to fulfil. But there are so many excellent samples from all over the world that may serve as models.

There may and, indeed, will be occasions where the cultural agency is expected to take the initiative and do things directly, more or less independently from the host country. However, we are convinced and have learnt from experience that discourse attitudes and participatory methods in need-oriented projects yield the richer and more rewarding results. It is a policy of give-and-take and a sharing of experience supplementing the communicative curriculum of negotiation.

Amongst the many dangers to avoid, one is to use the interested local teacher of English or teacher trainer as an envoy of one's own diplomatic purposes, like a fifth column, i.e. to regard teacher education in English as a tool in cultural policies. If the English language teacher is used as an instrument she/he might soon lose her/his original capacity to negotiate and bridge gaps both ways. Indeed, the local teacher who is committed to the culture and language of the target civilization always faces the danger of being regarded as somebody exotic and outside her/his peer group and society. It is therefore essential to see her/him as a local resource person and support her/him in doing her/his job as social and cultural interpreter.

First, one should learn from the local teachers what they feel are the values, views and needs of their societies. Only then should one use their foreign studies curriculum and growing competence to co-ordinate one's own views and intentions with theirs.

Views and needs, of course, can and should be developed or modified, if necessary. But, as in the learner-centred approach to language teaching, the non-native teacher should not merely be 'given information' or be 'instructed' but be *offered opportunities* to look for herself/himself, to experiment and to learn authentically, i.e. without further mediation. In this sense to 'prepare' teachers is to support them in preparing themselves.

This requires study and learning activities such as:

– becoming acquainted with
– becoming familiar with
– understanding
– interpreting
– valuing
– appreciating
– evaluating
– discerning
– comparing, etc.

directed towards real data and people, manifest and background information, traditions and trends, beliefs and facts etc., i.e. items and phenomena of existing, living British culture and society with a view to preparing teaching materials, conducting teaching projects, and devising and implementing syllabuses and curricula.

It is obvious that these activities can best be achieved in direct research and learning contact, i.e. when the teacher–learner can overcome barriers of mental/ideological and/or geographical distance. Some of the distance may be overcome at home and through the learner's own efforts, by way of studying books and using (audio-visual) media; a good part, however, can only be approached with the help of native speaker specialists and, indeed, by going to Britain itself.

From an INSET point of view it is evident that British Studies activities of the kind I have listed, while firmly rooted in initial teacher training, should become regular activities for practising English teachers. Teacher exchanges and INSET courses in the home country and in Britain should be regular, and of the kind that animate and activate teachers and offer opportunities for concrete encounters with English language and culture and have a spin-off for classroom practice.

It seems almost impossible to ask all this of a cultural agency like the British Council. And, indeed, it would be wrong to expect the British Council to occupy certain areas of educational work in a particular way. What is suggested is a feedback system or systems of networks where teacher training institutions and individuals abroad are linked up with centres of excellence and experts in Britain offering their back-up and support services. The role of the British Council in such a system of 'communicating tubes' would be one of professional mediator, not just of organizer or paymaster.

In West Germany, in recent years we have been very fortunate in establishing such a network serving teacher education – a network of ideas, people, materials and activities joining together the Hessian in-service education institute HILF (a spoken acronym meaning 'help' in German), the English language services of the British Council in Germany, UK professional institutions like the Lancaster University Institute for English

Language Education and language schools of the Bell Educational Trust, German institutions like the Hessian state curriculum institute (HIBS) and the English department of Giessen University, school and adult departments of radio and television stations (like Radio Bremen and Westdeutscher Rundfunk, Cologne) and some friendly publishing houses like Langenscheidt-Longman, Kamp and Hueber.

Networks of this kind do not simply exist; they are built up on certain principles. Firstly they are purely *functional* and *purpose-oriented*. Then they are *non-hierarchical*; their *members are autonomous* and determine the amount of interest and their factual contribution according to their own purposes and rules. And, there is *no order in roles or proceedings*; members may initiate or run projects and offer participation in the network. Moreover, the network itself is an *open form* of co-operation; it can be joined by new members and/or draw on sub-systems or other networks. *Networks do not 'belong' to any one member*, but they must be *specially sponsored and serviced*. They are *non-competitive* and based on the assumption that all members co-operate because they have *something special to contribute*, and indeed it is everybody's conviction that *if one unites one's efforts one can achieve* more.

These communicating networks can exist only because they are based on *personal links*, in that it is *professionals in their institutions who co-operate* rather than the anonymous institutions themselves. Basic attitudes are trust, open-mindedness and a sense of concrete co-operation.

To build and service networks takes awareness, time, energy and money and, sometimes, a good deal of lobbying in one's own institution. But what is so nice is that, if a project is successful, it has many fathers and casts a rewarding light both on individuals and on the institutions.

For a cultural agency like the British Council, in a foreign country, working through networks may also be a method of avoiding the danger of working with individuals outside or detached from the state education system of the host country, ignoring the sometimes inflexible or bureaucratic administration of schools and education. This may seem easier, and in some countries even necessary but, nevertheless, it does not lead very far. A lot of the local liaison work should be devoted to talking to school administrators and inspectors, trying to convince them of the necessity of concrete cultural co-operation, i.e. finding money for courses and projects using teacher time, and working with individual schools and teachers in officially-approved projects. Ideally the school/education administration should be made part of the networks. There are cases where the foreign cultural agency has a better chance of achieving this than the local English department.

One of the biggest problems in working for in-service teacher education is the lack of continuity. All too often, teacher courses are the 'on and off' type and the involvement of the cultural agency remains marginal. This applies to in-service courses in many countries staffed by visiting British specialists, or to the rare courses in Britain which have neither a proper preparation nor a sensible follow-up. It remains with the individual teacher whether she/he is capable of linking the course with the on-going work in school.

What is needed is an overall framework ensuring that INSET activities are connected and also regularly tying in with school and teaching projects. Of course, this is the task of the local school and education administration. The cultural agency, however, does not just depend on what the local situation might offer but, while avoiding on and off type involvements, ought to establish consistency and internal connections among its own professional activities both at home and abroad. The problems here are how long the periods of rotation of staff abroad should be and how deeply officers should penetrate the language and culture of the host country.

The network method again may be the most appropriate answer. It may ensure that activities in one country and the know-how gained there are available to other regions and at other points of time. The cultural agency then joins into networks and acts as mediator for British individuals and institutions.

In this paper I can only briefly and in closing refer to the network experience in teacher education in Germany and Europe on which my propositions are based.

The last few years alone have witnessed a variety of intriguing projects initiated or substantially supported by the British Council: the *Story's Way* project, video and print materials for the use of fiction in the advanced and adult English class; *Norwich Now*, a series of public television films on the life and people of an English provincial town; 'LIP', i.e. *Landeskunde* Information Packs, an on-going project to supply teachers with selected authentic newspaper and magazine texts on a variety of topics; and *Teacher Training Observed*, a most promising co-operative project, begun by the British Council in Cologne and HILF, documenting the yearly INSET 'outing' or expedition-intensive course in England, its preparation and local follow-up activities on video and film (pilot videos on the 'Lancaster Outing', 1982; West German Radio WDR Cologne films of the 'Norwich Outing', 1984).

A good deal of the motivation and know-how in projects of this kind has also gone into the INSET international and bi-national teacher workshops organized by teacher associations in the Netherlands, Denmark and West Germany with mixed course teams and participants from these countries, Britain and Scandinavia which have been held regularly on long weekends since 1979. The special method with these highly regarded and practical seminars on the communicative teaching and learning of

139

English is that English is not only the target language but also the means of work and international socializations during these courses (Skarrildhus 1981/1982; Vierhouten, 1981; Kerkrade, 1982; Hamburg and Skarrildhus, 1983/1984, forthcoming).

Finally, the Council of Europe series of INSET international courses for teacher trainers, begun in 1984 and already now very successful, should be mentioned.

On all these European teacher education projects the task for the British Council has been one of getting involved across the national borders of several host countries which, from a European point of view, seems to be very promising.

## Note

In my papers and proposals for the Council of Europe Modern Languages Project (CCC, Strasbourg 1979, seq.) I have dealt at greater length with some aspects of the communicative teaching of English, curriculum development and teacher in-service training. A full summary of continuous INSET activities of HILF and a typology of INSET courses is contained in my paper for the Georgetown University Round Table Conference in 1983 (GURT, 1983, edited by J. Alatis, H. H. Stern and P. Strevens). For the *Landeskunde* aspects I am using some passages of my unpublished paper for Robert-Bosch-Stiftung, Stuttgart, 1983.

# Commentator 1

## John Haycraft

I wonder whether Mr Edelhoff does not consider the German practice of having basic teacher training in Universities a mistaken one. After all, most teacher training is for school teachers. Isn't it therefore preferable for trainees to learn in the kind of environment which they have to get to know?

I myself favour teacher training being in a school where teaching practice and observation of classes are much easier. I regret that when comprehensive schools were founded in Britain, training colleges were not incorporated as well. Instead, teacher training, as in most countries, is isolated from the classroom in separate buildings and, as a result, training tends to be excessively theoretical.

I also feel that practice teaching is the corner-stone of training. International House courses have daily teaching practice, and because of this, theory can be translated immediately into practice. Thus, a theme such as the use of visual aids might be discussed one morning. The same evening, trainees prepare a lesson plan involving the use of these aids. Then, the following afternoon a practice lesson using them takes place.

Groups consisting of six trainers do micro-teaching with volunteer students for an hour and a half every day, and, later in the course, each teaches for longer periods. After each session, trainees discuss their own classes to see how far the theoretical ideas are valid and work with students, and ways in which their own teaching approach can be improved.

As a result, theory and practice are united and student reactions become a crucial factor. Also, trainees get used to the idea of discussing each other's teaching. The concept that criticism is malicious or an intrusion is replaced by the idea that it is a way of improving and sharing ideas. This is particularly important in a profession which tends to be defensive, and where teachers sometimes regard their classrooms as fortresses.

Another advantage of having teacher training in a school is that trainers can also teach normal classes. This means that their theoretical ideas are continually being brought down to earth by classroom realities and that they can also try out new ideas with students in a normal class.

As far as I can see, teacher training without regular classroom practice and observation is like trying to learn to play the piano by way of a course in the History of Music, with a few verbal explanations of how the fingers should be moved, or which keys represent which notes.

The model is already there in teaching hospitals, which are always

merged with those which take patients. It is a pity that our teacher training is still so far behind. After all, as we all know, training is the key to the
whole educational system and will determine the attitude of staff until
they reach retirement – in other words for scores of years.

# Commentator 2

John Trim

Christoph Edelhoff and I have worked together very closely in the Council of Europe's Modern Language Projects. It has been a great pleasure for me to see in practice the working methods which have enthused so many practising teachers from the countries of North-West Europe, and the constant guiding principles according to which the Council of Europe has promoted language learning, and which teachers and other parties to the 'partnership for learning' (administrators, examiners, publishers etc., as well, of course as the learners themselves) are invited to accept and apply in their own special circumstances.

The principles, which are closely related to the nature and purpose of the Council, can be summarized as follows:

## Permanent education

Education is a lifelong process, in which we are all learners and all teachers. Full-time initial education is a preparation to meet challenges, the nature of which is only fully revealed in adult life, when a more closely focused training is needed. The implications of this principle are particularly far-reaching for the learning and teaching of languages.

## Learner-centredness

Language education contributes to the steady and purposeful development of the learner in various dimensions: as a communicator, as a learner, as a member of various interlocking social groups and as an individual with a personal culture, values and beliefs. This development leads to an increasing autonomy of the learners, as their attitudes, understanding, knowledge and skills enable them to take charge of their actions as socially responsible, co-operative but free and self-directing agents. The needs, motivations, characterizations and resources of learners afford the basis for educational planning, involving the specification of worthwhile and feasible objectives, the use of appropriate methods and materials for learning, teaching and evaluation.

## Life-relatedness

Educational systems too easily become encapsulated, setting introverted goals and using cellular methods, evaluating according to criteria relating to a closed system. They should be opened up to interact with the rest of society.

## Participatory democracy

Within a supportive administrative framework, which takes into account the wider interests of society, decisions on goals and means should be taken as close as possible to the point of learning. This means that the necessary planning tools must be made available in suitably accessible form to teachers and learners, as a basis for informal choice of objectives and methods, by teachers and learners in consultation. This is the intention, for instance, of the 'threshold level' proposals.

## Communicative approach

Among the many legitimate objectives of language learning resulting from the needs and motivations of learners, priority attaches on a social scale to the learning and teaching of languages as a means and mode of communication, whether face-to-face or at a distance in space and/or time, in order to facilitate the freer movement of people and ideas in what has been a politically and linguistically fragmented continent. The communicative approach implies the avoidance of purism and formalism in teaching and testing.

## Learning by doing

It is not enough for the language classroom to be a place where young people are equipped with a knowledge and particular skills prerequisite for communication. It must also be a place where communication develops and is cultivated as an increasingly natural mode of action, as learners (and teachers) grow in confidence as well as in competence.

If these principles are to be put into practice, they must be wholeheartedly accepted and applied by a vast army of teachers – perhaps over 250,000 teach English in Europe. Unable to reach them all, the Council of Europe has launched a series of international workshops for teacher trainers.

As the programme proposed under 13.3 has developed,[1] it has become increasingly clear that methods such as those described by Edelhoff are successful in practice and are generally welcomed and enjoyed by teachers and teacher trainers from all European countries, including those who are not already familiar with the communicative approach. It has also become clear that there is no single pattern of in-service training. Workshops and INSET courses, like classroom teaching itself, vary widely according to the structures and traditions of the country concerned, and the values, attitudes, habits and personalities of teachers and their trainers, as of pupils and students. Personal qualities remain of central importance to good teaching and must be respected. Edelhoff has indeed emphasized the necessity of starting from where the teachers are.

Communicative methodology in teacher training is clearly widely successful, and the ideology which underpins it appears to be widely acceptable in many parts of Europe. The question arises, whether it is universally applicable. Different cultures take very different views of the roles, obligations and rights of teachers and taught. These views may be firmly entrenched in political and religious systems. What will happen when methods and procedures rooted in one view of human relationships are presented as models to societies whose educational systems are based on different premises? Acceptance, rejection or adaptation? Here too, English across the world raises some of the fundamental dilemmas of multicultural relations.

## Note

1  13.3: 'contributing to an intensified programme of in-service teacher training, including internationally organized, staffed and recruited in-service courses for language teachers, and facilitating the participation of serving teachers in such courses;' (Recommendation No. R(82)18 of the Committee of Ministers of the Council of Europe to Member States concerning Modern Languages).

# Theme IV    Summary of discussion

The model of In-service Teacher Education and Training (INSET) presented by the main speakers was one developed within a European context and designed to be consistent with a communicative approach to
language teaching currently favoured in this context. The question arose
as to how dependent the model was on the particular circumstances and
pedagogic assumptions it was designed to service, how far such a model
was generally appropriate in principle and applicable in practice outside
the circumstances of its origins.

It was recognized that if teachers are to follow an approach in which
learners are encouraged to negotiate the conditions of their own learning
in collaboration with the teacher and each other, then the education and
training of teachers should logically itself follow the same principle. The
point was made, however, that in many cases such a collaborative
methodology would be difficult to implement in that it would run directly
counter to the prevailing pedagogic orthodoxy which was sustained by
institutional policy. This might well in effect impose intolerable burdens
on both teacher and pupil. Learners would anyway naturally incline to
follow the familiar patterns of established custom even if institutions
could be persuaded into reform. If teacher preparation is to be consistent
with a feasible approach to teaching, then the collaborative model proposed would not be appropriate in these cases. There is also the problem,
it was noted, that one might be seeking to effect changes in pedagogy in
the English language class which were isolated from, and inconsistent
with, existing practices in other areas of the curriculum. So whereas it
seemed reasonable to adopt the same principles for the preparation of
teachers as these teachers would themselves be encouraged to apply in
their classes, it would be unwise to assume that these principles would
necessarily be those of a particular pedagogic approach.

There was general approval for the approach to INSET being proposed
as an *orientation* to teacher education but reservations about it as a
*method*. It was felt that there would be circumstances when it would be
inefficient, and indeed self-defeating, to rely exclusively on the natural
emergence of consensus through consultation and self-appraisal, when
there would be need for explicit guidance and the setting of specific

objectives in advance in order to give direction to discovery. The important thing was to ensure that INSET programmes encouraged teachers to
accept responsibility for their own subsequent development in terms of
the attitudes, skills, and knowledge required for effective teaching in their
own circumstances, and this implied a concept of INSET as a continuing
process of co-operation and support.

Another issue which was debated was the extent to which the INSET
model proposed was appropriate for pre-service teacher preparation. The
view was expressed, and subsequently challenged, that pre-service programmes were concerned primarily with induction, with the initiation of
students into the craft of pedagogy and that this called for the kind of
intervention and control associated with training rather than the creative
destabilization and critical self-appraisal associated with the education
objectives which the proposed approach to INSET had in mind.

# THEME V  LEARNER-CENTRED METHODOLOGY

## a)  Creativity and constraint in the language classroom

Christopher Brumfit

The purpose of this paper is partly retrospective and partly prospective. It aims to give an account of recent discussion about learner-centred methodologies, and to pursue that argument further with a more speculative exploration of issues likely to dominate future discussion.

Let me start by examining issues which will be very familiar to professional teaching methodologists, but perhaps less so to those whose interests lie elsewhere.

### Changing attitudes to language teaching

Educational institutions tend, for good reasons, to resist over-enthusiastic innovation, and for many years language teaching tacitly accepted the tradition inherited from classical education. Language was reified as a more or less definable system which existed independently of the user, enshrined variously in works of classic literature, grammar books, the best and latest textbooks, or the best and latest syllabus. Learners might slip and slither as they launched themselves on their journey, but at least the sea was frozen, the direction was clear and the guides dependable. Then the ice melted. Learners are no longer being led on a firm if slippery path, but they share with their teachers a volatile and buoyant, but unreliable and unpredictable linguistic environment through which they must negotiate their own tentative progress, while theorists debate whether structural syllabuses are the life-jackets of the future or the snow-shoes of the past. Prendergast, in 1872, like Palmer in 1922 and Hornby in 1954, has no doubt that language teaching is about establishing the fundamental sentence patterns of the language. Now, however, second language methodologists are following Halliday's first language lead in teaching 'how to mean' (Halliday, 1975).

It is easy to chart this shift in interest from recent language-related work, and we shall explore this in the next section. But it is rarely remarked how this shift also reflects very broad changes in our attitude to knowledge, authority and social cohesion in western European society. It is not simply that a fixed model of language reflects better a stable and

148

homogeneous speech community than a volatile and varied one, but the rise of the social sciences and psychology, the decline of hierarchic ideas along with the decline in literal religious belief, and the increased potential for emancipation of previously exploited groups such as women, peasants and workers resulting from advances in health care and political consciousness, have all led to fundamental shifts of sensibility. It is not that the world has become so much a global village as a global city, and – as Raymond Williams has noted – the city imposes different perceptions from the country:

> As we stand and look back at a Dickens novel the general movement we remember – the characteristic movement – is a hurrying seemingly random passing of men and women, each heard in some fixed phrase, seen in some fixed expression; a way of seeing men and women that belongs to the street. There is at first an absence of ordinary connection and development. These men and women do not so much relate as pass each other and then sometimes collide. Nor often in the ordinary way do they speak to each other. They speak at or past each other, each intent above all on defining through his words his own identity and reality . . .
> (Williams, 1973: 191)

Each of us has probably sat today in a bus or a train surrounded entirely by people we have never seen before and will never see again. In these city conditions, typified most characteristically by the departure lounge in an airport, language changes its purpose, becomes almost exclusively transactional, and fundamental communication takes place either in the closed circles of jargon-supported private groups, or through the elaborated medium of print. Increasingly we cannot avoid an awareness of the impossibility of communication, for we live our lives surrounded by people whose private references, personal needs and deepest aspirations are inaccessible to our communication, however sympathetic our intentions. In an effort to locate security within ourselves, for external security has been lost, concepts like 'authenticity' and 'autonomy' have been developed by philosophers; the characteristic political imagery of the age speaks of 'struggle', sociological imagery of 'negotiation'; we 'construct' our reality, for we cannot take it as given. This shift can be seen in symbolic acts within language in society – the substitution of linguistic diversity for authority and tradition in the western Christian churches – and even in language teaching: the disappearance of the last great monocultural language from the normal school curriculum, as Latin has disappeared.

It will be objected that this description, even if acceptable, is limited to the view from London. There is much truth in this claim, and I shall return to this point later. For the moment, though, it is worth noting that English is becoming the major medium of international communication in a very different sense from that of Latin's international role, and different again from the inter-cultural roles of other major world languages such as Arabic or Russian. But French, Spanish and Portuguese are international in the same ways as English.

## Shifts in theoretical feeder disciplines

Although core post-Chomskyan linguistics still thrives, it is probably fair to say that most commentators outside linguistics turned away from the narrowest tradition during the late 1960s and early 1970s. Yet, at the same time, the clarity of Chomsky's discussions of the scope of linguistics (Chomsky, 1964, 1965, 1968) enabled most language-related disciplines to establish a clearer framework for their concern with language, either by adoption and extension of Chomsky's ideas, or in opposition to them. The result of this ferment is that, in the kind of general terms that influence language teaching, a consensus has emerged about the nature of language which does not reflect accurately the specific position of any one discipline, but picks up general tendencies in all.

What is under attack is the autonomy of language, the reification of the analyst that results in decontextualized grammars and abstracted definitions. The notion of 'communicative competence' which underlies most current methodological discussion is itself derived from a heterogeneous collection of sources, including psycholinguistics (Wales and Marshall, 1966), anthropology (Hymes, 1971), pedagogy (Savignon, 1972), and (in name if not in substance) critical sociology (Habermas, 1970). All these trends increase our awareness of the social role of language. Thus, it is now freely admitted that our concern in language teaching should not be solely with the formal features of language, but also with the ways in which these formal features should be used in social interaction (Canale and Swain, 1980). Hymes's work defining the components of speech performance in relation to particular 'speech events' (Hymes, 1967) is widely cited. Work on variable rule systems within sociolinguistics (Labov, 1972; Trudgill, 1974), and on the various desires for convergence or divergence which may motivate unconscious variation (Bourhis and Giles, 1977) provide the beginnings of a theory of language in social life. In syllabus design the concept of speech as performance (Searle, 1969) has led to radically new views of syllabus specification (Wilkins, 1976); and Grice (1975) is a further much-cited source from linguistic philosophy, usually supporting the principle of co-operative interaction in conversation.

There is thus a fundamental concern with how language is made into messages, how it makes sense, rather than what form it has. Of course these two interact, and discourse analysts, particularly, are concerned with such interaction, but their influence on language teaching is probably stronger in general precept than specific implementation of detailed theory – though Widdowson (1978, 1979) has been active in trying to push towards the latter.

The message which emerges from all this activity to the teaching profession is not specific but it is clear. Language is more complex than was previously thought, particularly in its relations to personal development and social context. So far, there has been much (largely abortive) effort to solve language teaching problems primarily by reference to social context (Richterich, 1972; Munby, 1978) in terms of instruments for needs analysis. Personal needs have largely been left to teaching methodologists.

## Learner freedom

Early discussion of communicative language teaching tended to assume that if we changed the objectives from formal to functional or notional specifications, the methodology would naturally follow. Such hopes in fact concealed a fundamental argument between two different attitudes to teaching. One group (e.g. van Ek, 1975; Wilkins, 1976; Munby, 1978) still wanted to specify what was to be taught, but wanted the specification to be more socially sensitive than in a structural syllabus. The other (Allwright, 1977; Breen and Candlin, 1980) seemed more uncertain about the concept of a traditional syllabus at all. Since much of this work, in Britain at least, was an offshoot of work with MAs in Applied Linguistics and of British Council consultancies, and since the colleagues encountered in these circumstances were normally beyond or beside the stage of basic methodological teacher training, it is unsurprising that discussion was aimed more at advisors and consultants than practising teachers. Yet innovation which conflicts with the hopes and needs of teachers is unlikely to be successful, and it was at least arguable that change of a socially sensitive language classroom would be more dependent on teachers' management of their own classrooms than on adjustments to curriculum documents or examination syllabuses.

But teachers were not necessarily in a strong position. The over-strong claims made by confident audiolingual language laboratory salespersons had caused suspicion of theorists, many schools were confronting for the first time large numbers of unstreamed learners, and anyway schools in general were under attack from a vociferous if small deschooling body. 'Learner freedom' risked becoming no more than a slogan of political virtue in the post-1968 educational scene, and some of the earlier pronouncements of Krashen, for example, or of multicultural educators in Britain discussing ESL work, seemed to be unhelpfully anti-teacher.

Teachers do, however, have an expertise, for which learners (or their governments, or their parents) pay. Teachers know more about the varieties of learning possibilities than any one learner can. They know that there are different types of learner, that single learners develop in more or less predictable ways and vary in their motivations, that there are a range of materials, a range of techniques, and a range of activities possible for each learner. This understanding enables good teachers to abdicate responsibility as well as take it on, to withdraw as well as to intervene, to interact as well as to teach, and to participate as well as to judge and correct. Teaching is thus about the provision of appropriate freedom as well as the establishment of appropriate control. What Allwright (1976) classifies as 'samples' and 'guidance' with the target language establishes teacher inequality and control, for it depends on the teacher's professional expertise, but what goes on within 'management activities' may allow the teacher to provide complete freedom, though within limits which – ultimately – only the teacher controls. The question to ask here is the extent to which freedom *must* be curtailed, and the extent to which it is essential for language acquisition that learners should have their own independence.

In the days when (in theory at least) all errors led to more secure errors, freedom was directly counter to learning principles, and could not be countenanced without theoretical schizophrenia. Fortunately, recent views of the nature of language acquisition allow for more trial and error, and consequently for more classroom freedom. This is not the place to explore second language acquisition theories in detail, but it is worth noting that there are two essentials for successful language acquisition recognized by all theories. These are:

1  there must be exposure (either systematic or rich) to the target language;
2  there must be opportunities to use the target language for as genuine as possible communication, in conversation, or reading and writing, or listening.

Teachers would, I think, agree to add that there must be motivation to exploit these two essential conditions.

Beyond these, we can claim that we are dealing with conventions that are negotiable. But effective teaching without these conditions is impossible to conceive.

There has, in practice, been little disagreement that freedom for creativity is advisable for advanced learners. Even the most traditional language teaching has allowed freedom in reading, and to some extent in writing, for higher level students. Indeed, since freedom is much harder to constrain in interpretative activities, any course with a heavy reading or listening component has allowed unintended creativity. More recently, however, the debate has concentrated on the need for 'acquisition' in naturalistic conditions even for beginners. This may take the form of an argument for an 'acquisition-rich' environment with little or no selection and grading of linguistic forms, or it may involve a demand for negotiation of syllabus content with learners so that they have freedom in determining the teaching content (see discussion in Brumfit, 1984b, especially contributions by Candlin and Breen). What we need to be clear about is that any choice made by the teacher – to negotiate, to provide a structured syllabus based on any categories whatsoever, to refuse to structure at all – involves a restriction of the freedom of learners: a restriction which learners properly accept as inherent in the teaching contract. Learners whose self-perceptions demand traditional procedures, like some of those cited in one of the British Council's most interesting publications on language teaching (Pickett, 1978) need to be taken account of: 'I need always to have the grammar of a language laid out as a system for me. I cannot learn a language simply by induction' (p. 61), and 'I find that if I try to learn vocabulary I must concentrate on a word list and learn the items one by one . . . ' (p. 71). Freedom may be imposed inappropriately, either for individuals or for language learning principles, and – anyway – if it is imposed it is only limited freedom.

The point is that each collection of students involves the teacher in a different set of decisions to make, which can only be made on the basis of local understanding combined with professional judgement. Teaching any class involves generalizing from a wide set of possible options to a wide set of possible reactions by students, and the art of teaching consists of successful, because sensitive, matching of one set of generalizations against the other.

There seems little doubt that many learners benefit from having the input organized for them (Naiman *et al.*, 1978: 103; Rivers, 1979). What is equally clear, from the same sources and much other discussion, is that learners who never have the opportunity to improvise, to communicate naturally, or to aim at risk-taking by maximizing their available target-language resources in natural communication, either in comprehension or production, will be severely limited in language development. At worst, learners will be so constrained by the habits of their learning experience that they simply cannot participate in conversation, cannot remember the content of long stretches of reading, cannot construct written language fluently but only with painstaking and conscious effort. A weak argument for creativity will demand a substantial degree of fluency activity simply to give learners the experience of the kind of language activity for which they are being prepared.

But this weak argument is inadequate to confront the view of the nature of language outlined earlier in this paper. In this view, we may be able to learn the tokens of the language in a conscious manner, but learning a language is not learning tokens. Rather, it is using tokens in systems of meaning which are created by participants in interaction, constrained by conventional expectations. The tokens may be able to provide description and exemplification of the conventions, so formal learning of these may be helpful, but the integration of these into systems which are freely operable will depend on opportunities to create meaning with other users. And here creativity becomes essential to the acquisition process; it is not the result of acquisition, it *is* acquisition. The formal learning that so many learners find useful is a preliminary to acquisition, like possessing a dictionary, but only the process of activation causes assimilation, system-building, and the integration of meaning and context. Thus the formal work need not be eliminated, but it will need to be downgraded in importance. For some, such as Prabhu, this may not go far enough, and formal work could be rendered unnecessary if his type of procedural syllabus turns out to be widely successful. But however cautious we may be about the role of structured presentation and correction, it is very difficult to deny a major role for free interactive, productive and interpretative activities (see, e.g., Maley and Duff, 1982).

## Language and ideology

What has been outlined above, deliberately couched in general terms, commands wide acceptance among the professionally literate language teaching methodologists who exercise influence on training of teachers, materials development, curriculum design and evaluation. But there is a paradox inherent in this position. It seems somehow to be contentless — or, rather, it is committed to the notion that process *is* content. Yet, if language is indeed so closely bound up with personal and social conventions and needs, should these needs not be examined more carefully outside their linguistic manifestations? The Raymond Williams quotation with which I started my discussion continues to say:

> But then as the action develops, unknown and unacknowledged relationships, profound and decisive connections, definite and committing recognitions and avowals are as it were forced into consciousness. These are the real and inevitable relationships and connections, the necessary recognitions and avowals of any human society. But they are of a kind that are obscured, complicated, mystified, by the sheer rush and noise and miscellaneity of this new and complex social order.
> (Williams, 1973: 191)

These relationships and connections are brought to English classrooms by teachers as well as students, and they manifest themselves through the language, and the relationships, created in each classroom. But classrooms are not isolated from relationships outside school, and language classrooms are not isolated from classrooms for other subjects. To what extent can we separate our determination to provide a language acquisition which is 'created' in terms of 'individual functional needs' from our greater socialization into concepts like 'authenticity' and 'autonomy'? Is foreign language teaching in itself a sign of social instability, as was recognized by the Chinese emperors who made the teaching of Chinese to foreigners a capital offence? Or could it be an extension of communication from a socially stable environment? It is clear that there are circumstances in which linguistic conventions are not intended to be negotiated and participant-created, for example in certain legal or liturgical traditions. Although Bernstein's attempt to relate repertoires of speech styles to socially hierarchized family patterns ('personal' and 'positional' families: Bernstein, 1971) raises many difficulties, the principle is suggestive, for the extent to which language users are encouraged to approach interlocutors with equal rights to negotiate conventions will vary from society to society. A methodology which implies such equality may be able to ride on local political principle, as groupwork did in Yugoslavia in the 1970s. But such a methodology may equally be perceived as antagonistic in more authoritarian political situations ('Sir, you are anti-government', I was told when I introduced a seminar on groupwork in Franco's Spain).

Nor is the issue limited to the relatively straightforward domains of teaching methodology, content and subject matter of textbooks and syllabuses, or attitudes towards testing and evaluation. The emphasis on language interaction, and particularly on language as communication, is ultimately materialist in its concentration on the messages that pass to and fro (indeed the metaphors, 'transaction', 'tokens', 'exchange' are predominantly mercantile, as Bradbury, 1983, indicates). But how much comparable effort is devoted to the personal creation of the ideas that ultimately will constitute parts of messages? The emphasis on the literary classics of the grammar–translation tradition, the demand that students produce long pieces of expository prose in the foreign language, the encouragement of extensive reading, of formal debate, even of elocution: all these require an element of craft, of conscious (and not entirely negotiable) organization of material which implies that the material must be worth such effort in organization. Serious crafting demands serious thought about organization and content, conceptually as well as linguistically. Whatever other weaknesses there were in the earlier emphases, they were not as inherently trivial as some of the games which are now so much encouraged, nor as flippant about serious issues as some of the current exercises. Of course, the understandable desire of publishers to produce material for the largest possible market contributes to cultural blandness and an appeal to the lowest common denominator, but it is too easy to blame market forces at this superficial level. Deeply built into the view of

155

language as communication is the promise that once we have identified the hurdles to be leapt over, language is simply a matter of training in appropriate techniques. Over-emphasis on linguistic creativity, without any reference to what it is for and what it expresses, may be the most dangerous current constraint on the language classroom.

## Learner-centred teaching for learners

If we really want to be learner-centred we cannot be content-free. People, when asked what they believe in, do not answer 'activity' without reference to what the activity is for. They believe in political, social, religious ideas; they wish to create things, to understand things, to improve their own and others' behaviour. Unless language teaching can relate itself to some of these goals it condemns itself to marginality, in any culture. In broad terms, we may be able to specify such goals by asking what group a learner of English is making a bid to join: what does it mean to be a speaker of English in country X? I have explored this argument elsewhere (Brumfit, 1984a: 109–11). In this paper, however, I wish to conclude by outlining some implications of this position.

As Apel (1976: 60) has pointed out, understanding between different civilizations results in a mediation between syntactico-semantic language-*systems* and semantico-pragmatic language-*games*. The systems are conditions for effective communication, but the games are highly negotiable rule-systems which result from the human capacity to associate ideas to form structures for concept definition and development (see Widdowson, 1983, for a detailed exposition of this argument). It is the structures, or schemata, thus created which have to be negotiated as conventions for the discourse in the performance of language games. Here, human creativity is a necessary concomitant of fluent operation of the language system, and the dialectic relationship between the systems and the games constitutes the creation of meaning. Communicative language teaching has concentrated too much on the systems and too little on the games. There are understandable reasons for this. Some, like the fact that the teacher can control the systems, have been effectively attacked in the more radical language teaching literature (Gattegno, 1972; Stevick, 1980; Breen and Candlin, 1980). But others, like teachers' unwillingness to concede the ideological implications of a commitment to meaning rather than form, have scarcely been addressed (though see Candlin, in Brumfit, 1984b). Of course, from the point of view of international programmes and an international native-speaking EFL profession, such questions impose major difficulties. But if we are to understand language learning and language teaching more completely, they still need to be examined.

While, then, we have cautiously admitted a value in constraint and teacher control for some aspects of the acquisition of language tokens, we have insisted that freedom for creativity is essential if these tokens are to become value-laden within a cultural system for each learner. However, we have taken this argument a little further in asking that we investigate the *content* of such cultural systems more fully, to see language teaching as part of our social construction of reality. In our concern with product as form we neglected process. That balance has now been redressed. But product is also meaning, and meaning has its own processes, without which formal processes may be trivialized. If we wish learners to be central, we shall do them no service by diminishing their humanity. The concern for formal creativity was desirable in moderation, but isolated from a concern for serious meaning it degenerates into aestheticism. Scientific observation is more than the focusing of microscopes.

**Note**

I am grateful to Gillian Bourne for discussion of ideas implicit in this paper.

# Commentator 1

Merrill Swain

My first comment concerns the triviality-of-content problem. One of the fundamental points Dr Brumfit makes is that the content of learner-centred programmes deserves more attention. To quote from his paper: 'Whatever other weaknesses there were in the earlier emphases, they were not as inherently trivial as some of the games which are now so much encouraged, nor as flippant about serious issues as some of the current exercises.' He goes on to say: 'Over-emphasis on linguistic creativity, without any reference to what it is for and what it expresses, may be the most dangerous current constraint on the language classroom.'

What this leads me to suggest – in large part because of my involvement in immersion education – is that bilingual education is one possible solution to the problem raised. Any definition of bilingual education includes the key aspect that the second language will be used as a medium of instruction, implying that the content will be non-trivial.

It is true that when one speaks of bilingual education, one thinks of school-age children, not adults. However, in Canada now, there are experiments beginning which extend the concept of immersion education for second language learning to university level. Certainly, in principle, there is no reason not to extend the concept of bilingual education as a means of language learning and content learning to any age group. In the British context, however, outside of Wales the concept of bilingual education – even for school-age children – has not been extensively adopted.

Given Dr Brumfit's concern over triviality of content in some learner-centred programmes I would be interested in learning more about the relevance of bilingual education in the British context, or in the context of the British Council work both for school-age children and adults.

I wish to comment too on the expectations we have with regard to learner-centred teaching as compared with teacher-centred teaching. Immersion education in Canada has been labelled communicative teaching *par excellence*. In spite of this, it has tended to be highly teacher-centred. This has meant that teachers do much of the talking and students do most of the listening. Therefore it is, in my opinion, not surprising that immersion students perform more like native speakers of French on comprehension measures than on oral productive measures.

Recently, an experiment was carried out in Montreal by Florence Stevens where she directly compared a teacher-centred immersion programme with a learner-centred immersion programme – what she called an activity-centred immersion programme.

The students in the learner-centred approach had twelve and a half hours per week in French, whereas the students in the teacher-centred approach had twenty-one and a quarter hours a week in classes where French was the medium of instruction.

The results showed, among other things, that there were no differences between the two groups on measures of listening comprehension and oral production. I suspect that there were no differences in listening and speaking because both groups got equal opportunities to use these skills. There were, by the way, differences in favour of the teacher-centred group on measures of reading and general French achievement, which I assume occurred because in the teacher-centred classroom there was more time spent on activities related to these skills.

The question arises, then, what is it that we expect learner-centred teaching to accomplish that teacher-centred teaching does not? Is it simply a question of improving performance on those aspects of linguistic skills that are emphasized, or is there more to it than that? Personally, I think that learner-centred teaching allows for the possibility of using language for learning as well as using learning for language development, and therefore carries with it significant advantages over teacher-centred teaching. But I think the question implies a serious consideration of the issues Dr Brumfit raises in his paper – are we teaching only the language? Or are we teaching language in the service of content? Or are we teaching language so that it can serve as a tool for learning? Each it seems to me implies something different about the way language is taught.

Lastly I come to the role and nature of research in this field. Dr Brumfit talks about how teachers have an expertise that learners do not have: 'Teachers know more about the varieties of learning possibilities than any one learner can. They know that there are different types of learner, that single learners develop in more or less predictable ways and vary in their motivations, that there are a range of materials, a range of techniques, and a range of activities possible for each learner.'

I agree that these represent the kind of knowledge teachers have about the learners in their classes. What I think this statement reflects, however, is the inadequacy of the research paradigms that are used to investigate the influence of teaching on learning. Consider, for example, the research that has basically claimed that teaching doesn't make a difference. Such conclusions are clearly nonsense, and various attempts have been made in the literature to account, *post hoc*, for the results.

The problem, as I see it, is that the research is addressing simple questions because that's what the research paradigms being used allow researchers to do. But I don't think it has to be that way. Take, for example, the interesting conclusion of a Ph.D. student of ours, Nina Spada, recently reached by observing and measuring both the teaching process and the learners' product, and by using a combination of qualitative description and rigorous statistical analyses to get at the effect of the *interaction* among teacher behaviours and learners' informal contact outside of the classroom with the target language on a particular aspect of the learners' linguistic performance. The particular aspect of linguistic performance was grammatical performance. Spada found that if students were in a form-focused classroom, then more informal contact led to superior grammatical performance relative to those students who had less informal contact with the target language out of class. However, for students with more informal contact outside of class who had a more communicatively-oriented classroom experience, the extra informal contact gave them no advantage on the grammar test over their classmates with less informal contact. The implication of these findings drawn by Spada is that learners require opportunities for both formal and functional language practice and, if either one is lacking, they do not seem to benefit as much.

My final observation then is twofold: first, can research move us beyond the professional knowledge held by teachers? That is to say, has new insight been gained by a study such as Spada's which suggests some specific conditions under which formal or functional teaching will be particularly useful? And secondly, can research ever fully comprehend the intricacies of the *interaction* between learner variables, teacher variables and social/contextual variables in second language learning?

# Commentator 2

James E. Alatis

Dr Brumfit's insightful and incisive paper is not only thoughtful, but thought-*provoking*. Since I have been asked to serve as 'Commentator' at short notice, I know you will forgive me if my contribution is slightly autobiographical and anecdotal. It is much harder, and takes more time, to write a short paper than to write a long one.

Dr Brumfit's paper has made me think of those halcyon days when I was a Fulbright professor at the University of Athens, where I taught EFL and EFL methodology to Greek college students. This was my first introduction to the British Council, and my American colleagues and I shared the responsibilities with British colleagues in the English Department of the Faculty of Philosophy. I was the Language professor, and I used a book called *English for Greeks* based on *Structural Notes and Corpus* based on the *General Form* based on Trager-Smith's *Outline of English Structure*. It was (supposed to be) based on a contrastive analysis of English and Greek and was accompanied by a small instructor's manual called *Spoken English as a Foreign Language*. The manual emphasized the spoken language, avoided writing, used a complicated phonetic transcription; insisted that the teacher teach the *language*, not *about* the language, aimed at near-native pronunciation of a variable standard, with pronunciation drills, mimicry-memorization, pattern drills, etc. Double Unison Repetition, Single Unison Repetition, Individual Repetition, Cover the English / Cover the Greek. That was the routine! The pronunciation drills were based on 'minimal pairs' which were to be drilled in mindless repetition, without reference to meaning – translation was forbidden. Grammar was taught only inductively, the 'shut up and drink your beer' method of language teaching. The *Constraints* were many.

I taught only thirty-six days that first year. Being even then a compulsive 'workaholic', I worried that I wasn't earning my stipend, and I volunteered for 'extra duty'. It was decided that, when I wasn't teaching English to Greeks, I would teach Greek to American Fulbrighters. And again, I used a book that emphasized form over meaning, accurate pronunciation within a limited vocabulary, and the routine was, once again, Double Unison Repetition, Single Unison Repetition, Individual Repetition, Cover the Greek / Cover the English, pronunciation drills and pattern practices, inductive grammar.

I return now to Dr Brumfit's paper, and my comments. In the past, linguists were quick to insist upon the autonomy of their discipline. They did not wish the scientific study of language to bend to the winds of logic, philosophy or literary criticism. This principle of autonomy fostered the study of languages as a formal system – a conception which is summed up in the term 'structuralism'. Indeed, meaning itself, semantics, was frowned upon as too broad and unmanageable for rigorous, scientific study. However, now that linguistics has established its credentials as a mature academic discipline, linguists, particularly applied linguists, can afford to consider other disciplines which are relevant to language and language learning, especially the contributions of psychology, anthropology and sociology, in particular, out of which sprang the hemi-semi-demi-quasi-interdisciplines of psycholinguistics, anthropological linguistics, sociolinguistics. Out of these 'interdisciplines', in turn, sprang such concepts as communicative competence and research in first- and second-language acquisition. To continue in this genealogical vein, from these concerns arose such concepts as non-defensive, learner-centred, 'humanistic', communicative methodology, with greater emphasis on learner freedom. In the United States, at least, this evolution of thought has resulted in the emergence of a variety of 'models': Schumann's 'Acculturation Model', Krashen's input hypothesis and 'monitor model', Stevick's 'psychodynamic' model, etc. This, in turn, has resulted in a proliferation of new, 'non-conventional' methods and approaches, such as the Silent Way, Community (and Counselling) Language Learning, Suggestopedia, Total Physical Response, and even the Dartmouth method.

Dr Brumfit has provided us with a rich 'treasury' of information. I am particularly moved to comment on the suggestion that '. . . learners whose self-perception demands traditional procedures need to be taken into account', and 'each collection of students involves the teacher in a different set of decisions to make'. But this would lead me back to my Modern Greek class at Georgetown University, further discussion of that Creative classroom, and another anecdote!

I would like to end my remarks by suggesting that the teacher must learn to treat all theories, methods and techniques with a healthy proportion of scepticism. Whenever he is faced with the question: 'Which is the right method?', he must remember Palmer's answer: 'Adopt none exclusively, reject none absolutely.' Or Prator's 'Adapt, don't adopt.' Or, back to Palmer: 'Each variety has its uses, each has its place in the general scheme, and each in its turn may be the most rational one.'

Essentially, this is to advise teachers to adopt an attitude of practical common-sense eclecticism. There's certainly nothing original in that. It is not the only time I have done it, nor am I the only one who has. And now, I ask:

1  Earl Stevick has said that the distinction between acquisition and learning made by Krashen, whose early work Dr Brumfit characterizes as

'unhelpfully anti-teacher', is a most significant event, a major contribution to the field of language study. Would Dr Brumfit agree?

2  Is it cowardly (a 'cop-out') for a teacher-trainer to advise teachers to
adopt an eclectic approach, i.e. is eclecticism an intellectual obscenity?

# b) Coping with the unknown in language pedagogy

N. S. Prabhu

I want this paper to identify a particular sense of the term 'learner-centred methodology' and then to explore the implications of that view for language pedagogy.

It is perhaps useful to begin by making a distinction between 'learner-centred' and 'learning-centred'. One can say that learner-centred approaches are those which justify themselves essentially in terms of a concern for the learner – a concern which reflects the teacher's (or specialist's) sense of social, ideological or educational responsibility for his client. One form in which this is often expressed is the educator's responsibility to give the learner the best value for his money or effort. Careful analyses of learners' needs prior to course-design, matching the objectives or content of courses to learners' stated preferences or real-life needs (or couching syllabus statements in terms suggestive of real-life language-behaviour), designing courses to graded objectives so as to ensure a surrender value to each level of attainment, an emphasis on the use of realistic samples of language or authentic texts in the classroom can all be seen as expressions of this concern. It would be wrong to imply that this contrasts with an earlier lack of social or educational concern for the learner but the particular form in which the concern has been expressed in the past decade – viz. the ESP movement in general – and the primacy given to it in the theory of practice of language-teaching are certainly new and largely responsible for the new term 'learner-centred'.

This is not to say that ESP has been motivated solely by a social responsibility for the learner – some of the motivation has, for instance, been the teacher's own need to persuade the learner of the relevance of what is offered – but the educational argument for ESP has generally been in terms of economy and direct usefulness to the learner.

A different expression of this social concern for the learner is an argument for accommodating and protecting the learner's rights – an argument for a democratic sharing of control in pedagogy. Methodologies are thus proposed which allow (or train) learners to select their learning modes, use one another as learning resources, negotiate learning content with the teacher and generally take responsibility for the management of their own learning. The teacher is seen as only one of the resources available to the learner and the teacher's job as making the learner aware of other possible resources and encouraging his freedom in deciding which to use and in what manner. The ultimate goal is the autonomous learner and individualization, while groupwork in the classroom is an important first step in the direction. There is an interesting contrast between this concept of learner-centredness and the concept behind ESP. ESP can be said to increase the teacher's responsibility and control in deciding what is learnt and how, while a recognition of the learner's rights leads to a transfer of responsibility and control from the teacher to the learner.

What I am calling learning-centred methodologies, in contrast, are those based on particular perceptions of the nature of learning. Some of these – referred to generally as the 'humanistic approaches' – are concerned with learning in general and seek to create psychological (and physical) conditions in which memory is strengthened, personalities are engaged, mental and emotional needs are caused and met, attitudes considered favourable to learning are developed, strong associations are formed between the known and the new to help the retention of the new, and so on. What are involved here are hypotheses about the human mind as a learning device and the pedagogic procedures concerned are almost like an extension to human beings of the explorations made of the nature of learning in an earlier age by using animals.

A different form of learning-centredness – and the one I am concerned with in this paper – is that based on perceptions of the nature of language and, in particular, of language-learning as a distinct form of learning. Language can be viewed as a unique phenomenon – a defining characteristic of the species – and language-learning as being distinguishable in kind from other forms of learning. It would, in passing, be interesting to trace, in the history of language pedagogy, a recurrent tension between perceptions based on the uniqueness of language-learning and those concerned with learning in general – between language as 'skill' and language as 'knowledge', in one of their manifestations.

The uniqueness of language-learning was noted, some sixty years ago, by H. E. Palmer (1922), who said: 'We are endowed by nature with capacities for assimilating speech . . . These capacities are not limited to the acquiring of our mother tongue but are also available for one or more languages in addition' (p. 127). Palmer thus made a sharp distinction between our 'natural, spontaneous and universal capacities' for learning languages and our 'studial capacities' which operate in the learning of other subjects (including such 'skill' subjects as shorthand, piano-playing, typewriting and carpentry). Using a language, he said, involves 'unconscious obedience to some rules unknown to us' (p. 5) and in learning a language 'we learn without knowing what we are learning' (p. 44). Palmer therefore suggested that we 'design forms of work in which the student's attention shall be directed towards the subject-matter and away

165

from the form in which it is expressed' (p. 51) and argued that 'the utilis-
ation of his [i.e. the adult learner's] conscious and focused attention [on
language] militates against the proper functioning of the natural
capacities of assimilation'. Speculating on what processes might be
involved in such unconscious acquisition, he suggested that the student
had 'capacities for retaining unconsciously what he may happen to hear
(or read)' (p. 56) and that these retained 'compounds' gave him the 'working units' of language and the ability to engage in 'ergonic construction'
(in contrast to the more conscious process of 'grammatical construction').

Palmer's further observation that the system of rules we obey unconsciously in using a language is 'so complex and so vast that the learned
world has not yet succeeded in unravelling it or sounding its depths' has
since been brought home to us abundantly by developments in grammatical analysis. It is easy to look on Transformational-Generative
Grammar as being limited in scope to 'linguistic competence'. The fact is
that even such sophisticated instruments of analysis have not been able to
provide anything like a full account of linguistic competence, while every
successful instance of language acquisition in the world represents an
unconscious mastery of it. Perhaps the most valuable lesson for language
pedagogy from Chomskyan linguistics is a realization of how much more
complex language structure is than we had thought in the past, how little
we consciously know about it still – and, by the same token, how much
more than we thought is known unconsciously to every language user.
The exercise of what Palmer called 'studial' capacities is therefore not
only an inefficient way of learning a language; it is inherently inadequate
for the purpose since we still do not know consciously what we expect to
be acquired unconsciously.

Palmer saw explicit grammar in the classroom as having been the main
defect in earlier language pedagogy, since 'grammatical construction' was
totally unlike language use or natural language acquisition (1922: 119–
20). He saw value in training the learner's capacity to 'memorize without
effort' so that 'he may memorize a hundred or so real living sentences' and
by so doing 'acquire a hundred or so new habits or automatic actions'
(p. 49). Palmer was, however, very aware of the generative character of
language structure and went on to add that 'certain forms of *synthetic*
work exist which will enable us to form correctly an almost unlimited
number of foreign sentences; we shall see that the utilization of these
*studial* forms of work will carry us very far on our way to acquire the
language' (p. 48, emphases mine). The synthetic work was what he called
'ergonic construction', which formed the basis of the substitution table
and other forms of structure-manipulation. Among the other principles
which Palmer enunciated were those of gradation ('passing from the
known to the unknown') and accuracy ('Do not allow the student to have
opportunities for inaccurate work'), and, together, they formed the basis

of the Structural Approach which came to dominate second language pedagogy so much for so long.

The flux and ferment we are faced with in language pedagogy today is the result of a general disillusionment with the Structural Approach, but the new directions being explored are, to my mind, characterized by an avoidance of the issue of structure-acquisition instead of seeking alternative ways of bringing it about. Thus, notional–functional syllabuses aim at a more purposeful selection of grammatical material, thereby abandoning what value there was to Palmer's principle of 'gradation' – i.e. grammatical organization. They also hope to bring about a stronger form–meaning association in the classroom but take no stand on the issue of conscious v. unconscious learning. ESP courses aim to equip the learner most directly with the language most relevant to his needs – and can almost be related to Palmer's emphasis on the memorization of tokens, except that they don't seem to share Palmer's perception of the value of such tokens as 'working units' for 'automatic actions' – i.e. for an internal generative system. Communicative methodologies seek to create opportunities for the learner to engage in naturalistic language use so that he can bring into free, fluent play what language he already knows – or learn to cope with communication despite his language deficiency – but they make few claims about the acquisition of the structural base of language. Finally, pedagogic approaches based on a perception of language as discourse seek to highlight abilities of language use which lie beyond a mastery of language structure and, in so doing, play down the importance of language structure itself. Explorations of the nature of interactional capacity (as in Widdowson, 1983) are valuable but do not justify a brushing aside of grammatical competence as being merely a set of conventions or a system of rules too rigid to permit creativity in a certain sense. If one wished to challenge the centrality of grammar for language use, one would have to show either:

i)    that grammar does not matter, i.e. communicative competence in some sense which does not involve grammatical conformity can be an acceptable educational goal, or

ii)   that grammar is not a system, i.e. grammatical conformity follows from communicational appropriacy and grammatical deviance can be explained in terms of communicational inadequacy, or

iii)  that grammar is not a problem in pedagogy, i.e. it generally gets acquired easily, unlike communicative ability.

In general, those pedagogic proposals which base themselves on the argument that grammatical competence is not enough are providing justification for a widening of the scope of what is to be taught and learnt but are being ambivalent in their implications for the promotion of grammatical competence itself. The implication cannot be that we already know how to promote grammatical competence and most language learners do in fact acquire that competence sufficiently: Newmark's (1966) example of asking for a light in perfectly grammatical but inappropriate language is a synthetic one (and such examples are generally hard-found, anecdotal ones) while examples of grammatical deficiency abound in the language-teaching (and second-language-using) world; and nearly all courses produced for communicative language teaching have in practice felt the need to make provision for the teaching (or remedying) of language structure. The only other possible implication is that we have done all we can about the acquisition of language structure and that language structure is therefore to be taught, to the extent possible, by the procedures of the Structural Approach, though the Communicative Approach claims to be an alternative to that approach.

There is a further point to be made about grammatical competence. When statements are made of the form 'when grammar is taught, grammar alone is learnt', the word 'grammar' is being used with unhelpful ambiguity. If the grammar learnt is being equated with the grammar taught, then that knowledge of grammar cannot represent grammatical competence in the sense of an internally constructed and unconsciously deployed system – and one is ignoring Palmer's insightful distinction between 'grammatical construction' and 'obedience to rules unknown to us'. If, on the other hand, an internalized competence is in fact what one has in mind in saying 'grammar is learnt', then that grammar can hardly be equated with the grammar taught – or even assumed to be caused by the teaching of it. Moreover, there is at least a possibility that grammatical competence – in the sense of an unconsciously internalized system – leads not only to greater conformity to the system itself, when such conformity is not being attempted consciously, but to a readier deployment of the system in communication. The point I am making therefore is that arguments on the lines of 'grammar is not enough' may be taking too restricted a view of what grammatical competence involves and that the achievement of grammatical competence in a truer (more deployable) form may by itself mitigate the problem of communicative ability. If we agree with Brumfit that accuracy activity in the classroom leads to an ability which is not readily available for fluent use, the conclusion is not necessarily that fluency activity should supplement accuracy activity to make that ability more deployable: it is quite possible that a more deployable form of ability can in fact be promoted by means other than accuracy activity.

Palmer, as we have noted, suggested the use of 'ergonic construction'; as an alternative to 'grammatical construction' (although he was aware that ergonic construction – i.e. sentence construction based on 'working units' of syntax – was a form of 'synthetic work' which engaged 'studial' capacities) and added 'gradation' (of ergons – hence a structural progression) and 'accuracy' (error-prevention) as further principles of language pedagogy. I think it is these principles that we need to re-examine, in the light of our current perspective on language acquisition, in order to understand our disappointment with the Structural Approach.

Ergonic construction implies the belief that the 'working units' identified by the teacher (or borrowed by him from the linguist) are in fact units of the system which the language learner is hypothesized to construct unconsciously in his mind – the belief that we, as teachers, have conscious knowledge of the rules to which language-users show 'unconscious obedience'. It is a claim of isomorphism between the grammars constructed by linguists and the internal grammars of language-users – an attribution of psychological reality to linguistic models, which is more than any linguist has wished to claim. The fact that a successful model of linguistic analysis and success in learning a language are both subject to the same evidence (viz. conformity of their outputs to that of the language-using community) is not a relevant basis for this belief – even if we assumed that some model of linguistic analysis has in fact proved fully successful in those terms. What ergonic construction – or structural practice – implies is an identity of form between the analyst's construct and the unobservable reality; and one is justified in asking, in the light of results, if pedagogic procedures based on this unjustified assumption might not have acted detrimentally to language acquisition.

One of the most powerful current perspectives on language acquisition is the hypothesis of interlanguage development (Corder, 1981) which directly challenges the relevance of both deliberate linguistic grading and the principle of accuracy/error-prevention in language pedagogy. Grading implies that learning takes place part-by-part, in an additive sequence, while the notion of interlanguage implies that language development is holistic – a continual revision/elaboration of a transitional competence, prompted by new, conflicting language data. Further, since transitional competence is by its very nature not stable, not observable at any particular stage and not likely to be uniform to a group of learners, it is not possible to determine what piece of language data is relevant to it at what stage. It is of course important to make language data available all the time – that is to say, exposure to the language being learnt is necessary – but there can be no planning of an input-sequence; nor can input be equated with intake for any given learner at any given stage. Also, since the output of a transitional competence is bound to differ from that of a fully-formed competence, errors are a natural manifestation of language development and the principle of accuracy (in Palmer's sense of preventing errors – hence providing language practice) is misconceived.

Given the strong plausibility of the interlanguage hypothesis (in the sense that language-learning takes place through a series of approximative systems – whether or not one sees equal plausibility to the associated hypothesis of a discoverable in-built sequence), one can no longer expect language pedagogy to benefit from a planned linguistic progression, pre-selection of language for particular activities or language practice as such. The only important requirement is that language data be made available continually; and one can then go on to ask whether there are any conditions which are likely to make the data more effective – i.e. likely to increase the pace of interlanguage revision or, to put it differently, increase the chances of input becoming intake. Corder identifies motivation as the most important condition (*'given motivation*, it is inevitable that a human being will learn a second language if he is exposed to the language data', 1981: 8) while one of the suggestions Palmer made was focusing the learner's mind on the subject-matter ('The pupil must not be allowed to focus his attention on the structure of the language; he must keep his attention on the subject-matter', 1922: 51). What this suggests is classroom activity which brings about in the learner a preoccupation with meaning (or the message or content), since success in understanding things and success in saying what one wishes to say are both pleasurable activities for people – hence motivating, at least in the immediate context.

If meaning-focused activity is in fact the most important condition for the process of internal grammar-construction, we then have to regard structural progression and language practice as being not only not helpful to that process but as possible impediments to it. They promote what may be called form-focused work in the classroom, distinguishable from meaning-focused work in its having to fulfil predictions of particular language. Whenever classroom activity is based on pre-selected language (however well disguised that fact may be from the learner), a criterion for the success of that activity must be the fulfilment of that prediction; and the teacher's own awareness of that criterion is likely to lead to an attempt to ensure success in those terms – i.e. to an attempt to monitor language forms in a way that is unnatural in natural language use and certain to render the activity itself less meaning-focused. The nature of language is such that we cannot be engaged in genuine language use and simultaneously be scanning the language forms which emerge; and pedagogic attempts to set up classroom activity which constitutes both language practice (from the teacher's point of view) and meaning-focused use (from the learner's) seem to me a form of compromise likely to lose on both fronts.

What emerges from this discussion is that there are a number of things about language acquisition which we do not know and should not assume we do in language pedagogy. We do not know the form of the internal grammar we hypothesize and should not assume that it is the same as the linguist's grammar. We do not know the process of internal grammar-construction and should not assume that it is a linear one. We cannot say what any learner will learn at any given stage and should not assume that what is learnt is what we teach. We do not, that is to say, know enough about acquisition to seek to influence that process directly, and our best hypotheses at this time – viz. that the internal grammar develops as unconsciously as it gets deployed in language use and that the process involved is a holistic one – indicate a very indirect form of teaching, confined to ensuring availability of language data and attempting to bring about a preoccupation with meaning. Attempts in the past to do more than this – to control and regulate acquisition to a plan – turn out to have been based on unjustified assumptions of knowledge as well as disappointing in their results. If language is a genetic inheritance and language development an organic process (Palmer himself compared the process to learning to walk, in contrast to learning to cycle), it is indeed to be expected that attempts to influence that process indirectly will prove more beneficial than a more direct intervention. From a different point of view, there is a choice in language pedagogy between making minimal or maximal assumptions and, given the perception of language acquisition outlined in this paper, minimal assumptions seem the more promising.

I do not think there is any serious problem of feasibility with a methodology based on such minimal assumptions. Meaning-focused activity in the classroom can be attempted in a number of ways. One particular attempt – employing problem-solving tasks and without any language syllabus, pre-selection of language for particular activities or form-focused work – has been experimented with in southern India over the past five years (Prabhu, 1984), with tentative results which indicate that unconscious grammar construction does take place from such teaching and that the resultant ability is more deployable than the result of more form-focused teaching. Teaching a subject (such as science) through the language to be taught – thus regulating teaching in terms of the subject instead of in linguistic terms – is another possibility which has been suggested more than once in the past. Given the fact that subject-matter itself defines and regulates the language that comes into play in dealing with it, and the further fact that there are natural processes of simplification and negotiation which operate in any situation where communication is attempted between persons of different linguistic attainments, meaning-focused work in the language classroom is entirely practicable – and in fact simpler, in terms of the demands it makes on teachers and learners, than teaching which attempts to combine linguistic regulation with meaningful activity.

Where problems arise for such teaching – speaking from my own experience of the south India experiment – is in persuading teachers and administrators that an indirect attempt to promote acquisition is all we can usefully make in language pedagogy and that, given the nature of language and its acquisition, such indirectness is likely to be more beneficial than direct manipulation. There is a sense of insecurity arising from not knowing – e.g. being unable to say what piece of language one is teaching at a given time and accepting the notion that what gets learnt may be quite different from what one attempts to teach – and a resultant preference for security even when it is suspected of being based on unjustified assumptions. Perhaps teaching, like many other activities, seeks to define and justify itself in its own terms, submitting only to criteria of success which it can (or thinks it can) directly produce or control; and perhaps the uniqueness of language-learning, as compared to the learning of other school subjects or to the notion of learning in general, is specially in conflict with that propensity.

There is another point at which the concept of language development as organic growth conflicts with what educational administration (and perhaps applied linguistics too) seeks. Educational planning (especially the planning of language education in the modern world) finds the need to regulate (often reduce) the time given to language instruction – and finds it convenient to work on the assumption that language-teaching specialism can find ways of speeding up the learning process through more effective methods. And more effective methods are generally seen to be those that seek to influence the learning process more directly – and define criteria of success which suit such methods. Palmer noted this phenomenon and commented: 'If we are to obtain concrete and definite results in a limited space of time . . . we shall reluctantly be compelled to sacrifice a certain measure of soundness to the requirements of speed' (1922: 26).

Finally, not only do we not have specific knowledge about language acquisition; we do not know what sources might be dependable for such knowledge. Does one trust a successful learner's introspection when he says (for instance) that he always learnt languages by studiously memorizing lists of words – or a learner's rational view that if he is learning a language, he ought to know exactly what rules he should conform to? (How would we interpret the introspection of someone who is certain that he learnt to walk as a child by using a certain kind of push cart?) Does one treat theoretical constructs of language structure or language use as if they represented reality and could be used as operational models? Does one rely on empirical studies of first- or second-language acquisition, which too can make their perceptions only in terms of theoretical constructs? Or does one seek 'scientific' evidence from language-teaching experiments themselves, in spite of the severe limitations of an experimental design when applied to a variable-ridden human enterprise such as teaching? Perhaps one can do worse than to look to an evolving sense of plausibility in the profession, informed by what evidence and theory are available but shared and sharpened through professional debate. From the point of view of a particular sense of plausibility felt by Palmer and strengthened by subsequent experience, learning-centred methodology is perhaps largely a matter of coping with the unknown in language pedagogy.

# Commentator 1

## Richard L. Allwright

It sometimes appears that the picture for language teachers is so bleak that the best thing they can do is abdicate — get out of the way entirely. I appeared to have advocated that myself some years ago and had to write a paper on abdication and responsibility to spell out more clearly that I was not advocating total non-intervention, but a re-think of the *nature* of intervention, given the extent of the 'unknown in language pedagogy' (to quote from Dr Prabhu's title).

Dr Prabhu has been taking a similar line, I think. He is not advocating a policy of total non-intervention, but setting limits to the notion of what sort of intervention might be helpful to language learners whose aim is mastery of the target language system. He makes his arguments basically on the grounds of ignorance, our ignorance, about how to describe languages appropriately, from which it follows that if we design a language pedagogy based on linguistic description we are bound to be misleading our learners, not just wasting their time.

I would like to know how far Dr Prabhu would wish to take this line of argument, that linguistic descriptions are worse than useless for practical pedagogic purposes, because it seems that it is critical to his overall conception of the field. If he believes linguistic descriptions to be totally useless for pedagogic decision-making, then I would like to know if he considers language to be unique in this respect.

This problem of the harmful effect of supposing knowledge where ignorance is the case is related interestingly to Dr Prabhu's thinking on the issue of learner consciousness in language learning. Dr Prabhu argues that if the teacher raises linguistic descriptions to the level of consciousness he or she is bound to mislead since appropriate descriptions are not available. More intriguingly, I think, he pursues this argument and suggests that if learners attempt to explore consciously the language they are learning they will also mislead themselves, since it is inconceivable that they could verbalize insightfully about a language, and yet their attempts to verbalize their (mis)understandings will almost certainly pollute the natural processes of incubation.

I would like to know how far Dr Prabhu would take this line of argument also. Does he in fact see a positive contribution from learner consciousness, or is it wholly to be avoided? And, if so, is language, again, unique in this respect?

Dr Prabhu's minimalist position may seem wholly negative in relation to linguistic description and the associated issue of learner consciousness, but on the issue of intervention he is much more positive, claiming that we do know enough about the language development process to design instruction in a way that is interventionist on all other fronts. And he has designed and conducted an experimental project whose results, recently independently evaluated, support his contention that positive intervention is practically feasible, without dependence on linguistic description and learner consciousness, in the acquisition-poor setting of south India.

I would like to know if Dr Prabhu sees his project as the first, if major, step in providing a local solution to a local problem, or would he argue, on principle, that his arguments should hold in any setting?

# Commentator 2

## Henri Holec

Allow me, first of all, to thank Dr Prabhu for the very interesting food for thought he has provided us with in his paper; the process of second language acquisition has been the concern of a number of research workers over the last few years, as Pit Corder's state-of-the-art 1982 report to the Council of Europe witnesses; but the voices of didacticians concerned with the implications and applications of the insights so far gained still need to be heard more clearly.

The distinction made by Dr Prabhu between learner-centred and learning-centred approaches – although I would suggest a different labelling for reasons that will be made clear in my further remarks – seems to me a very useful one, not only for research purposes but also as a conceptual tool any teacher reflecting on his practice in the classroom can easily use to categorize the daily observations he makes about his learners; it might help him, for instance, to differentiate more clearly between lazy learners and slow learners and, possibly, to discover that some of his fast learners are very lazy and that some of his slow learners are very hard-working indeed.

It is also a distinction that highlights one of the fundamental reasons why one should never forget that acquiring a language is not a process which necessarily begins with, and certainly does not end with, the learner's physical stay in the teaching institution, and that, consequently, one should always be careful to assess the relevance of short-term teaching/learning objectives to the learner's long-term acquisition aims.

To come back to the labelling qualms I mentioned earlier: after reading the first two pages of Dr Prabhu's paper, I came to the conclusion that we had been thinking along the same lines as Dr Prabhu at our centre for research, at the CRAPEL (Centre de Recherches et d'Applications Pédagogiques en Langues) in Nancy, in our own research on the development of learner autonomy, i.e. the development of the learner's capacity to take charge of his own learning process. But, reading on, I soon discovered that the opposition between learner-centred and learning-centred did not focus on the same thing as our – and other didacticians' – opposition between learner-centred teaching and learner-centred learning. The reason why this is so stems, I think, from the fact that the word 'learning' does not mean the same thing in the two cases.

I think we should further distinguish between learning and acquisition, that is, between what goes on unconsciously inside the learner's head and results in his 'knowing' the language, or part of it (this is acquisition), and the more or less conscious behaviour he engages in, in the hope that this will bring about acquisition (that is learning behaviour). This distinction between learning and acquisition does not refer to what Krashen, among others, refers to when he opposes learnt knowledge to acquired knowledge. Just to make this clearer, let me draw upon another field of learning, say skiing. To acquire the ability to ski properly, people may engage in a number of activities: They may start by reading about the techniques involved and studying closely diagrams describing the different positions and movements of the arms and legs when turning, stopping and what not; they may then start practising, possibly rehearsing, different positions and movements before trying them out on a real slope; they may even do things like running or swimming to build up their muscles, and so on and so forth. All these activities will eventually lead to their being able to achieve what they aimed at when they began.

Now, I'm not saying that language learning is like learning to ski; I'm just trying to point out the fact that learning and acquiring are not one and the same thing; some people acquire without really learning, others learn without acquiring, and others again acquire and learn without there being any systematic relation between the one and the other (they acquire a lot without learning much, or vice versa; or what they acquire bears little or no direct relation to what they learn).

So, given this distinction between learning and acquisition, what is 'teaching'? Teaching is not directly concerned with acquisition; as has often been repeated, teaching does not cause acquisition. Teaching is concerned with learning, the relation between the two being variously interpreted – from those who think teaching should build and provide all the learning the learner should engage in willy-nilly, to those who think teaching should help learners discover, mainly by informed trial and error, the types of language activities that suit them best, i.e. that bring about, for them, acquisition that conforms to their expectations, finally to those who think that teaching should provide the framework the learner needs to define his learning behaviour.

In view of this, I would like to ask Dr Prabhu the following: shouldn't we devote more attention than we are doing at the moment to the relationship between learning and acquisition on the one hand and between teaching and learning on the other, in order to overcome the depressing feeling *we* get at times that teaching is useless and that we don't get the learners we deserve, and that *learners* get at times that learning is useless, that teachers are frauds and that the best way of acquiring a language is to be born with it?

# Theme V   Summary of discussion

As with Teacher Preparation (Theme IV), discussion here dealt with the two related issues of validity and feasibility. How far was a learner-centred methodology pedagogically valid in principle on the one hand, and how far was it applicable in practice on the other?

There was debate on the distinction between learner-centred and learning-centred methodology. The former, it was suggested, had to do with bringing about a certain kind of social environment in classrooms whereby learners took the initiative for learning as a realization of their own personal constructs. Learning-centred methodology had to do with the setting of tasks which would engage the learners in the kind of problem solving assumed to be conducive to learning, but without commitment to any basic change in the traditional roles of teacher and learner in the classroom encounter. Learning-centred methodology, so defined, did not carry the sociological and ideological implications of learner-centredness.

The concepts were, however, mutually compatible. Both were based on the assumption that language was learnt contingently by the engagement of learners in activities not directly focused on the language itself but requiring the use of language for their achievement. This assumption was questioned by a number of participants. Doubts were expressed, for example, as to whether it was indeed the case that such activities inevitably led to the internalization of the language system. Again, the question was raised as to how the activities were themselves to be selected and ordered. Since there was no available scheme for analysing tasks in terms of their complexity or implicational connections, it would seem likely that their use would be predetermined by a prior selection and ordering of language items. A suggested alternative would be to relate language learning directly with other subject areas in the curriculum which did deal with the organization of activities in the specification of course content. It was recognized that such proposals would mean the imposition of control which would not be in the spirit of learner-centredness. On the other hand, some organization was felt to be necessary to ensure the learners' sense of security.

A central issue, then, was how far could the learning process be left to

178

the learner without being directed by deliberate intervention. It was possible that the avoidance of such intervention was only apparent and was in effect a tactical manoeuvre to make learners think that they were in control when they were in fact being subjected to subtle manipulation. The point was made that it is not possible, in principle, to learn anything at random by free-ranging discovery procedures: there needs to be an established frame of reference which gives these procedures a purpose and meaning. In practice, it is often necessary (and consistent with the socializing process of education) to provide such frames of reference to ensure the effective use of learner initiative.

There was a general recognition that it was desirable for language teaching to create conditions for the genuine participation of learners, but it was felt too that extensive classroom research was needed to establish what range of practices was consistent with such a view, how far they were effective (and indeed how their effectiveness could actually be evaluated) in the circumstances of particular teaching/learning situations.

# THEME VI  LITERATURE TEACHING

## a) The teaching, learning and study of literature

H. G. Widdowson

Whatever progress there might be to report on approaches to the teaching of English literature abroad, it has had little if anything to do with developments in English language teaching. Generally speaking, the prevailing assumption has been that the approach to English literature teaching in a mother tongue context will be transferable, with some minor adjustments, to foreign parts, and will have no particular relationship with how the language is taught. The two activities have traditionally been seen as belonging to two different pedagogic domains, one drawing its inspiration from linguistics and the other from literary criticism: they may occasionally co-occur, but they do not compound. My purpose in this paper is to deplore this separation and to propose a reconciliation for the future.

As far as English language teaching is concerned, literature has over recent years been generally purged from the programme, together with other undesirable elements like grammar and translation, on the grounds that it makes no contribution to the purpose or the process of learning the language for practical use. It is supposed that people do not usually learn English these days for cultural enrichment, as a means of access to the aesthetics of verbal art; that such a purpose belongs to a more élite and leisured age, one which could afford to be less concerned with the exigencies of practical need. To most teachers in these days of the Threshold Level and ESP, when value tends to be uniquely connected with cost, the idea of literary purpose for language learning seems rather quaint.

With regard to the process of learning, literature would appear to be disqualified on two counts. First, its obscurity introduces undesirable difficulty, which disrupts the gradual cumulative process of language learning and undermines motivation by the imposition of pointless complexity. Secondly, this obscurity is frequently associated with eccentric uses of language which learners are required to accept in their receptive understanding but to reject as models for their own productive performance. Thus they are obliged to be creative in their reception of language but conformist in their production. Obviously there is the danger that learners will, following a natural inclination which teachers would in other cases wish to encourage, derive production from reception and carry literary eccentricities into their own repertoire. Learners are prone to be non-conformist anyway and to give literary sanction to their errant ways, is, it can be argued, only likely to make matters worse.

With regard to language teaching, then, neither the purpose nor the process of learning would seem, on the face of it, to provide much justification for the inclusion of literature. Actually the strength of the case for exclusion is undermined by the principles of communicative language teaching, as I hope will become apparent as I proceed, but the opinion that opposes literature is still very widely pervasive for the reasons I have given. And one has to acknowledge, I think, that language teaching has done reasonably well without it. It has developed at an impressive pace. Whatever one may think of particular pedagogic proposals, or the manner in which they have been transposed into techniques and materials, there is no doubt that the last fifty years has been a period of dynamic development in English language teaching, a period of enquiry and exploration, of changes in perspective and approach, of recurrent reappraisals of practice and its theoretical warrant. Excessive claims have of course been made, changes too hastily implemented; fervour inspired by revolutionary and prophet has sometimes led to excessive enthusiasm at the expense of thought. It may be that all this vigorous activity only creates the illusion of progress and that we are really no further forward than we were fifty years ago. Be that as it may, there has been an exhilarating eagerness to explore, a commitment to enquiry, a sense of movement, to use a phrase from Thom Gunn, whereby

> One is always nearer by not keeping still.

Prompted by this line of poetry, we turn now to English literature teaching overseas. Here we find a very different state of affairs. There is no comparable dynamism, no interest in innovation, no quest for underlying principles. Things go on much as they always have done. The only approach that appears to be practised is one imported long since from a first language context and imposed by force of habit without regard to appropriacy. And this approach is heavily protected against the influence of language study and language teaching. It is difficult to give a fair account of the reasons why this should be so since any debate on the matter tends to degenerate into polemical confrontation. Instead of a dispassionately argued case, what we very commonly get is the expression of a fixed conviction that the integrity of literature as an aesthetic object can only be experienced directly, cannot be explained and is bound to be irreparably damaged by any attempt to treat it as a use of language. And that's that. Literature seems here to be conceived of in much the same way as Lady Bracknell in *The Importance of Being Earnest* conceived of ignorance:

> 'I do not approve of anything that tampers with natural ignorance.
> Ignorance is like a delicate exotic fruit; touch it and the bloom is gone.'
>
> (Act I)

The desire to protect literature from the tampering of language study and to keep it preserved for aesthetic contemplation sometimes finds expression in pronouncements of a quite surprising emotional intensity, where vehemence of feeling is matched only by incoherence of argument. One such expression has appeared in a recent issue of the *English Language Teaching Journal* (Gower, 1984), in the form of a review of a pamphlet by Brian Lee entitled *Poetry and the System*. The review itself has little or nothing to commend it, but it is worthy of note because it appears in a journal which has long since presided over developments in our field, and because it is indicative of attitudes which are well rooted in tradition, which still stubbornly prevail and which sustain the isolation of literature from language teaching against which I am arguing in this paper.

The review reveals the resistance to language study that I referred to earlier and condemns any application of linguistics to literary study on the grounds that it must of necessity be damaging to the essential power of literature to evoke feelings and disclose the truth of life. Any study of the language of literature tampers with the ineffable. This is the Lady Bracknell attitude. The reviewer asserts, without supporting argument, that:

> The spirit of literature is alien and inimical to the systems and methods
> of science . . . and linguistics and stylistics are of *no use to us at all*
> [emphasis in the original].

The fear of the destructive force of rational thought which underlies this review predates Lady Bracknell, however, by a long period. The deep suspicion of anything intellectual and a preference for truth which is revealed through visceral sensation rather than cognition can be traced back at least to the Romantics. One thinks, for example, of Keats:

> I am certain of nothing but the holiness of the heart's affections and the
> truth of imagination – what the imagination seizes as beauty must be
> truth.
>
> (Letter to Benjamin Bailey, 22 November 1817)

> O for a life of sensations rather than of thoughts.
>
> (Letter to John Hamilton Reynolds, 22 September 1818)

Or of Wordsworth:

> Sweet is the lore that Nature brings;
> Our meddling intellect
> Mis-shapes the beauteous form of things:
> We murder to dissect.
> ('The Tables Turned')

Now it may be that the case that literary works are an expression of intuitive awareness controlled by some deep sense of connection inaccessible to intellect which conscious analysis on the part of the artist can only distort. It may be that the creative artist has a particular gift for what C. S. Peirce referred to as 'abduction', a process of inspired guesswork or intuitive inference distinct from both induction and deduction, 'an instinct', as Sebeok and Umiker-Sebeok put it 'which relies upon unconscious perception of connections between aspects of the world, or, to use another set of terms, subliminal communication of messages' (Sebeok and Umiker-Sebeok, 1983: 18–19).

But this does not mean that literary criticism or literature teaching must be informed by the same subliminal perception, accountable, like Keats, only to the holiness of the heart's affections and the truth of the imagination. On the contrary, it is logically impossible for them to be so informed. For the creative artist's subliminal perception can only be expressed by a uniquely appropriate use of language that represents that perception. Any paraphrase or commentary will inevitably recast it in conventional terms and thereby alter its artistic character. As soon as the critic makes statements like 'The poem is about . . . ' or 'The poet says that . . . ' or 'The poem expresses this that or the other', the meaning is transposed into a conventional key and its uniqueness vanishes. Literature teaching cannot be a matter of re-creating the literary work by duplicating its effect. It can only set up conditions whereby people can feel this effect for themselves. If the teacher inclines to a literary critical approach he will seek to create these conditions by focusing on the message expressed: if he is linguistically inclined, he will focus on the language used to express it. Neither approach can capture the essence of the original: all that either can do is to provide access to it. A study of the language of literature is no more alien or inimical to the spirit of literature than is literary criticism. The issue is how far either of them can help in making the spirit accessible.

One might of course claim, without too much respect for logic, that in dealing with the message, the literary critic comes into more intimate contact with literary truth so that his exegesis may approximate quite closely to the original. The critic may then be seen as a kind of literary translator producing versions hardly less creative than the works from which they derive. Only a small step along this line of argument is needed to conclude that there is really no essential difference between literature and criticism. Such a suggestion is indeed made by the author of the review I have referred to. He says:

> Although it might be called 'criticism' – not exactly 'literary criticism' – it is really as close to being *literature* as anything intended as 'literature' written today.

This would appear to put Brian Lee in the same Parnassian company as say Philip Larkin, Graham Greene, William Golding, Harold Pinter. It seems to be an extravagant claim. And one might be disposed to dismiss it as an isolated aberration. But this conception of criticism as a *literary* activity is in fact a very pervasive one and, as we shall see, has an important influence on how the subject of literature teaching is defined. It breaks surface again in Ian Robinson's *The Survival of English*. This time it is F. R. Leavis who is singled out as the critical creative artist. He alone, apparently, meets the exacting standards of great literature. These standards would appear to be related primarily to the promotion of decent living, robust moral health and worthy principles of a similar sort which one would normally associate with the Boy Scout Movement. Robinson is also, as one might expect, a fierce and quixotic opponent of linguistics.

Now it may be that literature teachers and literary critics would be as embarrassed as everybody else at these intemperate attacks on linguistics and excessive claims for criticism. Nevertheless, they do seem to me to be symptomatic of a way of thinking about literature and literary studies which has prevented the development of an effective pedagogy for English literature teaching overseas – and in this country too if it comes to that. This is not at all to deny the very considerable achievements in the *study* of literature. But I am concerned with teaching as a means of promoting the *learning* of literature, and this is a different matter. This distinction between study and learning is, to my mind, a crucial one and I believe that the lack of progress in literature teaching can in large part be attributed to a failure to recognize it.

By study I mean enquiry without implication of performance, the pursuit of knowledge about something by some kind of rational or intuitive enquiry, something, therefore, which is given separate third-person status. By learning I mean getting to know how to do something as an involved first-person performer. Study, in this sense, is action which leads to knowledge and extends awareness, whereas learning is knowledge which leads to action and develops proficiency. The difference is quite clear in respect to language study and learning, as is apparent in the ambiguity of the term *linguist*. On the one hand it can mean someone who studies language as exemplified in different languages, but who may well not be able to perform in any of them except one – a linguistician, a linguistic scientist. On the other hand the term may mean someone who is proficient in the use of several languages, but may have studied none of them – a polyglot.

In language teaching too the distinction is clear, and it is now generally accepted that the pedagogic objective here is to develop proficiency: the focus is on learning, not study. This is not to say that a conscious awareness of aspects of the language might not contribute to this purpose, that study might not sometimes serve the cause of learning. Indeed the relationships between these two activities is a fundamental issue in pedagogy in general. But of course one cannot begin to consider how they are related without first recognizing that they are different.

With regard to literature, however, it seems that there is no such recognition. The most common assumption appears to be that literature teaching is concerned exclusively with study so that students are expected to make critical observations about literary works, *on the supposition that they have already learned how to read them*. Not surprisingly, students find this difficult to do. One solution (an obvious one, one might think) would be to teach them how to read literature as a necessary preparation for studying it. But this is not the preferred solution. The usual procedure is to instruct students in a sort of simplified version of literary criticism so that they may be given access to significant aspects of the work they are studying without having to go through the bother of learning to read it for themselves. So it is that over recent years in this country, there has been a proliferation of little booklets of potted critical judgements which students can use as an effective prophylactic against any personal contact with actual texts. These booklets thus become part of the study of literature and enable students to make critical comments as if they had read the original. So, in a sense, they learn to perform without competence. Overseas there is, if anything, even greater reliance on this kind of surrogate for experience, or literary substitute, since, the originals being in a foreign language, the demands made on reading and consequently the appeal of avoidance are even greater.

In this approach to literature teaching, then, critical comment is elevated to a status not much less prestigious than that of the original literary work and much more influential. The most immediate source of reference and inspiration is not poetry or drama or fiction but the pronouncements of critics.

Literature is not directly experienced through actual reading, for this is altogether too difficult, but is just used as exemplification. Such a study of literature is in fact analogous with the study of language. If, for example, a non-native speaker wanted to study the English language, I would not expect him to start by directly confronting data, but by consulting existing descriptions by established authorities – such people as Quirk,

Svartvik, Leech and Greenbaum, because to study linguistics is to study language as described by linguists. And so it is with literary study: one studies literature as described by literary critics. But if this non-native speaker wanted to *learn* English, he would be well advised to go for guidance elsewhere.

So where would one go for guidance in the learning of English literature, or the literature in any other language for that matter? Apart from a few isolated indications there is in truth very little guidance available. Indeed the very idea that literature needs to be learned as well as, and perhaps as a prerequisite to its being studied seems not to have been seriously considered. So I would like to use this occasion to stimulate a debate on the matter by suggesting what a pedagogy directed at the learning of literature would have to be concerned with.

To begin with, it must be clear about its commitment to learning. I defined learning earlier as acquiring the ability to carry out a first person activity in which one plays the role of participant performer. There is no place here for secondhand response. But how, it might be asked, can one learn literature in this sense? The concept of linguistic performance is easy enough to understand and accept. But what can literary performance mean, except creative writing?

It can mean creative reading. Performance is not confined to production but means also the interpretative processing of what other people say and write. One can perform by being covertly engaged without necessarily being overtly active as a participant. This is the case when we read. And it is in this sense that literature is performed by the reader.

The task for literature teaching, then, is, I would suggest, to develop a pedagogy which will guide learners towards an independent ability to read literature for themselves, as a precondition for subsequent study. This would allow for the possibility of learners being able to evaluate the critical judgements of others against their own experience of literature and so make criticism an extension of their own interpretation rather than a replacement for it. In this way there is the chance that literature teaching might achieve what I assume to be its educational purpose: to develop a capacity for the understanding and appreciation of literature as a mode of meaning, rather than the accumulation of information and ideas about particular literary works. For too many people at present, literature is confined within the classroom and is equated with the set texts taught at school. This, I suggest, is, at least in part, because they have never really learnt how to read it.

What, then, is involved in learning how to read literature? One way of approaching this question is to consider how literature reading might differ from reading of an ordinary, everyday kind. Essentially, I think, reading something in the normal course of events is a process of recognition whereby we engage schematic knowledge of the familiar world.

There will be occasions when what we read refers to unfamiliar events and concepts, but we will usually count on our existing knowledge to serve as a framework within which the unfamiliar can be accommodated. What we read, therefore, is incorporated into the schematic structure of our knowledge, resulting in the recurrent reformulation of conventionalized reality. This process uses language as a means for establishing and extending the conventional bases of belief in what is factually true and actually real. In ordinary reading, we might say, we use language as a means to recognition in two senses: on the one hand to bring what is referred to within the bounds of what is familiar and at the same time to acknowledge the legitimacy of the conventions upon which familiarity is based. Reading is, in a way, an act of conformity.

Now literature does not refer to conventionalized reality, but represents a reality which cannot be accommodated within the schematic structures of what is factually true or actually real. It represents a kind of alternative reformulation in a different epistemological dimension (see Widdowson, 1984). In consequence, we cannot, when we read it, just use the language to plug us in, as it were, to what we already know. The language must itself create the contextual conditions for understanding, it must build its own schematic framework. Now, obviously, this framework must bear some resemblance to that which operates on the ordinary conventional plane, or otherwise it could provide no basis whatever for understanding, but it is distinct from it, dissociated, self-enclosed.

The language of literature is required then not to confirm an existing order of reality which can be recognized as conventional but to create an alternative order of reality within its own self-generated context. It follows from this that the reading of literature calls for a much closer attention to the actual language than would customarily be the case when reading. For, when we read in the ordinary way, once our schematic knowledge is engaged we can usually take short cuts, checking on the indications of direction from time to time, pausing to take linguistic bearings when on unfamiliar ground, but generally moving at considerable pace with minimal attention to the language. But in reading literature, we cannot treat the language in quite so casual a way because it is not just a collection of clues; it is the only evidence we have.

Consider, for example, how we need to react to the following opening of a short story by Somerset Maugham.

'The Unconquered'

He came back into the kitchen. The man was still on the floor, lying where he had hit him, and his face was bloody. He was moaning. The woman had backed against the wall and was staring with terrified eyes at Willi, his friend, and when he came in she gave a gasp and broke into loud sobbing. Willi was sitting at the table, his revolver in his hand, with

> a half-empty glass of wine beside him. Hans went up to the table, filled
> his glass and emptied it at a gulp.
>
> 'You look as though you'd had trouble, young fellow', said Willi with a
> grin.
>
> Hans's face was blood-stained and you could see the gashes of five sharp
> finger-nails. He put his hand gingerly to his cheek.
>
> 'She'd have scratched my eyes out if she could, the bitch. I shall have to
> put some iodine on. But she's all right now. You go along.'

*He came back into the kitchen.* Who is this? The use of the third person
pronoun would normally presuppose shared knowledge of the person
referred to. It would act, therefore, as a device for recognition. Here it
obviously cannot act in this way since there is nobody to recognize. And
where has this person come back *from*, and what was he doing there, and
where is this kitchen, and why should all this be worth mentioning anyway? This first sentence, in apparently making reference to shared knowledge of a familiar world, actually creates conditions for its own self-
enclosed context to be realized by subsequent reading. We are projected
forward towards the satisfaction of a need for the knowledge which the
opening sentence implies we already have. We read on.

> The man was still on the floor, lying where he had hit him, and his face
> was bloody. He was moaning.

Again, the use of the definite article here presupposes shared knowledge
which we as readers do not have, so we are provoked to read on to satisfy
this unfounded presupposition, thereby, as it were, giving it warrant. We
now have two recognizable figures we need to identify by subsequent
reading: the man who came into the kitchen and the man whom he hit,
lying and moaning on the floor. And now a third figure appears:

> The women had backed against the wall and was staring with terrified
> eyes at Willi, his friend, and when he came in she gave a gasp and broke
> into loud sobbing.

Who is this woman? Why is she terrified? And who is Willi? And whose
friend is he? *His* could be referred to either of the men who have been
mentioned.

> Willi was sitting at the table, his revolver in his hand, with a half-empty
> glass of wine beside him. Hans went up to the table, filled his glass and
> emptied it at a gulp.

More contextual information is provided: a table, a revolver in Willi's hand, the name of the man coming into the kitchen, Hans and Willi: German names. Is this significant in any way? And the wine on the table. Does this help to create the required context which will enable us to make meaning out of all this?

> 'You look as though you'd had trouble, young fellow', said Willi with a grin.
>
> Hans's face was blood-stained and you could see the gashes of five sharp finger-nails. He put his hand gingerly to his cheek.
>
> 'She'd have scratched my eyes out if she could, the bitch. I shall have to put some iodine on. But she's all right now. You go along.'

Another 'she' now appears on the scene, not, one supposes, the one previously mentioned but another one, who has scratched Hans's face in whichever place he came back from into the kitchen. Why did she do that? What has she got to do with the woman sobbing and the man moaning on the floor?

And so it is that as we read this short story opening, the assumption of shared knowledge which is carried by the normal use of linguistic expressions like third person pronouns and the definite article, provokes questions whose gradual satisfaction creates an internal self-enclosed context within which meaning can be achieved. In reading we pay particular attention to the implicational or projective power of the linguistic expressions. We are engaged with the writer in creation of a represented context. One figure is sketched in, then a second, then a third until there are five: three men, two women. A detail here and there: a half empty wine glass, a revolver and, foregrounded in detailed relief as it were, gashes on a face caused by five sharp finger-nails.

How might teaching encourage students to realize this context-creating use of language as they read? One way might be to present them opening paragraphs of short stories piece by piece, much as I have done, and ask them to infer information that is presupposed to be checked out against the developing context, and so to anticipate significance. Another way might be to present them alternative versions of the openings to see what different reactions they evoke. In the present case, for example, we might offer the following in parallel with the original:

> Hans came back into the kitchen, went up to the table, filled his glass and emptied it at a gulp. His face was blood-stained and you could see the gashes of five sharp finger-nails. The man was still on the floor, lying where he had hit him, and his face was bloody. The woman had backed against the wall and was staring with terrified eyes at Willi, his friend, and when he came in she gave a gasp and broke into loud sobbing. Willi was sitting at the table, his revolver in his hand, with a half-empty glass of wine beside him.

'You look as though you'd had trouble, young fellow', said Willi with a grin.

Hans put his hand gingerly to his cheek.

'She'd have scratched my eyes out if she could, the bitch. I shall have to put some iodine on. But she's all right now. You go along.'

Other techniques are possible. The point is that they should be accountable to the principle that literature reading is a matter of realizing the contextual significance of language. I am not saying that the reading of literature will always require a conscious close scrutiny of language as a necessary condition of understanding. Practised performers of literature have developed an instinctive sensitivity to the subtleties of linguistic expression and have a feel for significance. That is to say, they have learnt how to read it. I am talking about those who have not yet learnt, and who need guidance. It is also true, of course, that some kinds of literary reading call for a closer concentration on language than others.

The openings of short stories, for example, generally call for a quite intensive focusing. They have to create the context for their own significance within a narrow compass and the first paragraphs are important in that they have to engage the reader in sketching out the setting, the characters, in establishing the narrative perspective and in putting the story in the appropriate key. Once readers are initiated into this unique schematic framework of the created context of the fictional narrative, then this naturally enables them to read in the normal way they would employ with referential reading but within the confines of the represented reality of literature. Even so, one can never know when the ability to use language for new contextual representation might be called on, when the particularities of linguistic choice suddenly become significant for a proper understanding of what the writer wishes to convey.

There is one kind of literary performance which sets a high premium on close linguistic processing, where language is given a particularly high representational value. I refer to lyric poetry. Here the compass within which a context has to be created is, of course, even more narrowly constrained. In this case, every word is likely to be charged with significance, not only as a function of its syntactic and semantic properties, but also because of its phonological shape. Learning to read poetry is a matter of developing an awareness of this significance. What approach to teaching might afford the most effective guidance to this end?

Let us suppose that, with due notice paid to questions of linguistic difficulty and cultural appropriacy, we wish to teach the short poem by Thom Gunn entitled 'Considering the Snail'.

'Considering the Snail'

The snail pushes through a green
night, for the grass is heavy
with water and meets over
the bright path he makes, where rain
has darkened the earth's dark. He
moves in a wood of desire,

pale antlers barely stirring
as he hunts. I cannot tell
what power is at work, drenched there
with purpose, knowing nothing.
What is a snail's fury? All
I think is that if later

I parted the blades above
the tunnel and saw the thin
trail of broken white across
litter, I would never have
imagined the slow passion
to that deliberate progress.

This poem is a convenient one for my purposes since it will enable me to illustrate the distinction I made earlier between learning and study. For this poem is one which has been selected for treatment in a collection of exercises in practical criticism (Cox and Dyson, 1963), which can be fairly taken as typical of the study-oriented approach to literature teaching which prevails both here in this country and overseas.[1] The study of this poem begins as follows:

> This is a most unusual poem. At a first, quick glance it might seem just a vivid, descriptive poem. But soon we have to acknowledge that the deliberate rhythms create a most original music, and that the lucid, muscular language has a compelling power.

What we have here is a set of conclusions, ready made for immediate student ingestion, but no sign of any observation or argument to support them. In what way is the poem unusual? What are 'deliberate' rhythms? What does it mean to say that the language is 'lucid' and 'muscular', what are the particular linguistic properties that characterize lucidity or muscularity? And why do we have to acknowledge these qualities, on what compulsion must we? And what does 'compelling power' mean? Cox and Dyson go on to ask:

> How does this description of a snail become so charged with meaning?

191

This is indeed the crucial question and we might expect that the authors will now proceed to explain, and so give some meaning to the phrases they have been using. But they do not. What follows is a general discussion of Thom Gunn's work, and its prevalent themes, and some very general observations about the meaning of this particular poem like, 'throughout the poem we feel the strong will of the snail', ' . . . the "pale antlers barely stirring" frighten us with the mystery of life, so delicately constructed and yet linked to so blind a purpose', 'The "green night", "wood of desire" and the earth darkened by rain symbolize the nightmare blackness that surrounds the modern consciousness'. And so the student is provided with an *ex cathedra* exegesis with the imprimatur of critical authority but is given no indication whatever as to how the actual language in the poem realizes these meanings. He is just told that the language is lucid and muscular and has compelling power and that the poem is about the mystery of life and the modern consciousness and so on, and no connection between the linguistic expression and the poetic message is suggested at all.

Exercises of this kind might teach students a number of handy critical expressions for use in examination answers – 'muscular language', 'compelling power', etc. – but they have no relevance whatever, as far as I can see, to the problem of teaching students how to read poetry, how to become aware of the way the language is being used to create the kind of significance that Cox and Dyson claim to have discovered.

What exercises can, then, help students learn how to read poetry? Let me just briefly mention one possibility. This involves quite simply providing students with alternative linguistic expressions within the context of the poem, and requiring them to choose the ones they prefer and to give reasons for their choice. This is a simple enough procedure but it has the merit of drawing the attention of students to the way the meanings they can derive from the poem depend on the particularities of linguistic choice, how one alternative creates a context of significance which another fails to do. The Thom Gunn poem presented in this way might look like this:

'Considering the Snail'

A
The snail ^moves_pushes through a green
This

                    heavy
night, for the grass is sodden
                    weighty

with water and meets over

The bright path ^it_he makes, where rain

has darkened the earth's dark. It/He

moves/pushes in a wood of desire,

pale antlers barely moving/stirring

as it/he hunts. I cannot tell　　　　as it/he hunts. Knowing nothing,

what force/power is at work, drenched there　　　I cannot say what force/power is at work,

with determination/purpose , knowing nothing.　　　drenched there with determination/purpose .

What is a/the snail's fury? All

I think is that if later

I parted the blades above
the tunnel and saw the thin
trail of broken white across
litter, I would never have
imagined the slow passion
to that deliberate progress.

With reference to the alternatives set out in this way, the students can be made aware there is an ambiguity in the first verse, in that we do not know whether he is talking about the snail as a particular individual creature he is observing at a particular moment, or about snails generically. Or is he doing both at the same time, thus achieving a representational meaning which is beyond the scope of conventional reference? The alternatives *A/The/This* draw attention to the possibility. Again, the snail, whether particular or general, is associated with a human pronoun *he* and not the non-human *it*. Is this significant? Does it perhaps indicate a closer association with the human first person pronoun of the poet's assumed voice? In the second verse, *power* and *force*, *purpose* and *determination* might be regarded as synonymous in many contexts. Are they in this one? Which word in each pair is to be preferred, and why? Does the choice have anything to do with the words occurring at the end of the last two lines? In the second verse again, the phrase 'knowing nothing' has been shifted in one version. What is the effect of this? It removes an ambiguity. In normal referential language use would one regard this as an improvement? Is it an improvement in this case? And so on.

Presenting alternatives in this way provides students with the opportunity, enhanced by teacher guidance, to be involved in the actual process of reading poetry and to realize for themselves the significance of linguistic choice in the expression of poetic meaning. If later they choose to use expressions like 'muscular language' and 'compelling power' there is at least a chance that such phrases are expressive of a genuine personal experience of the poem and are not just the counterfeit currency of critical jargon.

I have argued in this paper that the task for literature teaching is to develop in students the ability to perform literature as readers, to interpret it as a use of language, as a precondition of studying it. Let me stress again that this does not mean that literary study, as I have defined it, does not have a crucial role to play in education here and overseas, but only that students need to be prepared properly to engage in it as a genuine critical enquiry leading to personal appreciation, and not just as a trafficking in fine phrases and packaged judgements. Literature learning, if you like, preludes not precludes literature study. I believe this to be true whether the literature is in the mother tongue or not, whether we are talking about literature in English for speakers of English or speakers of other languages. With speakers of other languages, however, the learning of literature in the way I have suggested has the additional advantage that, with due regard to the need for careful selection and presentation, it can be closely related to language learning since it calls for the particular intensive use of the procedures for realizing meaning in context which are required as a resource for ordinary discourse processing when meanings cannot be easily inferred by reference to existing schematic knowledge. In other words, literature reading provides the means for the purposeful practice of procedures of interpretation which need to be engaged for reading in general.

As far as English literature teaching overseas is concerned, therefore, it can, in my view, only have meaning and purpose if it is integrated with the teaching of English language. I have given only an indication or two as to how such an integration might be achieved. But I hope this will suffice at least to provoke an enquiry into how the two domains might be drawn together by pedagogic principle so that there is some prospect of more progress in the future than there has been in the past.

## Note

1  I am grateful to Colin Sloley for drawing my attention to the Cox and Dyson collection and for stimulating my own interest in this particular poem.

# Commentator 1

Jina Politi

Some three centuries ago, a non-conformist petitioned the English Parliament to abolish speech. Jonathan Swift, as we all know, grossly misunderstood the significance of that plea against logocentrism. Two centuries later, Oscar Wilde cried out for the abolition of tyrannical fact. Had these two been listened to, humanity might have been happier today, and Robinson Crusoe (who I believe is the unacknowledged founder of the British Council) might have found less arduous employment than teaching Friday English. So, communicate we must, and in English at that, though I should state at the outset that personally I adhere to the old line of globe-demarcation between civilized/uncivilized and consider every non-speaker of Greek a barbarian.

Had, therefore, Professor Widdowson been a learner of the language of Aristotle, his rhetorical strategies in this otherwise very interesting paper 'The teaching, learning and study of literature' might have been less transparent. For his argument is marked by a contradiction: namely the case is put forth in one long *argumentum ad hominem* (for who would like to be classed as ossified and antique?) for a revolutionary change in the teaching of English literature that will fill the developing globe with sweetness and light. Yet the rhetoric of persuasion relies on as traditional and conservative a method as the one that is being attacked.

I shall briefly expose it: Professor Widdowson rests his argument on the age-old opposition Ancients/Moderns, and expresses with an unwonted degree of vehemence his enmity against the Ancients, Dyson, Cox *et al*. At the same time he evangelizes for a radical modernism which I am afraid has already grown too senile to enter yet again the state of matrimony — if one is to date its birth back to the Russian formalists, the Prague School of Linguistics, Ferdinand de Saussure, William Empson, or Jonathan Culler for that matter. Thus the opposition is rendered rhetorically ineffective. For, alas, critical theory moves at as fast a pace as technology, and if, even before we had time to set it up, we heard the sad news that 'The Language Lab is dead' simultaneously with the good news 'Long live the micro-computer' (for technology, like kings, has two bodies), so it is with critical theories: stylistics, structuralism, semiotics, meta-semiotics, speech-act theory and so on, whilst teachers and learners all over the globe rush breathlessly on towards the infinities of Zeno's paradox. But let us, together with Thom Gunn's snail, move on. The opposition Ancient/Modern is associated by venerable tradition with another opposition, that of Head/Heart. Naturally Professor Widdowson attacks headless enthusiasm and, in a manner not dissimilar to that practised by

Bishop Sprat in his encomium of the Royal Society's Manifesto for Language,[1] feminizes aesthetic approaches to literature and invests linguistic approaches to it with a healthy, male vigour. Being a gentleman, Professor Widdowson then picks on some English critics (and not on foreign ones, known and unknown) who, together with all their colleagues overseas, seem to be falling into one fallacy after another: the aesthetic fallacy, the intentional fallacy, the affective fallacy, the 'boy-scout' fallacy, the heresy of paraphrase. But because English literature at university level does not and cannot consist simply of a naïve application of linguistic techniques to literary texts, or of naïve expressions of critical opinions, but does and should involve research and scholarship – in short, the teaching of a much richer and infinitely more varied discourse – it is for their significant contributions to this discourse that some of us regard with respect Professors Dyson and Cox, and deplore the ease with which they are held up to ridicule. Now, if I am sceptical about the readings proposed by Professor Widdowson, it is not because 'I fear the destructive force of rational thought', but rather because there is too little of it. The result is that both text and learning process are impoverished. For beyond the obvious linguistic explanation of a simple literary convention for the creation of suspense, which aims to arouse in the reader an appetite for consuming more of this readerly text, little is said about the opening paragraph of 'The Unconquered'. As for the games proposed on Thom Gunn's 'Snail', their purpose, in the final analysis, is to assert that whatever is (on the page), is right.

The type of learning proposed by Professor Widdowson might make life easy for a computer teaching the subject. But the serious learner might in all justice ask a teacher – if one still happens to be around – not together with Sartre 'What is Literature?' but 'What, after all, *is* English literature, and has there never been such a historical discourse in that country?'

And now to a question: What of the 'green night'?

## Note

1 See Jina Politi, 'Fall and redemption of language in the seventeenth century', *Epistimoniki Epetirida tis Philosophikis Scholis*, University of Thessaloniki, Thessaloniki, Vol. 18, 1980, pp. 271–82.

# Commentator 2

Lloyd Fernando

The value of Professor Widdowson's paper is that it summarizes the view of a sympathetic linguist, with strong literary interests, on the relation between language and literature. It allows us to study constructively what it is about literary critics and criticism that has repelled linguists in the past. From such an analysis we can move on thereafter to a more constructive phase in our relations.

Professor Widdowson contrasts the linguist with the literary critic as follows: The linguist employs 'rational thought' in his endeavours; the literary critic prefers 'truth revealed through visceral sensation rather than cognition'. The critic's preference is tellingly illustrated by extracts from an essay in a 1963 critical text which are, admittedly, quite horrendous. How Messrs Cox and Dyson came to load upon a competent but not otherwise striking poem by Thom Gunn such a weight of meaning about the modern consciousness, I cannot fathom. It does not comfort us one bit that we could easily cite by way of riposte some equally horrendous passages masquerading as scientific writing published by some linguists. If linguists and literary critics are to be friends, that is no way to proceed.

But the fact remains that in Professor Widdowson's kindly and gentlemanly way (and I mean no irony whatsoever by that) the literary critics are shown up to be the fools, the visceral reactors – to adapt an image thrown up in this conference, they belong to the forces of darkness – while the linguists plainly belong to the forces of light and reason. There is a very disappointing logic hidden away behind all this. It is that there are no inherent reasons for joint labour by linguists and literary critics in the study and teaching of language up to its fullest forms of expression. Rather the relationship arises out of necessity because the literary critics need the linguists to help them with sober 'rational thought'. This is a pity.

Anyway it is not true. Not only are linguists not entitled to appropriate the term 'rational thought' exclusively for themselves, their 'rational thought' is of a fairly elementary kind. I am not playing any semantic game here merely to score a point. It seems that linguists sincerely believe they are scientists, whereas they are in fact social scientists. The 'gradual cumulative process' of linguistic discourse is not, however hard one may try to make it so, rigorously mathematical or logical. Linguistic discourse is open-ended. The same is true of good literary critical discourse. But an important difference is that, by choice, linguists have in their discourse restricted meaning to one sentence at a time. In other words meaning advances in a sequential or linear pattern in separate distinct steps. But for critics, *overall* meaning emerges, as well as linear meaning, from the simultaneous echo and re-echo of meanings at different points in the entire sequence.

Now this is what I think Ezra Pound meant when he defined literature as an 'ideogram'. As in a Chinese written character certain strokes of the brush may convey little or nothing at all; it is the completed character, the whole ideogram, that reveals the full meaning in a single impact. The good writer, whether poet, playwright or novelist deals with meaning in this ideogrammatic sense. A disciplined critic knows he must perform his task bearing this in mind. In this process, even if the viscera are involved, so is the brain. In my view, the 'rational thought' of the linguist has severely prejudiced their study of language because the main schools paid little attention to meaning at all in the first instance, and now when they are ready to do so they are unable to grasp or find a place for ideogrammatic meaning.

The second half of Professor Widdowson's paper deals with the method of teaching literature. I can only beat my breast and say yes, there are too many packaged judgements, yes, students learn the judgements not the works, and so on. The exercises Professor Widdowson proposes to counter this are very useful. We can add to them the creative writing and imitation exercises proposed by Professor MacCabe in a previous paper. I am also greatly impressed by the exercise involving alternative linguistic expressions for Thom Gunn's poem.

I have thought about this second half very hard, but I fear I cannot get it out of my head that there is absolutely nothing new here. In fact the methods advocated by Professor Widdowson were first developed about fifty years ago with I. A. Richards's *Practical Criticism*. Since then the method of 'close reading' (which is how the technique came to be referred to), to which the method proposed by Professor Widdowson is akin, became the dominant critical method, and we have had a long line of distinguished practitioners of the art: besides Richards, Leavis and T. S. Eliot, one can name D. W. Harding, L. C. Knights, Cleanth Brooks, and William Empson. From my own undergraduate days, I remember Leavis's essay on Keats's 'Ode to a Nightingale', Harding on Jane Austen, and Empson's *Seven Types of Ambiguity* convincing me that literary criticism was certainly not the last refuge of scoundrels but instead required disciplined regard for the text, the page, the structure and the word to grasp the overall meaning.

The usefulness of Professor Widdowson's examples is to remind us that these honest methods have certainly not lost their relevance yet, and if they have been dropped in the language teaching situation then they should be brought back immediately. But what is even more delightful is that after all has been said and done, literary critics and linguists are agreed on this fundamental teaching technique. In the interests of evenhandedness we should ask what have been the more significant disappointments linguists have experienced through failing to take literature and literary content into account in their theory, and as a practical aid in language teaching.

Professor Widdowson's paper deals with language as an aid to literature teaching. But one must also consider literature as an aid to language theory, learning and teaching.

Regarding the interesting distinction between the study of literature and the learning of literature, must one assume that the student must overcome nearly all linguistic difficulties before being introduced to the work as a work of literature? The point has already been made earlier that students already have a knowledge of literary expressiveness in their own language which can be put to use. My own view is that even when faced with difficulties in a text, students make their own 'secret pact' with the language when they encounter something in it that appeals to them. That mysterious source of motivation for learning a foreign language has been seriously underestimated.

# b)   Issues in the teaching of English literature in Nigeria

Ayo Banjo

The institutionalized teaching of the English language in Nigeria dates back to the middle of the nineteenth century, well before the country formally became a colony of Britain. The records suggest that the few primary schools founded at the time were, to all intents and purposes, an extension of the educational system in Britain, and whatever literature books were read at the time must have differed in quantity rather than in type from those read in Britain. When grammar schools started to be opened in the country towards the end of the century, they too compared similarly with their counterparts in Britain, and indeed in the rest of the British Empire.

Fairly early in the present century, however, new approaches to the teaching of the English language in Nigeria came in the wake of new strides in the science of modern linguistics. As noted elsewhere (Banjo, 1970: 64) Professor Westermann visited Southern Nigeria in 1929, though his mission was to advise on 'the problems of orthography for the vernaculars'. As for reading materials, there is evidence in the Report on the Education Departments for the Southern Provinces published in 1935 that West's Readers were in use in schools. The same Report confirms the impact that linguistics was already having on the teaching of the English language when it notes:

> It has been suggested that there is need for a functional English Grammar based on a careful study of West African languages, and of local difficulties.

Even though many of the suggestions made over the decades for the improvement of the teaching of the English language in the country were not implemented, it would nevertheless be true to say that the teaching of the English language in Nigeria has always been more advanced than the teaching of English literature. The reasons for this are not far to seek. For one thing, the growth of structural linguistics in the United States of America and Great Britain early in this century soon revolutionized the teaching of English, first as a foreign language, and later as a second language, throughout the world. For another, the necessity to adapt the teaching of English as a second language to the local setting in linguistic and sociological terms was generally recognized by the middle of this century, with the result that there has been a continual effort to produce the ideal English language course book.

In contrast, no comparable theoretical framework for teaching English literature to speakers of English as a second language has emerged until recently when stylistics came to the rescue. Indeed, the status of English literature in a second language situation has never been very clear, at least in Nigeria. As recently as 1979, the Nigeria English Studies Association held a conference at the University of Lagos on the theme of 'junior literature in English' where, among other things, the relationship between literature and language teaching in Nigerian primary schools was examined. A considerable amount of time was spent debating whether the only use for English literature at the primary school level was as an aid to the teaching of English language, or whether English literature at this level should be treated as an end in itself, ideally to supplement whatever literature teaching has gone on, or is going on, in the indigenous Nigerian languages.

This, indeed, remains a major issue in the teaching of English literature, not only at the primary but at the secondary school level as well. The dilemma arises from the fact that while literature is indisputably a particular use to which language is put and indeed constitutes a register of language which consequently is part of the communicative competence of any speaker of a language, it is equally true that literature has other non-utilitarian uses which are usually categorized as aesthetic. Literature in the latter sense has its independent educating influence, and demands a particular approach to its study which in the traditional sense has to do with the examination of theme, plot and characterization, in addition to language, though, of course, it can be argued that all these aspects of literature are subsumed in language, in which they are realized.

This issue is in turn closely related to the problem of methodology. If literature teaching is viewed solely, or even mainly, as an aid to language teaching, then it is likely that the number of literature texts prescribed will be small and close reading will be emphasized, whereas if the more autonomous view of literature is adopted, a rather large number of texts will be prescribed and children are likely to participate more in class discussions. In order to identify the view subscribed to by a number of grammar schools situated around the University of Ibadan, a small study was conducted. These schools were seven in number, and six of them belong to the public system in which no fees are charged while one of them is a private fee-paying school run by the University itself and drawing pupils from different parts of the world (School 7 in the table below). The number of literature texts read in each class in each of the schools is shown in the table below (Table 1):

201

TABLE 1

| School: | 1 | 2 | 3 | 4 | 5 | 6 | 7 |
|---|---|---|---|---|---|---|---|
| No. of books in | | | | | | | |
| Form I | 3 | 3 | 2 | 2 | 2 | 2 | 5 |
| Form II | 3 | 3 | 2 | 2 | 3 | – | 5 |
| Form III | 3 | 3 | 2 | 3 | 1 | – | 5 |
| Form IV | 3 | 5 | 2 | 3 | 2 | – | 6 |
| Form V | 3 | 5 | – | 6 | – | – | 6 |
| Sixth Form | – | – | – | – | – | – | 11 |

Table 1 shows that in the first three years of grammar school in Schools 1 to 6, only two or three books are read annually. In School 7, however, five books, or roughly twice as many as in Schools 1–6, are read. This illustrates the difference between the two categories of schools and is a pointer also to the difference in methodology. School 7 in fact contains a fair number of pupils who are native speakers of English while the over-whelming majority of the rest are bilinguals with English dominance. Hence the teaching of English literature in School 7 approaches more nearly the practice in the first-language situation. It may be as well to add that the main literature teacher in School 7 is also a native speaker of English. School 7, however, is not typical of the Nigerian grammar school, and it can safely be assumed that only two books are read annually in each of the first three years of the typical Nigerian grammar school.

Incompleteness of data makes it less safe to attempt a generalization in relation to the last two years and the Sixth Form, but the difference between Schools 1 to 6 on the one hand, and School 7 on the other, is evidently maintained, except that School 2 is somewhat out of step with the remaining schools in its category. The difference between the two categories at this level is, however, surprising, since the fourth and fifth years are the period when pupils all over the country are prepared for the School Certificate examination. It is possible that while Schools like 1, 3, 5 and 6 limit themselves strictly to the requirements of the examination, those like 2, 4 and 7 manage to do more than the absolute minimum. Only School 7 has a Sixth Form, and it is evident that a certain amount of wide reading is encouraged at this level as well.

The second major issue at the secondary level is that of typology. The choice here is between texts by English authors and those by Nigerian (or African) authors. Our survey reveals that the same texts tend to be used in schools. The choice is almost invariably as follows:

Form I:   a)  *Akin Goes to School,* by C. Ajayi and M. Crowder
          b)  *Collected Poems, Book 1,* by O. Taiwo

Form II:   a)  *The Children of Ananse*, by P. Appiah
             b)  *My Father's Daughter*, by M. Segun

Form III:  a)  *The Incorruptible Judge*, by D. O. Olagoke
             b)  *Wedlock of the Gods*, by Z. Sofola

Form IV:  a)  *The Merchant of Venice*, by W. Shakespeare
             b)  *The African Child*, by C. Laye
             c)  *The Gods are not to Blame*, by O. Rotimi

Form V:   a)  *Things Fall Apart*, by C. Achebe
             b)  *Animal Farm*, by G. Orwell
             c)  *Selected Poems*, by T. Vincent and K. Senanu

The above list reflects the dramatic changes that have taken place within the last fifty years in the English literature curriculum in Nigerian schools. African authors now dominate the classroom and only few schools now prescribe some of the other plays of Shakespeare or *The Adventures of Tom Sawyer* or even *Gulliver's Travels*.

The assumption is that literature texts by Nigerian, or at least African, authors are more easily accessible to Nigerian pupils than texts by other authors. This has, however, not proved entirely true in practice for two main reasons. The first is that the number of Nigerian or African authors consciously writing for young people is negligible. The result is that, in most cases, texts set after the first year or two were neither written in the first place for children nor have they been adapted or abridged for children. Thus *Wedlock of the Gods* is a popular text in Form III. *The Gods are not to Blame* and *The African Child* in Form IV and *Things Fall Apart* in Form V. These same texts are set for degree examinations in Universities. The situation is even more untenable with regard to poetry. The anthology popularly used even in Form I must present considerable conceptual problems for the children. It is therefore not enough for the authors to be Nigerian, the level of the literature also has to be appropriate. The second reason is that even adult highly-educated Nigerians do not always find the best Nigerian literature readily accessible. The reason for this, in turn, is partly that written literature is still something fairly strange to the Nigerian cultures, and partly that African literature is neither exactly like the oral literature with which children and adults alike are familiar, nor like the kind of English literature which most educated Nigerians are acquainted with. Most of good Nigerian poetry written in English, as well as some good fiction (such as Wole Soyinka's), turns out to be a conundrum for most highly-educated Nigerians, for the act of literary creation in a second language situation is necessarily a bicultural and bilingual process for which few consumers are adequately prepared.

Given these difficulties, the teaching of English literature in Nigerian schools is understandably a laborious process. For this reason, many Nigerian children are switched off literature for the rest of their lives.

The most senior literature teacher in each of the seven schools visited was asked a number of questions relating to the attitudes of teacher and pupils to the teaching and learning of English literature. The questions and responses were as follows (the number of teachers making the response is indicated in brackets against each response):

i)      Which do you enjoy teaching most?
        Poetry (1)    Fiction (2)    Drama (4)

ii)     Which authors do you enjoy teaching most?
        African (6)    British (2)

iii)    Do you relate the teaching of literature to the teaching of language?
        Yes (5)    No (2)

iv)     Do you encourage the reading aloud of literature texts?
        Yes (4)    No (3)

v)      Which do you spend more teaching time on?
        Language of texts (1)    Content (7)

vi)     Would you like to see more African authors prescribed?
        Yes (6)    No (0)

vii)    Which do your pupils do best in?
        Poetry (0)    Fiction (4)    Drama (3)

viii)   Which literature do your pupils do better in?
        African (5)    British (1)

The correlation between the responses to (i) and (vii) is hardly surprising, neither is that between (ii) and (viii): the responses to (vi) are predictable. But the lack of correlation between (iii) and (v) is a little puzzling while again, the responses to (iv) are hardly surprising, given the background in oral literature brought to their task by teacher and pupil and an understandable desire on the part of the teacher to use the opportunity of the literature lesson to revise work already done in spoken English.

With this as background, we may now consider the situation at University level. The major issues here are typological and theoretical. The University of Ibadan, which is the oldest University in Nigeria, started off as a College of the University of London. At the very beginning, therefore, the English Honours programme was identical with the programme in London itself, and although the College became an autonomous University in 1962, serious reforms of the programme did not take place until about five years later. First, two alternative syllabuses were introduced, making it possible for students to obtain an Honours degree with specialization in either English Language or English Literature (in the newer Universities, the latter was to evolve into Literature in English, dominated by African Literature of English expression). Old English continued to be offered at Ibadan as an optional course, until the early 1970s when it no longer attracted any students. The syllabus of the Language specialization had, by then, come to concentrate on the study of contemporary English based on modern linguistic principles.

Meanwhile, the literature syllabus was fast undergoing a change of character. While the study of literary criticism continued – and continues – to draw on literature from different parts of the world – and particularly from the United Kingdom and the United States – texts set for study have become predominantly African. Indeed, in the early 1970s there was a debate as to whether any Shakespeare texts should be set for study. While most people see this as a natural development some anxiety has been expressed over the possibility of an English Literature Honours programme which does not include the 'classics' of English literature and which does not pay enough attention to the history of the development of English literature at least from the sixteenth century. Moreover, the problem of accessibility is present at this level, too. The three poets most widely prescribed are Clark, Okigbo and Soyinka, but while Clark's lyrical and sonorous verse does not present too great a problem to the undergraduate, the works of Okigbo and Soyinka often breed despair.

The second major issue is, in fact, closely related to this. The problem that any reader has with some of the best African literature stems, to be sure, partly from a lack of adequate cultural preparation which has already been referred to. But more important is the fact that an appropriate approach to the criticism of African literature is still in the making. How does one 'talk' about this new literature?

When African literature of English expression first came to be studied at the University level, the only critical tools available were those fashioned specifically for English literature of British or American origin. It is true that some of the early African writers in fact tried to fit their writings into the mould of the metropolitan literature. But it quickly became clear that such writers were not to be too highly regarded. The search was therefore on for a viable theory of African literature of English expression – for the formulation of an African literary aesthetics. The situation has given rise to two schools of thought perhaps most strongly represented by Chinweizu *et al.* (1975) on the one hand, and Wole Soyinka (1975) on the other. While the former advocate a purist view of Nigerian literature of English expression, one which would make the literature more widely accessible as a result of the familiarity of images and references, the latter advocates a literature which faithfully reflects the modern bilingual and bicultural writer's situation. The two views can be illustrated from Nigerian literature, but there is no doubt that

Soyinka's view is the more influential, at least in University departments of English.

A major breakthrough in the criticism of African literature is represented by Izevbaye (1968) who approaches the problem from a purely literary point of view. More recently, a stylistic approach has been explored, by Osundare (1979) working on fiction, and Johnson (1981) working on drama. Perhaps a synthesis of these two approaches offers the best promise, for in talking about African literature, it is as necessary to be aware of the African world-view (including the African idea of what is beautiful) as it is to be conscious of the peculiarities of the act of literary creation in a second language situation. While waiting for the day when the synthesis will be enshrined in a coherent theory, many Universities, including Ibadan, adopt a two-pronged approach in the training of their students. By making literary criticism and stylistics compulsory for all English Honours students, it is ensured that the students gain an insight into the aesthetic as well as the stylistic peculiarities of African literature.

# Commentator 1

Svetozar Koljević

In the discussion of the teaching of literature we have to assume, of course, that literature can be taught. The assumption is large enough at the best of times, but the situation becomes even more interesting if the basic critical tools, the fundamental approaches to the literature which is presumably taught, are still in the making. We have nothing like this Nigerian problem in Yugoslavia; if we felt like replacing British and American literature in an English university syllabus by Yugoslav literature in English, we could not do it. Even if the spirit were willing, the flesh would be weak. However, English literature also, fortunately, leads a perfidious double life in Yugoslavia. First, it is very much alive and kicking in Serbo-Croat and other translations; as Yugoslavia has been, since 1945, one of the leading countries in the world as regards the number of translated titles, almost all of English literature that is worth translating, and perhaps a little more, has been rendered in Serbo-Croat, and other languages used in Yugoslavia. And much of it – like Eliot's ideas of tradition, Joyce's avant-garde attitudes and 'atavistic catholic stylistics' – have proved to be hot political and literary issues in the local battles of the books. The Watergate aspects of *Hamlet* (who should spy on whom and on what moral grounds) has provided the basic pattern for a contemporary political comedy set in a Croatian village in the middle of nowhere. On the other hand, in the English Departments, English literature has led its own independent academic life (if life is not too strong a word), even if the insistence on close reading and the unavoidable 'passages' has sometimes led students into a situation not unlike that of Salman Rushdie's young Doctor Aziz who examines a girl-patient through a perforated sheet and tries to imagine the bits together. The urge may not be always as strong.

So there are two sets of critical tools and assumptions in the response to English literature in Yugoslavia: one – local, lively, and irreverent, but always applied to English literature in translation; and the other – well-informed, academic, largely English and American by origin (I. A. Richards, T. S. Eliot, F. R. Leavis, W. Empson, N. Fry *et al.*), and usually confined to the English Departments and literary periodicals. Are the two sets of critical tools in Nigeria – one applied to English English literature and the other to African literature in English – also very different? What is the difference and what is its general cultural significance?

# Commentator 2

## Maurits Simatupang

I would like to begin by saying that I was entirely unfamiliar with the Nigerian situation before I read Professor Banjo's thought-provoking paper. But having read his paper, I still cannot claim to have a clear picture of the English literature teaching situation in his country – and I must be the one who is at fault.

Coming from an EFL country, I must also admit that much of what has been said regarding the existence of other 'Englishes' which have their own norms worthy of our recognition, has enlightened me on the arguments put forward for such a claim, and also on the unpleasant experience (if I may say so) other people must have had in the past as regards the English language, or at least their own varieties of it. We were under the British Colonial rule ourselves, and there were Indonesians, though not many, who lamented the day the British had to waive the rules, and they would say 'Oh, we could have spoken English much, much better had Raffles stayed a little bit longer'.

I would now like to address myself to one of the issues raised by Professor Banjo in his paper: it seems to me that it is still worth our effort to look again into the idea of having one's literature (if it is indeed intended to be such) written in someone else's language. This statement, of course, can be meaningful only if we can prove that a person cannot be truly bilingual and truly bicultural at the same time.

The implications of this statement are arguable, of course, but by dismissing them altogether, we may run the risk of overlooking questions, the answers to which might eventually enhance our understanding of what, for instance, literature really is, the relation between literature and language, and the nature of literary language. The statement can also prompt a more specific type of question, such as: does a piece of writing about something peculiar to a certain culture in a language alien to that culture have the possibility of being considered a literary product of that culture? It seems to me that whatever answers we may give to these questions will somehow modify our definition or concept of, say, English literature, or any other literature, or perhaps literature in general.

To my knowledge, this matter has not been explored and discussed exhaustively. I might also venture here to suggest that the reason for using the name 'African literature of English expression' might perhaps be prompted by a desire on the part of non-native speakers of the language to have a share in the ownership of the English language. This of course is just a wild guess on my part, but nevertheless it might be worth exploring, and should there be any truth in it at all, the production of literature of this kind, to my mind, should be welcomed, supported, and encouraged because it would certainly help spread the use of English, unless the owners of the language wish otherwise. But one still may ask, 'Do they after all have the right to decide what to do with the thing they have already exported?'

In his paper, Professor Banjo, to deal with the African literature of English expression, has also suggested that the synthesis of two approaches – namely, a purely literary point of view and stylistics – may perhaps offer the best solution. However, we may still ask whether such a synthesis could ever be realized. A Sapir/Whorf view would lead us to conclude that, without breaking its own rules which are jealously guarded by English grammarians, English can never express certain ideas which are not part and parcel of English culture. It would perhaps be claiming too much to settle for a compromise here, unless of course we are prepared to accept the existence of the Englishes Professor Kachru speaks about in his paper.

# Theme VI  Summary of discussion

This theme of literature teaching stimulated lively debate. A good deal of this was devoted to the defence of practical criticism and the rejection of linguistics as irrelevant (or worse) to the study of literature. Although of considerable interest in itself, this argument was criticized as not actually bearing upon the main issue, which was not what contribution literary criticism or linguistics might make to the study of literature as an academic discipline, but how one might devise an effective methodology which would teach learners in general, and not only the élite pursuing specialist studies in the subject, to read literary texts so that they could realize meaning for themselves. The methods of literary criticism and the methodology for literature teaching were not the same thing.

There was no necessary implication, it was pointed out, that literary criticism could not be used as a basis for an appropriate methodology and that the approach through language which had been proposed was the only one possible. But if literary criticism were to provide such a service, then this would need to be demonstrated. It was not enough to assert its validity as self-evident. If the use of potted critical notes as a primary resource for learners were to be avoided, the question was what alternative should take their place?

It was noted that I. A. Richards himself had concluded that literary criticism could not be taught as such; he had therefore turned his attention to the teaching of reading instead. But how were learners to be encouraged to read literary texts in English? It was reported that an experiment in Germany had indicated that learners were favourably disposed to such literary texts as did not depend for their interpretation on extraneous information but must be understood in terms of their own self-contained context. Furthermore, it appeared that the learners' experience of literature had a beneficial effect on their language learning. It was suggested that more research of this kind was needed so as to discover the basis for learner preference, the factors which cause difficulty in interpretation, the effect on learners of different types of text, literary and otherwise, and in general the way in which the learning of language and literature could be seen as complementary.

The point was also made that distinct issues arose with literature in

English by writers (for example in anglophone Africa) who were influenced by cultural traditions other than those which informed the classical canon of English literature. Such texts might well require different criteria for interpretation and appreciation, and the methodology for teaching the reading of literature would need appropriate adjustment. It would also need to take account of the learners' experience of literature mediated through television and film. These media provide abundant illustration of the multiple resources and the self-enclosed character of literary representation.

It was clear from the discussion that there were several possibilities to be explored for developing a methodology for the reading of literature, so as to make it an experience of general educational value. This did not preclude (it would indeed lay the foundation for) the study of literature as a legitimate activity in its own right for those who had the inclination and opportunity to pursue it.

# THEME VII    ENGLISH FOR SPECIFIC PURPOSES

## a)    ESP – The Heart of the Matter or the End of the Affair?

John Swales

> To an ethnographer, sorting through the machinery of distant ideas, the shapes of knowledge are always ineluctably local, indivisible from their instruments and encasements. One may veil this fact with ecumenical rhetoric or blur it with strenuous theory, but one cannot really make it go away.
>
> (Clifford Geertz, 1983: 4)

As readers will recognize, my title borrows from the works of one of our most distinguished novelists – and one whose career has itself spanned the half century of British Council activity in the field of English that we celebrate this week. I also hope the Greene-tinted question in the title announces a serious attempt at the original request 'to take a bold stand with regard to future developments'. In fact, offering evaluation rather than description is, at least in principle, made easier by a recent flurry of publications delineating past and present ESP progress and practice. At the year's beginning there was Coffey's state-of-the-art review (1984), usefully informed by much 'insider' British Council knowledge, and 1984 sees the publication of no less than three teacher-directed general books on English for Specific Purposes (McDonough, 1984; Kennedy and Bolitho, 1984; Swales, 1984). One other book on ESP has recently appeared, but of rather different character and orientation (Widdowson, 1983), and I will need in the course of this paper to offer some perspective on Widdowson's extensive discussion of ESP principle.

In more general terms, I hope to make an undoubtedly personal, and possibly idiosyncratic evaluation of ESP's current strengths and weaknesses, its future opportunities and the threats to those opportunities. In so doing, I shall need to reconsider the historical influence of English Language and Linguistics studies on ESP and I shall want, alternatively, to press for closer relationships between ESP and the Sociology of Science, Cultural Anthropology and Research Communication Studies. This in turn will raise questions about the preparation and training of ESP practitioners and touch, if fleetingly, on interactions between ESP and its parent profession of English Language Teaching.

The ESP situation-type that I shall use for illustration is that of English Language Centres offering Service English courses for undergraduates

212

not intending to specialize in English or English Language teaching: or, in the jargon of my field – English for Academic Purposes. It is my impression that many of these ELCs in many parts of the world survive in straitened circumstances; and it is my feeling that one important but insufficiently recognized cause of present retrenchment and loss of morale has been that most ELCs have adopted a dangerously inhibited view of the constituencies they are designed to serve. Inspired by quite legitimate developmental and educational aspirations of 'doing the greatest good for the greatest number', ELCs have concentrated on building bridges between school and university via ranges of pre-sessional, foundation and in-sessional programmes. Precisely because much of this work world-wide has been correctly adjudged as a considerable improvement on pre-ceding arrangements, the damaging limitations of what are essentially first-year undergraduate ESP materials writing and teaching schemes are only now becoming apparent – in Southeast Asia, in Africa, in Latin America and in the Arab World.

Of course hindsight is easy, but perhaps we should have paid more attention to the difficulties of those teaching language in Literature Departments or to the plight of English Composition lecturers in American colleges of Arts and Sciences. That we did not pay due attention was, I suspect, because we felt (and often with justification) that *our* type of Service language was different – more sensitive to needs in the manifold senses we understand that term today, more innovative and exciting in methodology, and more capable of contributing to our understanding of the use of English itself. It was surely impossible that host-institutions could fail to be appreciative of such transcendent virtues.

Alas, it has proved only too possible. As a result, ELCs, as well as other ESP units in commercial and occupational settings, are losing confidence in their future as the issue of the status of ESP work, and of those engaged in it, once seen as a temporary problem solvable by goodwill and sensible innovation management, has emerged as a permanent difficulty. Thus, in tertiary circles and in many occupational settings, the low and/or uncer-tain status of the ESP unit has become a major structural weakness with deleterious effects on staffing, on motivation, on initiative, and on pro-gramme maintenance (Mohammed, 1984; Barmada, 1983; Swales, 1984). It is also becoming clear that within tertiary environments lec-turers cannot prosper by Service teaching alone. In the heady early years of important projects long-term structural problems tend not to be antici-pated, especially as they may not directly concern expatriate specialists working to fixed term contracts. In subsequent years, opportunities decline and threats multiply – not least in the dispersal of the carefully-nurtured cadre of qualified and motivated ESP staff. The fashionable 'timed project' certainly provides better managerial control, but does not of itself strengthen a fragile post-Project future.

The problems raised by the uncertain viability of long-running ESP work have been tackled in a number of ways. The oldest and perhaps standard answer is to argue that ELCs can gain the respect and reputation they need in order to prosper in a tertiary environment by research and publication. This solution was long advocated by Jack Ewer (1981) among others, but in 1984 I am not so sanguine about the effectiveness of visible research as a vehicle for ameliorating status, however valuable it continues to be for the internal health of ESP enterprises.

A second approach is to dissolve the problem in a quasi-Wittgensteinian way by reconceptualizing the situation. Thus Cooke and Holliday (1982) undertake an 'inverse Munby' whereby a Means Analysis identifies the constraints within which the ESP programme will have to operate and then investigate ways of turning those constraints into advantages. Analogously, Andrews (1984) ingeniously argues that subject lecturers who opt to persevere with English, take time to develop their students' English vocabulary, offer instruction on writing up etc., are in their lecturing activities, *de facto* members of the ESP Department. However, although such cognitive refigurations are splendidly anti-defeatist, they are essentially ways of coming to terms with problems rather than of resolving them.

A third type of initiative is to graft a 'respectable' constituency onto the mass undergraduate root-stock, most typically by adding ESP-oriented teacher training to the ELC's range of activities. This is certainly a route taken in Britain (pioneered at Lancaster and Essex and extended to the Master's level at Aston), a route being followed today in Alexandria and Bangkok, and one in various stages of active consideration and experimentation in a number of other better-established ESP centres. The advantages to ELCs of obtaining degree- and diploma-awarding status are obvious, as are the easy availability of appropriate teaching practice situations, the opportunities to assemble a group of potential recruits and the chance to influence for the pragmatic better postgraduate Teacher Education in its broader national context. The difficulty, as we say in Yorkshire, is 'in setting your stall up' especially if the Departments of English, Linguistics or Education are already active in the market place. Earlier I referred to the dangerously narrow and inhibited view of Service English work commonly held by colleagues in my profession. Although I would be the first to congratulate ELCs that establish a balanced combination of research, specialized-teacher training and general service English, I remain of the opinion that EAP activity world-wide has tended to over-concentrate its resources on the first two years of undergraduate programmes and has self-destructively neglected graduate students and staff. In other words, ELCs have all too often locked themselves inside an extensive world of basic training and all too often locked themselves out of the world of scholarship. It is one of the major contentions of this paper that ESP would benefit from exploring this latter world with a good deal more determination and expertise than it has brought to bear up until now. Specialized personnel providing English language support for staff and researchers are more likely to come into contact with energetic and senior members of their host institutions and thereby to accrue a valuable capital of goodwill and respect eventually repayable in enhanced ELC status. Immediately it may be objected that such a partial shift towards the élite is wasteful of expensive ELT specialist resources, but I hope that my observations so far have made at least a preliminary case for a greater 'political' realism and opportunism in ESP planning, not because such an orientation is admirable in itself, but because it is for the long-term benefit of the whole range of an ELC's activities.

The ESP profession would seem, however, to be under-prepared for such an enhancing Service English role. In the first place, it is out of touch with work in Research Communication Studies and with its highly numerate offshoot, Scientometrics. As humanists, we may well be shocked by having our scholarly worth measured by citation indices, or by the rumours in America that it is now possible to find researchers who will cite your work on payment of a fee. We should be more appalled, however, by the lack of consideration given to matters of language in this sizeable literature. The relationship between the language chosen for pub-lication or presentation and the writer or speaker's proficiency in that language, and the further relationship between the choice of a language and its visibility, audience-size and prestige, are almost universally ignored. A couple of instances must suffice. Blickenstaff and Moravcsik (1983) (the latter a leading figure) in their investigation of the pro-fessional profile of participants in an international meeting, did not include a questionnaire item about the language proficiencies and prefer-ences of those participants. Schubert *et al.* (1983), having recently analysed the proceedings of more than five hundred international scien-tific meetings, concluded:

> The distribution of the participants of international scientific meetings depends on [*sic*] the geographical location of the host country, and in addition, the similarity of efforts for scientific development (e.g. in the developing countries), the organizational structure ('open' or 'closed' nature of the scientific communities), the economic situation (travelling expenses can influence the participation rate) and in some cases, political considerations may also have an important role.

I would imagine that practically all of the participants in this seminar would also have wished to raise the issue of a possible connection between the language or languages formally accepted for particular international meetings and the distribution of participants, both as auditors and speakers. But if this literature is linguistically 'unaware', it is at least partly so because *we* have ignored it.

There are, however, two useful recent papers by Baldauf and Jernudd (1983) that do take up the question of language-use patterns in the periodical literature. They first establish that English is the dominant language in the literature they scanned. The figures are summarized in the following table:

PERCENTAGES OF ABSTRACTED PUBLICATIONS ORIGINALLY WRITTEN IN ENGLISH

|  | *1967* | *1981* | *(Total articles abstracted in 1981)* |
|---|---|---|---|
| Chemistry | 50 | 67 | 252,409 |
| Biology | 75 | 86 | 300,024 |
| Physics | 73 | 85 | 167,618 |
| Medicine | 51 | 73 | 258,941 |
| Mathematics | 55 | 69 | 35,907 |

Even making allowances for English-language bias in the abstracting services, the proportion of articles published in English has increased substantially in the last fifteen years. Other European languages have declined whilst Japanese has increased, but in 1981 only reached the 10 per cent level in chemistry. Despite the predominating position of English, the numbers of publications are so large – around a million papers in the five disciplines surveyed – that there remains a very considerable literature in other languages. Baldauf and Jernudd then examined the relationship between language use and location in a small section of the Fisheries literature and concluded that 'English language dominance appears to be the result of the large number of scientists doing research in English-speaking countries, English national language countries, or for international organizations or forums'.

If we accept these findings – and I have brutally condensed Baldauf and Jernudd's discussion – then the larger picture of the increasing pre-eminence of English may well be gratifying to participants in a Seminar entitled 'Progress in English Studies', but the smaller picture of the locations of active and visible researchers is decidedly disconcerting. This smaller picture suggests that research is the preserve of countries where English is either the national language or the official language, of countries with an international language of scholarship or of those individuals who go to international meetings. Baldauf and Jernudd's figure of only 40 'unexpected' English-language locations out of 884 Fisheries papers indicates, for example, very low levels of research activity in the so-called lesser developed countries (LDCs) of the Arab World, Latin America, Southeast Asia and perhaps francophone Africa (Davies, 1983). A survey of my own more than corroborated this pattern in that I found that out of 632 articles in Medicine and Economics only five of Third World provenance were incontrovertibly written by non-native speakers of English (Swales, 1985).

Such a suggestion is *prima facie* unlikely, given the wide consensus that publication in respectable journals should be an important criterion for promotion in academic and research fields. An alternative hypothesis would therefore be that research in non-anglophone LDCs is indeed being done, but little of it is finding its way into the journals that come to the attention of major (and highly efficient) abstracting services. Either way, we seem to be faced with further evidence of North–South imbalance, due presumably to an interlocking multiplicity of factors among which we might find additional language hurdles facing non-native speakers of English, editorial gatekeeping bias, and a generally less supportive research environment. And either way, we are faced with serious questions about the effectiveness of the massive investment by hard-pressed LDCs in doctoral scholarships held by their nationals in the USA and Europe, and about the long-term scientific and developmental value of research scholarships and visitorships offered to LDC nationals by American, British, Russian and European governments and other sponsoring agencies.

I began the case for the teaching of 'Research English' by arguing that such an initiative offers hope to over-stretched and under-promoted ESP lecturers. I have closed it with an argument placed on an altogether different dimension – and one considerably more significant by several orders of magnitude. On the limited evidence available, more support for Research English would seem necessary if full advantage is to be taken of efforts to transfer technology, to establish joint research programmes, to maintain international contact and so on. In a very small way, my own Unit has experienced the need for such support as a result of its link with the University of Córdoba under the '*Acciones Integradas*' scheme. The report by Bloor (1984) provides a vivid but unnerving picture of Spanish academics edging their way through English papers via continual recourse to bilingual dictionaries, and expressing considerable anxiety about the substantive and linguistic accuracy of the English translations of their abstracts – translations they are required to submit along with their Spanish papers.

It would thus seem that the scientific paper – or more broadly, the scholarly article – is a crucial genre. And certainly contemporary ESP research shares an interest in genre-analysis with literary colleagues, especially those of a structuralist persuasion (Hawkes, 1977). The scientific paper is not only an extremely important genre because of its size (several million exemplars each year) but also because it is the vehicle whereby private and localized research work is turned into a public account. *Tout court*, papers are the products of the knowledge-manufacturing process. It is therefore now necessary to review what we understand of this process and product.

Within the field of Applied English studies, both from a linguistic and an ESP starting point, there has been a fair amount of investigative activity in this area (Barber, 1962; Huddleston, 1971; Sager, 1980), which in recent years has moved with the times and overlaid syntactic and lexical investigations with those of a textual or discoursal nature (Dubois, 1982; Swales, 1983). A further overlay has been provided by the use of specialist informants who can offer expert insight into the textual product (Selinker, 1979; Tarone, 1981). More recently, Huckin and Olsen (1984) among others have investigated tapping the introspective and retrospective reflections of the original author as to both product and compositional process. (However, as my literary colleagues know particularly well, the opinions of the original author, although revealing, do not necessarily reveal truth in the terms that the enquirer may hope to construct or reconstruct it.)

There also exists a quite separate tradition of enquiry into such matters, falling within the general field of the Sociology of Science. Bazerman (1983), in a recent 142-citation review of the literature entitled 'Scientific Writing as a Social Act' makes no reference to any of the work summarized in the previous paragraph, and nor do any of those linguists cite any of the work cited by Bazerman. And this despite the fact that Bazerman has section headings with such titles as 'The Writing Process', 'Textual Form', 'The Dissemination Process' and 'Audience Response'. Similarly, Knorr-Cetina (1981), in her lengthy account of the processes by which laboratory notes are transformed into a publishable paper, can observe 'at present, there are not many analyses of writing in the natural and technological sciences'. Gilbert and Mulkay (1984), in their fascinating socio-discoursal account of what has 'really been happening' in a controversial area of biochemistry, can refer to 'the relatively few previous studies of formal scientific texts', one of the very few known to *us* being Peter Roe's monograph (1977). And yet work in this sociological tradition can offer further overlays to our utilizable perceptions of the genre of the scientific paper. Certainly my own work on Article Introductions would have been greatly enhanced if at the time I had had the initiative to search out such papers as Gilbert's 'Referencing as Persuasion' (1977). And as a Parthian shot at this topic, let me refer to the well-attested difficulty of finding suitable subject matter for study skills courses aimed at multidisciplinary groups of undergraduates or pre-postgraduates. These difficulties will certainly intensify as we move to programmes for more senior, more settled and more specialized members of the academic community. Yet we appear to have a multi-targeted arrow to hand that will cover the wide ground of interest we are seeking – the very literatures I have been referring to in Scientometrics, the Sociology of Science and the genre-analysis of the scientific paper.

In essence, my description of layers and overlays has been an argument for 'thick description'; and the biography of that phrase in this context is itself quite 'thick'. Here then is an English teacher's version of the anthropologist Geertz's reading (1973) of the original paper by the linguistic philosopher, Gilbert Ryle. Consider, more or less says Ryle, a group of boys rapidly contracting the eyelids of their right eyes. In the first boy this is an involuntary twitch; in the second, a conspiratorial signal to a friend. A third boy, unimpressed by the second's performance of the signal, now closes his right eyelid in parody. A fourth boy, unsure of his communicative competence in this domain, practices a wink at a moment sufficiently opportune as to be undetected by his friends. And so on. These specks of behaviour, the blink, the wink, the parody and the rehearsal are all physically the same and thus the I-am-a-camera observer will record them all as identical. Yet the difference is great. The fact that four boys have rapidly contracted their right eyelids is 'thin description'. The fact that four boys have performed quite different acts, distinguishable by the strength and direction of communicative purpose, and by the extent to which the acts depend on social and cultural convention is 'thick'.

On the whole our descriptions of the disciplinary and occupational matrices within which our Service work is set have been too thin, and principally because our own training and preoccupations have themselves been too firmly set within the matrices of language and discourse. We have given text too great a place in nature and believed a thick description of text is the thickest description of them all. However, it is not only texts that we need to understand, but the roles texts have in their environments; the values, congruent and conflictive, placed on them by occupational, professional and disciplinary memberships; and the expectations those memberships have of the patternings of the genres they participate in, be they monographs, textbooks, lectures, examination papers, memos, minutes, testimonials, case-notes, or presentations at fiftieth anniversary seminars. The ESP practitioner therefore needs some appreciation of the *conceptual structures* of the disciplines and occupations he or she is called upon to service and support. To seek, if you will, the skull beneath the textual skin. However, the practitioner also needs something else; an appreciation of the *conventions of conduct* that organize vocational and organizational life. And that is why I now retract my intemperate youthful derision of diplomatic claims that going to cocktail parties was 'work'. Today, taking tea in laboratory technicians' cubby-holes or in to-me-exotic staff rooms equally seems a natural part of the job, but a part frustrated by lack of education in ethnographic sleuthing and sociological thinking.

So far this evaluation has had a critical (indeed self-critical) character. However, there is one area where we are already on the way to thick description – that of the learning environment. Within our own tradition, there has been important work on lectures (Murphy and Candlin, 1979), classrooms (Sinclair and Coulthard, 1975; Dhaif, 1983), demonstrations (Hutchinson, Waters and Breen, 1979), case-study sessions (Charles, 1984) and so on, much of this research associated with the Departments at Birmingham and Lancaster and with the looser grouping of *Lecturers and Tutors to Overseas University Students*. Contemporaneously, there is burgeoning an equally valuable literature devoted to longitudinal case studies of individual overseas students (Schmidt, 1984; James, 1984). Of perhaps greater interest have been developments in team-teaching, whereby subject teachers, ESP teachers and students can develop a better mutual understanding of the educational processes in which they are differently engaged and of how those processes are mediated by language (Johns and Dudley-Evans, 1980; de Escorcia, 1984). In addition to this 'in-house' activity, it is also clear that in this area at least the ESP profession is in contact with the work of those educational researchers concerned with the tertiary level, as Widdowson's (1981) important lead article in the Festschrift for Louis Trimble demonstrates. Nor do I today have much anxiety about the level of contact between advanced work in ESP (as prioritized here) and the teaching of First Language Communication Skills (Williams, 1984).

In effect I am proposing a view of English for Specific Purposes as an applied nexus with lines of communication to a considerable range of co-disciplines in the Social Sciences and Humanities and with a contribution to make, in interdisciplinary and educational terms, to those disciplines. Promiscuity is the preferred state, even though traditionally ESP has had a scrupulously monogamous relationship with the linguistic sciences. If that preference is correct, then the consequences for the preparation of future ESP practitioners are indeed controversial. The opening paragraphs of this paper certainly corroborate the need already well canvassed in British Council environments for training in management skills. Latterly, my conclusions imply either an extension of postgraduate and post-experience training into multidisciplinary studies or, if extension proves impossible, a reconsideration of priorities. To take two instances, and these more illustrative than substantial, phonology may have to make way for the Sociology of Academic Life, and Semantics – in any case ruthlessly eroded by Pragmatics – for ethnographic and educational research techniques.

Such considerations also suggest that ESP will continue to drift away from its mother-ship of English Langue Teaching. Although I do not welcome this tendency, there is every reason to suppose that whilst general language learning theory operates within its own classroom-bounded universe of discourse, ESP is required to operate within the multifarious universes of discourse denizened by other occupations, disciplines and professions, and it would be struthious to deny this fact however much one may want to veil it 'with ecumenical rhetoric, or blur it with strenuous theory'. Albeit in a somewhat different way, I also do not welcome the accusations of the wider profession that ESP is overbearingly 'élitist' or indeed 'tendentious'. It seems to me that ELT desperately needs to garner all the specialisms it can. Of course, promotion beyond the general classroom is certainly achievable by moves into administration or teacher-training, but ESP can provide another opportunity for upward mobility, one calling upon wide-ranging intellectual and linguistic sensitivities and, moreover, one still involved with direct teaching. To undermine this opportunity reduces the chances of 'promotion through the ranks' and this set against a background in which many commanding positions are already occupied by officers seconded from elsewhere and where the recruitment offices for the ELT profession are besieged by those with little to offer except themselves and the fact that they are native speakers of the language.

I have spent much time attempting to make a case for 'thick description' as leading to a better grasp of the ESP situations within which we work – and a further aspect of thickness that I have not had space to develop is the need for ESP practitioners to be familiar with the now-substantial literature of their specialization. For a similar purpose, Widdowson has long advocated the need for 'thick theory', not so much as something to have and to hold but, as he modestly puts it, 'in the hope that it might prove of some service for the clarification of current ideas and practices in the field'. There is no opportunity here to offer a reasoned discussion of the elaborate and complex argument that Widdowson develops in *Learning Purpose and Language Use*, nor a chance to consider any of the interesting meta-questions that such a theory raises, such as whether we should view Widdowson's thesis as a logical proof prone to collapse if one of the axioms proves untenable, or rather as an educational philosophy that survives virtually intact even if we judge it as being only 'mostly right'. Nevertheless, an evaluative position-paper (as this purports to be) needs at the very least to react impressionistically to the first full statement of principle about an important educational activity now some twenty-five years old.

On the positive side, the long and impressive discussion of *language use* is fully convincing. Similarly, the realignment of methodology and course design placing the former 'at the very heart of the operation with course design directed at servicing its requirements and not the reverse' is, in my opinion, important, welcome and long overdue. Nor, I imagine, will there be much dissension from Widdowson's avowed purpose of developing student *capacity* (crudely glossable as 'creative communicative effectiveness') as the prime educational objective, particularly in English for Academic Purposes situations.

However, Widdowson's argument is premised on a distinction between training and education and predicated on an ESP methodology derivable from and dependent on that operating in the student's particular specialist area. There is, I believe, room for legitimate doubt about both premise and predicate. A difference between training and education is more sustainable, I suspect, in lower and earlier levels of education than in subsequent ones. Certainly at the post-experience level, the problems of deciding what is Yin and what is Yang are formidable, not least because *experience* itself – and reflection on and utilization of it – creates triangularity rather than polarity. Particularly in relation to the higher-order communicative skills, the three elements seem inextricably blended, as Atkinson's (1984) analysis of political oratory makes clear.

More central perhaps to my argument at this point is Widdowson's view that methodology should be concerned with 'appropriate procedural activity'. Methodology's purpose is thus to stimulate problem-solving activities of the kind which are 'congruent with the student's specialist preoccupations' and for which language is needed as a contingency. Hence ESP pedagogy is a dependent activity, 'a parasitic process'. It seems, however, that Widdowson's thick theory takes us rather farther out than we really ought to go; it makes us too independent of general ELT methodology and too dependent on the methodology of the target discipline. As I have argued elsewhere (Swales, 1984), it seems to me unfortunate for both teachers and students for us to insist on methodological constraints of this kind – in effect, to deny variety in the relationship between ESP classroom discourse and target discourse. The difficulty lies with the strong and theory-driven assumption that there should be 'congruence' between Service English and Subject activities. In my terms, 'thick description' ensures that whilst our ESP classroom activities are *informed* by specialist preoccupations, the pedagogical shaping of those activities is not necessarily *determined* by specialist preoccupations. Nevertheless, Widdowson's emphasis on 'procedural activities' is a valuable one, even though – and especially as – the motivations of most ESP students are instrumentally geared to successful ends, to understanding the book, to answering the examination question, to winning the contract. Certainly, this paper has shared Widdowson's concern to shift attention from engaging students in the right text to engaging them in the right task. Indeed, one consequence of this shift is the resolution it offers to certain sorts of practical constraint. Here is a very able British Council Officer (Crocker, 1982) on this topic

> Although students valued 'relevance' in the language course, the prospect of requiring instructors, whose control of English covered the

domains of general educated social use, to handle samples of use well outside normal domains (texts on international law, company contracts etc.) was sufficient to preclude (matters of principle aside) initiating any task with inspection of a sample legal text. Instead, straightforward language exercises of variable content were chosen, which required students to identify, explain and then rectify ambiguity.

The resolution arises, of course, from the recognition that law students need to develop exceptional skills in disambiguation and that these skills can be developed, if necessary, with texts of the 'Flying planes can be dangerous' variety as with any other.

In this paper I have drawn upon investigative, theoretical and pragmatic considerations to put forward a case for the downgrading of both textual matter and subject-specific matter. In compensation I have argued for 'local knowledge', for a renewal of connection with the textual environment, and for greater attention to the tasks that specialized environments require of their occupants. I have seen our aims as perceiving and then pedagogically mobilizing interactions between language use, learning purpose, professional sub-culture and prevailing educational style. I have tried, in at least one genre, to relate these interactions to wider geo-political and geo-linguistic issues, and to show how both prudence and responsibility may require us to give greater attention to Research English and to the business of its creation. As for my title and its original disjunctive question, readers who have followed me so far will recognize that what I should have written was:

ESP – The End of the Matter but the Heart of the Affair.

# Commentator 1

Husain Dhaif

John Swales's paper in essence represents an ongoing and significant shift in ELT methodology in general and that related to ESP in particular; a shift which started at the end of the last decade and which legitimately focuses on the learner and, more importantly, on the cognitive and behavioural profile of that learner. In fact the British Council publication *Projects in Materials Design* (*ELT Documents Special*, 1980) strongly underlined the necessity for such a shift both in pedagogy and materials production. The point is that our pedagogy in ESP has for a long time taken its cue from the discipline which the language is supposed to serve. In so far as English for Science and Technology (EST), for example, is concerned, the underlying assumption seems to be that since science is a universal area of enquiry with identifiable communicative acts which are neutral to any specific language – and I am here referring to Professor Widdowson's model – it is assumed that it is possible to produce teaching materials which will be suitable to any EST group of learners irrespective of their learning contexts and/or cultural backgrounds. Thus the springboard of such materials is the discipline and its communicative acts rather than the learner and what he brings with him to the learning situation. In this context the letter 'S' in the term 'ESP' is very much related to the discipline which the language is serving rather than the learner who wants to use that language to function in that discipline.

Given this state of affairs, I would like to suggest that a mismatch often exists between that pedagogy, the teaching materials and the learner. I also believe that such a mismatch usually takes place not at the linguistic level but at the cognitive/behavioural level. That is to say, the mismatch often exists between the teaching and learning strategies prevailing in the learning context on the one hand and those preassumed by the teaching materials on the other.

One reason why such a mismatch continues to exist is perhaps that the learning strategies developed by the learner are usually deeply rooted in the learner's cognitive repertoire and are therefore difficult to alter overnight through the English language class. They are also the by-products of a set of cultural and educational factors.

Research by Selinker *et al.*, and Dudley-Evans *et al.*, has shown that foreign learners of EST, for example, coming from certain cultural backgrounds, find it difficult to understand authentic scientific texts because they lack the cognitive skills which are required for negotiating meaning in such texts. I believe that the solution to such a problem does not lie in conditioning the learner, as our present ESP pedagogy seems to be advocating, but rather to explore an alternative approach which is guided by careful and systematic investigation into what the learners have, do or can do in the learning process. In other words, our pedagogy should take its cue from the behavioural and cognitive domains of the learning situation and be related to the learning strategies prevalent in that situation. I think it would be helpful here to extend the notion of 'learner freedom' discussed in Professor Brumfit's paper and to suggest that it is perhaps necessary to view that freedom as being related not only to what the learner wants to learn but also to how he wants to learn. In this respect one cannot but agree with John Swales that we need to create a closer relationship between ESP pedagogy and cultural anthropology. But let me now try to enlarge the circle of the 'learner freedom' concept to accommodate an important issue which John Swales raises in his paper – that of the predicament of non-native scholars and researchers who want to publish their research and to participate in international conferences but who are deprived of that right through lack of proficiency in English language. I think it is a question of attitude towards culture in general. It seems to me that we in the so-called developing countries are constantly being asked to justify our research worthiness by publishing it in English. I think there is a need for the developed countries to take a more appreciative look at research written in the native languages of some of the developing countries, and I wonder if we should not consider the translation theory as one of the solutions to this problem. It is a well-known fact that the Arabs translated a lot of works in science and literature from other languages such as Farsi and Hindi when they realized the richness of such works.

One of the papers cited by John Swales as evidence of the dominance of the English language in scientific meetings, seminars and publications indicates that out of 97,693 papers in the Fisheries Periodical Literature, 76,456 were written in English. This seems to be convincing enough evidence, but I think I would also like to know how many of those papers were initially written in languages other than English and then had to be translated into English. I would like to end my remarks by saying that I share John Swales's call for 'Research English', but must pose a question: since this type of skill-oriented programme will only be required by an élite group of specialists in each field with very specific needs, how cost-effective is it, knowing that one of the fundamental criteria for evaluating ESP courses in developing countries is the ability to provide a financial short cut?

# Commentator 2

Anthony Howatt

The first point that I should like to make is to welcome John Swales's proposal for the extension of ESP into the research field. The notion seems to me to make admirable sense and he has marshalled some persuasive evidence on the potential scale of need in this area.

What I intend to do now is to consider one or two of the pedagogical implications of the proposal, and perhaps the simplest thing to do would be to put a question directly at the outset and follow it with some observations on why I think it may be a pertinent one. It concerns the intended scope of Research English (RE) teaching in relation to the needs and purposes of the potential customer for such services: should we assume that the primary focus of RE teaching would be on the research scientist as a consumer of specialist texts (an emphasis which is consistent with the general direction of the bulk of English for Academic Purposes (EAP) teaching hitherto) or should we assume, as I think John Swales's paper is leading us to assume, that the focus would shift to the scientist as a primary producer of such texts, with all that that implies in terms of personal and professional vulnerability, and the consequent weight of responsibility placed on the shoulders of the RE teacher?

Since it is likely (and in many ways reasonable) that RE teaching will be seen as an extension of EAP teaching, albeit at a more specialized level, it is worth exploring this contrast briefly. The first point which arises concerns what Firth and Malinowski might have called the context of situation. It is evident that in the case of EAP teaching the three main participants, the student, the subject teacher and the EAP teacher, all belong to the educational community, and the language that is produced (essays, projects, theses, etc.) is addressed to and, more importantly, evaluated by other members of this community. For this reason, among others, the 'standard model' of EAP teaching has been able (legitimately) to put the vexed question of the subject-matter on the back burner.

When, however, the EAP student graduates, as it were, into the professional world, becomes a scientist-at-work rather than a scientist-in-training, he moves out of the educational community into a professional one — and the English teacher cannot follow him. In this new context, it seems to me, the subject-matter issue comes into sharper focus; it is upgraded rather than downgraded since it is the main distinctive feature which identifies the professional world of the RE client from other possible professional worlds.

One obvious practical effect of this is that the RE teacher will need to know more about the subject-matter rather than less, and he will need to cultivate a concern for precision as to how exactly the language expresses the propositional and conceptual content of that subject-matter and the ideational structure of the material the client wishes to communicate to his fellow professionals.

It seems, therefore, that John Swales's illustrative comment on the preparation of RE teachers that 'semantics (may have to give way to) ethnographic and educational research techniques' is not entirely convincing. Consider, for instance, the example of abstract writing which is, I should have thought, a clearer example than most of an exercise in 'applied semantics', concerned as it is with questions of equivalence in meaning between two stretches of text. Moreover, the need for precision is likely to exert pressure on the teacher to co-operate bilingually with the learner-client. Although the preparation of RE teachers may well include the sociology of science, it might equally usefully include training in the concepts and procedures of translation.

One final point. The membership of a professional world implies the adoption of a specialized mode of discourse (a 'discourse dialect' so to speak), which cannot be acquired by the RE teacher who with experience can expect only to become a competent user of 'standard academic discourse'. (The analogy with the school teacher of standard English to pupils who speak a non-standard variety comes to mind.) However, even if this 'dialect' cannot be acquired, it has to be learned, and learned accurately, if the teacher is to be of much use. What this seems to imply is a strong argument for the development of specialized linguistic descriptions for pedagogical purposes of this kind.

Since these comments apply with greater force if the learner is aiming to be a producer rather than a consumer (though they may apply to both in different ways), could I reiterate the original question: which of the two would provide a primary focus for courses of RE instruction, and would the selection of the former carry any of the pedagogical implications I have tried to indicate?

# b) ESP and beyond: a quest for relevance

Blanca A. de Escorcia

## Introduction

Although my main concern in this paper will be with the situation of ESP in South America, I do not intend to write a state-of-the-art report. Rather, I want to take up a few issues that have recently dominated the field, and examine them more closely in the South American context.

Three very distinct patterns of development have emerged in South America, as exemplified by the ESP operations in Chile, Brazil and Colombia.[1] Although in all cases there is a clear tendency to follow the general world-wide trends in the profession, each country has solved problems in different ways.

For the purpose of this paper, I will take the Colombian situation as a starting point and try and place it in the wider perspective of the other countries. My main concern will be to examine closely the concept of needs, its incidence in the development of methodologies and the implications of this relationship for Teacher Training.

## Needs and needs analysis

In the context of ESP, needs analysis has become the dynamic impulse underlying course design, the justification for the S and for the P, the driving force that has motivated teachers and course designers throughout the world ever since the magic acronym ESP came in.

I think it is time to divest the concept of its magic connotations and to bring it back into proper perspective. In other words, I want to show that the concept of needs does not suffice to account for decisions taken in course design within the reality of language teaching throughout the world and specifically in Latin America.

We may consider, in the light of this statement, two basic categories within ESP, mainly EAP, developed at the universities around reading comprehension as the basic skill, and EOP, which responds to the demands of the community at large, and which includes familiar areas such as English for Executives, for Bilingual Secretaries, for Long-Distance Telephone Operators, for Air Traffic Controllers, and the like. We note that, in the latter area, where needs are immediate and motivation strong, teaching is in the hands of traditional teachers, with little time or inclination to do any research, with a characteristic lack of knowledge of the content areas they are handling, and consequently with a total dependence on traditional textbooks designed for general language teaching.

In the universities, on the other hand, where most of the ESP expertise resides, with better-trained teachers and the possibility of obtaining resources for research, students are in general less motivated, more uncertain of their needs. Whether we adopt the systematic exhaustive approach towards needs analysis in the Munbian tradition, or a more eclectic, intuitive one, the same picture seems to emerge systematically: English is the language that most people need for their careers (about 90 per cent of the answers to questionnaires confirm this fact) and reading comprehension is the skill most widely accepted as responding to this need. These results are overwhelmingly confirmed in all needs surveys which have been carried out in universities throughout Latin America. I am not questioning here the validity of the surveys nor the reliability of the results. Instead, I want to examine them more closely in the context of the situation as it really is at our universities.

First of all, I think it is necessary to make a distinction between *real* and *ideal* needs. Every student in a Colombian university is aware, in an abstract general way, of the necessity of studying English. He knows that a great deal of the literature in Science and Technology is mainly available in English. He also knows that an ambitious professional who wants to do graduate work will often have to find his way to a university in the USA. But, on the other hand, he is aware of the fact that very little pressure will come from his teachers to use resources in English, specially at the beginning of his career, and that he can easily finish his studies and become a reasonably acceptable professional without a large amount of English. A real need is only felt, in most cases, towards the end of the careers, when more specialized up-to-date reading material has to be handled.

Taking these factors into consideration, it would be reasonable, convenient and most relevant to offer English courses to students in the last part of their study programmes. But administrative decisions, which are not made by the ESP teacher nor by the Language Departments, determine that English should be offered in the first semesters of the programme, in order to get rid early of basic cumbersome requirements and get down to more important areas of specialism as soon as possible. Thus, although ideally English is known to be useful and desirable, the students do not feel a real immediate need for it at the time they are being offered their ESP courses. I am sure this is a generalized, well-known problem in

229

other parts of the world and there is no need for further elaboration of the issue.

However, if we accept the implications of the distinction between real or immediate needs and ideal or deferred needs, it should be obvious that the concept itself is not very useful and that we have to find other ways of making English immediately relevant to the student. Besides feeling that the foreign language is necessary, the student has to want to learn it by relating it to more personal concerns. This is specially crucial when we consider the student's previous experience in learning English. For six years in secondary school, he has been told that English is necessary and good for him without being able to relate his classroom experience to the types of situations in which he would really have a use for the foreign language: watching foreign films, listening to popular music, reading English comics and magazines, etc. Even the most recent innovations in the secondary school curriculum which include a strong reading component in preparation for their 'future' needs at the university, is not enough to motivate students who, in extremely high percentages, will drop out of school or never go on to higher education anyway. At the university, the incoming student is usually placed in the category of false beginner (this term to be understood as that no previous knowledge of English can be taken for granted), he is highly unmotivated by the prospect of starting all over again and can only think of English in terms of ideal, deferred needs. This is the situation that we, as ESP teachers, have to face and that good, solid specialized materials alone cannot totally solve.

One of the ways in which this problem could be handled would be to introduce as a component of the beginners' course a motivating element to increase the student's awareness of the role of English in his future professional life. This could mean, amongst other things, simple devices like visiting the library and getting acquainted with books in English on his subject and, in general, becoming aware of the existence of such resources in the foreign language. This 'needs awareness' technique must, of course, be encouraged and complemented by similar moves from the specialist teachers who must be persuaded to recommend from the beginning reading material in English which complements their own courses. Again this may sound like a simple measure, but it is not at all trivial if we consider that specialist teachers have for a long time doubted whether or not English courses can adequately prepare students to handle specialized literature. One way of breaking this vicious circle would be to encourage the students to be the initiators of the process and ask the teacher for a bibliography of works in English to complement their courses. A more sophisticated variation of this approach has been the successful attempts made at team-teaching, which have forced specialist teachers to think very seriously in terms of using more resources in English for their classes.[2]

But whatever devices are used by the resourceful teacher to bridge the gap between real and ideal needs, this distinction raises a more fundamental question: How does content specificity relate to immediacy of needs? It seems to me that it is more relevant to take a 'restrictive' view of topic content when dealing with EOP areas than when handling EAP situations. A long-distance telephone operator, for example, has very immediate well-defined needs, i.e. to be able to carry out certain conversational routines of a very specific nature. The decisions to be made in designing a course for such a group of students will be basically determined by a very restricted view of language use. But, on the other hand, in the situation of EAP, where needs are of a rather distant, ideal nature, content specificity could be more relaxed, to the benefit of the development of learning strategies of a more far-reaching nature. This conclusion has also been reached from an empirical approach to the problem, as reflected in the materials development projects carried out in Brazil and Colombia. Handling students at the beginning of their study programmes, often mixed groups with respect to their specialization, has led to the design of materials with a 'common core' component aiming at the development of strategies for coping with reading in general and with scientific discourse in particular.

## The role of methodology and materials in the learning process

Some of the problems usually associated with methodology in ESP are no longer an issue in Latin America; such is the case, for example, with authenticity. The use of authentic texts is emphasized everywhere, the problem being rather how to relate authenticity to relative simplicity in terms of language. This, of course, involves taking into account other aspects of the reading process like shared knowledge, shared experience of the world and of the topic, etc. A great deal of research into the language of scientific texts has been carried out recently in Latin America, contributing to increase the ever growing knowledge of the characteristics of scientific discourse amongst ESP practitioners.[3] Detailed descriptions of the lexis and language characteristics of certain disciplines lead to a better understanding of the workings of science and help build up a feeling of self-confidence in the teacher who, traditionally, has been exclusively oriented towards the humanities.

But ESP is not a matter of relevant content alone, nor of the ordered presentation of linguistic items. Authenticity also means the development of personal learning strategies to approach the particular task of interpretation and further application of texts to real life situations. In this respect, a great deal of effort has still to be made. For there is usually a basic discrepancy between the good solid knowledge of scientific discourse provided by research and the application of those results in the production and presentation of materials. If we are really concerned with the learning process, with the development of sound, individual strategies for learning, if we are concerned with changing unhealthy study habits, with turning our students into independent beings, going against the age-old educational tradition of memorization and repetition of teacher-transmitted knowledge, then our task as ESP teachers has wider educational implications. Both the role of teacher and student have to change, and this will necessarily imply, amongst other things, a radical change in methodology, including the organization and presentation of materials on the one hand, and classroom management techniques on the other. Classroom management is a two-way relationship and it does not make sense to throw the burden of learning upon the student if the proper conditions are not created. The teacher has an extremely important role to play in order to change trends in education. Traditionally, language teachers have placed their trust in commercially produced textbooks, assuming, uncritically, that the burden of methodological decisions is on the author and that anything that appears in print must necessarily be good to use. A more critical attitude, however, is taken by the ESP teacher who is much more conscious of the specificity of his teaching objectives. In the last few years, there has been a proliferation of ESP textbooks covering all kinds of possible areas and levels. Nevertheless, once they are produced and thrown onto the market, they tend to lose a good deal of their validity. They never seem to quite fit *my* particular situation, *my* particular group of students. This is not necessarily a negative reflection on the materials, but rather on the restricted view of specificity that some practitioners have come to adopt. They tend to think in terms of differences rather than similarities. And yet, there is a lot of common ground underlying all academic writing that we often fail to acknowledge in our eagerness to present extremely specific materials. I am not advocating here a return to General English, not even the use of ESP materials that are comprehensive enough in their topic content to suit everybody and to satisfy nobody. What I am saying is that area specific materials, designed to satisfy the needs and interests of particular groups or students must and can be used for the development of generalized strategies that can be applied in other situations and that will be of a more educational value to the student than just learning a restricted language in a restricted and totally predictable context. In other words, ESP should be the springboard to English in general and not the other way around.

This position has, of course, implications not only for the types of teaching materials that we want to select or produce, but for the kinds of activities we want to use them for. The development of reading as a process, and of strategies for the interpretation of different kinds of meaning in text, should be a priority in our courses, especially if we are up against traditional learners' characteristics of rote-learning and word-by-word translation. Flexibility should guide the teacher to provide an adequate balance between meaningful content and 'real life' strategies. No single textbook as yet written and available on the market could ever bring together the necessary mixture for all people in all situations. Should we decide to adopt a particular text or series of texts, we are still left with the task of complementing it to accord with our particular objectives. In this sense, a custom-made course could include a set of common-core materials constructed around some kind of minimal 'text-attack strategies', possibly provided by a commercial text, complemented by modules including more specific materials, both with reference to topic and functional content. In any case, materials production should be one of the most encouraged activities of the ESP teacher. Although a time-consuming and not well rewarded job, it is however most gratifying to the teacher, it helps him clarify criteria of organization, it forces him to look at his task more rigorously, and it encourages research in theoretical and practical areas. In short, materials production must be developed as the source and justification for many in-service training activities.

Another crucial point of materials selection and methodology in general in ESP is that of matching authenticity of texts (in topic, level of content and language knowledge, authenticity of tasks, etc.) with systematization of linguistic structure. Since there is no guarantee that particular linguistic features will be grasped from exposure to one single text, systematization must consist of presenting a series of texts with relevant features in common. Whether with respect to conceptual or rhetorical organization, a typology must be used which will allow the student to assimilate common characteristics underlying particular areas of discourse and match them with the schematic framework he brings into the task. Only by being exposed systematically to authentic models of language will the learner be able to exercise fully his cognitive capabilities with respect to language learning.

To sum up, methodology is not a matter to be taken lightly. Only when a great deal of research has been carried out on psycholinguistics, matters of L2 acquisition and learning in general, on specific learning styles in particular, on institutional and individual attitudes to language learning, on the relationship between elusive needs and real expectations, on every aspect of classroom management, will we have the tools for the adequate implementation of specific contents.

## Teacher Training

With the exception of Chile, which includes an ESP component in some undergraduate Training programmes,[4] most South American countries only have specific training at graduate level or in-service. The status of ESP or 'service' courses has been so low until recently, that the job is often offered to new, inexperienced teachers in Language Departments who consider these courses as part of the 'initiation rites' they have to go through before going into the real business of teaching English Literature. Fortunately, the image of the ESP teachers is changing fast and, in some cases, they have taken the lead in Applied Linguistics research in their Departments and are helping to produce radical changes in attitude towards language teaching in general. In spite of this considerable progress, most ESP teachers are still 'in-service' trained and share the general features of the general language teacher, whose weaknesses can be characterized as follows:

1 Fair-to-low level of proficiency in the language itself. Most English teachers in South America were brought up in the structuralist tradition of pattern practice, grammatical correctness and synthetic approaches to language teaching. Their ability to use the language for communication is not always up to a desirable level and they tend to perpetuate in their teaching the methodologies with which they themselves were taught. Although it would be unfair to overgeneralize this pattern and although it is true that most university teachers involved in ESP have an excellent command of English, it is still valid to say that higher standards of language use would be necessary for people working in ESP areas, specially those involving oral production.

   This is not a trivial matter, since using authentic models of language in the classroom involves a native-like capacity for language use.

2 No conscious awareness of study skills and strategies. Within the general educational tradition of rote-learning and teacher-oriented transmission of knowledge, no deliberate attempt is made to encourage the development of study skills and reading strategies in the schools. In EAP it is a crucial matter that the teacher himself should be at least a good, efficient reader, since he can hardly convince his students of the desirability of developing something he does not himself believe in.

   In Colombia, attempts are being made to train secondary school English teachers to learn reading strategies to be applied in the new English curriculum. However, it is felt that the origin of the problem lies at a still lower level and some seminars and workshops have been offered to train L1 teachers to develop those strategies in L1 in the primary school. It is also felt that the development of sound reading strategies in L1 at the primary and secondary levels would, in fact, contribute, amongst other things, to a better understanding of language organization in L2 and to a redefinition of methodological principles in ESP in the South American context.[5] The issue is quite complex, since breathtaking educational changes do not happen overnight and in-service 'remedial' training only reaches select groups of people in the main urban areas.

3 Inadequate knowledge of 'principles'. Although most undergraduate teacher training programmes include a Linguistics component, the courses offered in this area are, in general, too theoretical and not adequately suited to current trends and developments in Language Teaching. Therefore, the teacher finds it difficult to adapt himself to the demands of specific teaching situations as presented in ESP courses.

In addition to these problems which affect English teachers in general, the ESP teacher has to face specific difficulties he has not been trained to cope with:

## 1 *In relation to content*

– Negative attitude towards Science due to a lack of familiarity with its contents, its activities, its language. This produces feelings of anxiety and insecurity, of being at a disadvantage in front of the students.

## 2 *In relation to course design and methodology*

– Lack of analytical training that will allow him to look at language globally, not in isolated unrelated chunks.
– Difficulty in relating needs to specific skills to be taught.
– Difficulty in designing objectives for the course that will match more general educational aims.
– Lack of familiarity with psycholinguistic aspects of L2 learning which would help him prepare materials and improve his classroom techniques.
– Negative attitudes towards error with an emphasis on correctness rather than fluency, which inhibits the development of communicative abilities.

If we take the position that all language teaching should be purposeful, most of the changes needed in Training for the ESP teacher must necessarily affect the General Language Teacher as well. The improvement of personal skills; a knowledge of analytical tools for the description of different kinds of discourse; a principled approach to the development of methods and techniques; a perception of the relationship between needs, course objectives and educational aims; general principles of course design; the importance of evaluation procedures in relation to learning strategies; a principled way of overcoming 'unhealthy' habits towards

235

language learning; a positive attitude towards unfamiliar subject areas. These are only some of the aspects that should be included in Teacher Training programmes at an undergraduate level. The basic tools provided in this process could then be put to work by the ESP teacher in any situation he might be confronted with. In-service training should then be directed to more specific problems presented by the language of the specialism or the nature of the tasks involved in specific areas of interest.

## Conclusion

I have not tried to be exhaustive in my presentation and analysis of the problems involved in ESP teaching. Rather, I think it is a matter for discussion and interpretation how these issues are viewed by different people in different circumstances. ESP, like all language teaching, should be based, in my view, on very strong principles and a lot of flexibility for their methodological adaptation, taking into consideration the multiplicity of the variables involved in each case.

As an example of this 'adaptability', it will be useful to compare the three basic ESP projects in South America taken as the inspiration for this paper, and analyse them with reference to the following parameters:

1  *Aspects which have to do with theoretical positions and their implementation*

   – General principles (communicative approach; notional–functional; linguistic, etc.).
   – Specialist language problems viewed as an extension of general linguistic structure or as specific problems of 'register' in general.
   – Methodological approaches and practical decisions.
   Relationship between strategies and linguistic structure.
   Comparative emphasis given to formal aspects.
   The role of grammar in the interpretation of texts.
   Emphasis on differences or similarities.
   Relationship between teaching and evaluation.
   Practical criteria for course design and materials production.
   Relationship between needs and topic content.
   Criteria for dividing up teaching units.
   Relationship between texts and exploitation exercises.

2  *Aspects related to the manner of implementation of the projects*

   – Centralized v. institutional developments.
   – The role of 'outside' v. 'national' expertise, and more specifically the British Council contribution.

– The existence and role of Resources Centres.
– Modalities of Teacher Training (undergraduate, graduate, in-service).
– The role of Language Departments.

A detailed analysis of this topic would, by itself, generate another paper.

## Notes

1 For overall reports on the state of the art in these countries, I have taken as specific points of reference:
For Chile: *EST/ESP Newsletter*, June 1979; *Oregon ESP Newsletter* Nos. 79, 80.
For Brazil: *The Especialist*, No. 9.
For Colombia: *Oregon ESP Newsletter*, No. 81; Report on the First National ESP Seminar, Bogotá, April 1984.

2 Two very distinct team-teaching operations exist in Colombia, one of them at Universidad Pedagógica Nacional, the other at Universidad del Valle.

3 The Chilean team have been pioneers and most dedicated researchers on the language of Science.

4 See *EST/ESP Chile Newsletter*, June 1979.

5 Cf. the research project carried out at the Colombian Ministry of Education under the coordination of KELT adviser John Wood.

# Commentator 1

## Alan Moller

The study of English for Specific Purposes (ESP) lies predominantly in the domain of the expanding EFL circle. Learners are obliged to learn English in order to use it in some immediate or future task or set of tasks. They work with texts in English and interact with teachers using English in the learners' own, non-English-speaking environment. In this situation they begin to function as students of English as a second language in the world of English as a foreign language. This leads to problems of motivation and needs discussed in Blanca de Escorcia's paper.

She rightly points to the conflict between 'real and ideal needs' of the learner and the difficulty in experiencing the relevance of those needs, largely through the lack of immediacy – a major problem for the teacher of English for specific purposes. At least one situation is known to me where the students, who are to begin their undergraduate studies in a new medium, English, within six months, still fail to see the immediacy of their needs. Blanca de Escorcia's suggestion is that in such situations a 'common core' component should be introduced, with subject specialist English added. Yet is this really satisfactory? Will this solution effectively motivate the learner? Does this really correspond to what the learner perceives his needs to be at this preliminary phase?

I question the adequacy of the solution to the problem and of the basis on which it has been reached. We can safely assume that the results of needs analysis, register analysis and discourse analysis available to the course designers have been taken into account, but to what extent has account been taken of the students' own perception of their needs at the pre-immediacy stage and to what extent have their future instructors' or employers' desiderata been taken into account? If the perceptions of the latter do not coincide with the course designer's diagnosis, how should this difference be resolved?

Another question arises, this time in relation to evaluation. In his survey article Coffey (1984) reminds us that teaching English for specific purposes is essentially the offering of a service to the principal beneficiary – the student or *customer* – and to the agency, institution or individual sponsoring the course – the *client*, and he refers to the course designer/teacher as the *curriculum worker*.

It seems that two of the reasons for our present quest for relevance of courses in English for specific purposes are that there has not been sufficient collaboration between client, customer and curriculum worker and that there is insufficient evidence of the success, or lack of success, of these courses both in the short and longer term. Do we know to what extent the customer's abilities in English have improved as a result of the course? Do we know to what extent the client is satisfied, or dissatisfied, with the outcomes of the course? Both customer and client will look for data before passing judgement. The customer will need to have his or her improvement in English proficiency – or lack of it – confirmed by the results of the assessment procedures adopted. Pre- and post-testing are indicated here. The knowledge that students have improved their English, as demonstrated by scores on pre- and post-tests, in previous courses is a motivating factor, as is the gaining of high scores in progress and achievement tests during a course.

This information can also reassure and encourage clients. But clients will need further evidence of relevance. They will need to know how the course, or training, has affected their students' or trainers' performance in their special tasks, i.e. in their studies or in their jobs. This will involve follow-up studies which are admittedly often very difficult to set up. One of the major problems experienced by an ESP project with which I am acquainted has been precisely in this area. It has been impossible to show the client in a valid way the extent of the linguistic progress achieved by students by the end of their courses because of the diversity of type and quality of tests used. It has also been impossible to make statements supported by data as to the success or otherwise of the courses because no follow-up studies have been conducted. The most satisfied clients have been those working closely with both the curriculum worker and the customer.

So, I wonder whether in addition to refining the understanding of students' real needs in ESP, and in addition to refining the methods, materials and supporting linguistic research, and improving the training of teachers, establishing systems of evaluation in the broader sense of programme evaluation and in the narrower sense of developing appropriate language, tests could be an important factor in the quest for relevance in our ESP programmes.

# Commentator 2

Odette Boys Michell

Initial appearance and later development of English for Specific Purposes (ESP) programmes has taken place in most Latin American countries. In a few, such as Chile, developmental work came early, whereas in others, such as Brazil and Colombia, it came later. In a few of the other countries ESP programmes are not known to have developed in a significant way. But where it is practised, ESP has invariably experienced rapid growth.

Several contributing factors have brought about the development of ESP in the subcontinent. Of these, two stand out quite clearly. The first has been the uncontrollable and rapid growth of English as the lingua franca of the world, so that the ever-growing number of locally-trained scientists, technologists and professionals at large need to be able to cope with it in their professional journals and other publications. Second, and more important, is the incapacity of the school English language programmes of the countries concerned to provide its school leavers with the language and language-related resources necessary to cope with the English language demands that present-day professional life calls for. Unfortunate as this latter situation is – and it certainly is – one need only consider the human and financial resources involved – it has, on the other hand, led to the growth of ESP.

This unprecedented growth of specific purpose English language teaching has injected a feeling of success and optimism into ESP practitioners in Latin American countries. Such a positive attitude of mind has been, in a few cases, encouraged by experienced teachers who have proved able to 'adapt' and not simply 'adopt' many of the ideas that have come to the developing non-English-speaking countries through the UK/US-dominated ESP literature. Beneficial as the expansion of ESP literature has been to the overall development of the field, it has on the other hand been unfortunate that only a small proportion of it is of direct relevance to the realities of the ESP classroom in an EFL country. In the conference-room context of an English-speaking country it is often hard to appreciate fully the great differences that exist between the needs, characteristics and motivations of students of ESP in English-speaking countries and those in an EFL situation; most case-studies reported in the professional literature relate to graduate students doing ESP courses in university settings in English-speaking countries and not to the typical undergraduate student of the EFL country. In such circumstances, great discriminatory skills are required of the ESP teacher in order to apply only what is directly relevant to his particular teaching situation.

Overall, ESP has grown in the past and is likely to continue to do so in the years to come. However, despite this overriding feeling of optimism, signs of unrest are beginning to appear. Thus, in a few cases, ESP courses do not seem to be coming up to expectations. Factors of a socio-economic, theoretical, pedagogic or educational nature are coming into play, and need to be remedied soon if ESP is to continue playing the important role it is called upon to perform. Some critical ESP reviews in the last few years anticipated that such a situation might arise.

Given this possible uncertainty, ESP practitioners, researchers and theoreticians in both the developed and developing countries must make every effort to clarify key issues of a theoretical and practical nature and set guidelines for future action. It is earnestly hoped that the ESP practitioners of Latin America will choose wisely amongst the several priority areas that call for immediate attention. And since it is unlikely that all sectors can be tackled simultaneously in view of the still limited financial and human resources available for ESP and the daunting size of the tasks involved, a choice must necessarily be made.

In setting guidelines for future action, the following all-important areas appear worthy of priority attention:

*Teacher training*, both pre-service and in-service, particularly since local effort and foreign aid are still far from meeting real needs.

*Classroom methodology*, including important matters of student motivation, the applicability of learner-centred methodology, the management of learning, etc.

*Research*, including the often neglected but still important area of linguistic description of the main registers that ESP is concerned with, about many of which little is yet known. Considering the linguistic uncertainty that affects numbers of non-native ESP teachers, such work still seems of high importance.

*Textbooks and teaching materials*, including a decision whether or not to continue stimulating teacher-production of materials – as has happened over the last ten or fifteen years – or whether instead to start emphasizing the systematic and permanent evaluation/analysis of the ever-growing number of textbooks appearing on the world market today.

*Syllabus design*, including a revision of the different alternative stages involved in this all-important process.

*Testing and evaluation*, including not only classroom testing but the even more important aspect of overall evaluation of ESP programmes.

*Informational networks*, through setting up local clearing-houses of ESP materials of different types, along the lines set up at the University of Aston in Birmingham.

*Public relations*, an often overlooked yet important aspect if the 'image' of the profession is to improve, however slightly.

In the context of the conference, the speaker was asked which of the above she thought should receive priority attention in the Latin American context and, having decided that, to suggest possible modes of implementation. If an attempt to answer this and other related questions is made, the desired 'quest for relevance' and the continued growth of ESP still required in Latin America is more likely to succeed, and some contribution to 'Progress in English Studies' will have been made.

# Theme VII    Summary of discussion

The realization that effective pedagogy should take more account of the particular disposition of learners and their conditions for learning was evident in the discussion on this theme, as it had been in previous sessions. It was suggested that the teaching of English for Specific Purposes could no longer be thought of as the transmission of a restricted competence specified by reference to terminal needs, but had to associate language with sets of behaviours which constituted the sub-cultures of particular areas of enquiry and activity. The main source of reference for ESP, therefore, ought to be ethnographic rather than linguistic, its main purpose being to encourage learners to negotiate communicative outcomes within the conventions of their sub-cultural specializations.

Some concern was expressed, however, that such a perspective might lead to undue neglect of linguistic considerations. The point was made that there were language items at all levels of linguistic description which were specifically marked for particular conceptual and communicative meanings in certain domains of discourse and that these were not subject to the same degree of negotiation between participants. Indeed, it was suggested that communication in general was frequently not a matter of the discovery of meanings of language items in reference to contexts but was a matter of recognizing meanings predetermined and projected directly into use. There was a risk of supposing that meaning was solely a matter for free negotiation and that nothing in the way of prior linguistic knowledge was relevant to communicative behaviour.

Another area of discussion was the relationship between ESP and general English teaching. If ESP was concerned with guiding learners towards the realization through English of culturally appropriate behaviour, then it was difficult to see how it could be distinguished from the communicative teaching of English in general, the only difference being perhaps that ESP was provided with ready-made contexts of use, recognized as relevant by learners, whereas general English teaching had somehow to contrive them. It was also argued that to the extent that ESP was concerned with areas of experience and a formulation of reality of disciplinary sub-cultures different from those associated with primary cultural values, then its objectives could be seen as similar to those of literature teaching and could therefore enter into the same reciprocal relationship with English teaching as had been suggested in the discussions of Theme VI.

There were two further points of contact with discussions on earlier themes. One had to do with evaluation. A preoccupation on the part of ESP practitioners with behaviour appropriate to the pursuit of particular specialist objectives made it difficult to envisage what kind of assessment could be devised to measure its success. The achievement of such objectives might not be, and might not be seen as being, principally a matter of language use at all. In any case this achievement should be seen as a return on teaching which could not be calculated by measuring actual teaching investment. A second point had to do with teacher preparation. If the business of ESP were to be the development of culturally appropriate sets of behaviour, then teachers would presumably themselves need to be familiar with them and this would involve extensive knowledge of the content and communicative conventions of the subject areas served by particular ESP courses.

What was of particular interest in the discussion as a whole was the way issues in ESP brought into sharper relief problems of language teaching as a whole and in particular the problem that recurred as a continuing matter for debate: the extent to which language learning could or should be determined by authority or left to the autonomous initiative of the learner. The consideration of such a question places language teaching and learning squarely in the context of education in general where it rightly belongs.

# THEME VIII  RETROSPECT AND PROSPECT

The last session of the Conference was devoted to the identification of what appeared to be the most salient issues arising from the preceding discussions and the indication of any significant omissions or imbalances of emphasis. In the first part of this session, points were presented by rapporteurs on each of the themes of the Conference. These rapporteurs were, in order of presentation, Dr T. J. Quinn, Dr Khalil Hamash, Professor Arne Zettersten, Dr Elite Olshtain, Fernando Castaños, Elizabeth Moloney and Tony Cowie. In the concluding part, there was a presention of views expressed by people who had been asked to identify and report on matters of particular significance. These reporters were Dr Roger Bowers, Professor Adriana Calderón de Bolívar, Professor A. M. Daoud, Enrique López Quiroz, Tony O'Brien, and Professor H. Piepho.

The work of the rapporteurs has been built into the summaries of discussion sessions. The broader issues are summarized here in the form of papers drawn from the presentations of the leaders of the two groups of reporters, Professor Calderón de Bolívar and Dr Roger Bowers, and that of the Co-ordinator of the discussions of this last session, Professor John Sinclair.

The first paper is a set of statements, based on Professor Bolívar's presentation, and it deals with particular issues from different perspectives. The second, prepared by Professor Sinclair, presents a personal perspective on the business of the Conference. The third paper, by Dr Bowers, also offers a personal perspective but in the form of an overview which relates the particular issues raised throughout the Conference to a set of more general recurrent themes.

# 1　Individual issues

Adriana Calderón de Bolívar

The controversy between linguistics and literature was thought to be rather unenlightening. This was in part at least because a distinction was not made between English teaching at the secondary level, at the tertiary level for students learning English for its use in other disciplines, and at the tertiary level for students who were pursuing literary studies and in particular a study of English literature. The relationship between language and literature in each of these cases has to be seen in very different terms.

It seemed particularly profitable to follow through the suggestion that research on an international scale should be undertaken to enquire into the relationship between the interpretations of literary critics and the responses of learners to literature at different levels of language proficiency.

Innovation and reform in teaching and learning can, it was felt, be best brought about by co-operation involving theorists, teacher trainers and practising teachers not only through national, but through international, networks of information and interaction.

Related to this, it was thought that the nature of universals, established 'paradigms' of approach and principles of learning and teaching should be explored in more detail with specific reference to regional, local and individual constraints. It was felt that some of the generalizable components of a theory of the learning and acquisition of English has sometimes been too hastily rejected in discussion because they appeared not to be in accordance with the standards of teacher training, school administration, instructional habits and so on of particular pedagogic circumstances. The international and intercultural applicability of methodological principles and approaches to in-service teacher training needed to be carefully explored.

Whereas several countries in Africa and Asia are using and cultivating English as a second language in a virtually bilingual setting, other countries are aiming at a bilingual situation as a planned process, developed by explicit instruction. It would be valuable to relate the experiences and experiments in these different kinds of sociocultural setting in a systematic way by means of the network of contacts, encounters and exchanges referred to earlier.

Although there was discussion on the cultural implications of English learning and use, it was felt that translation, both in theory and practice, could have been given much more attention as an area of intercultural mediation and appreciation of values.

A question arose as to what criteria needed to be considered in the design of curricula which related the teaching of language and literature. There could be conflicts in deciding on what literature was to be included between criteria of cultural and linguistic appropriateness.

There was also the general question of how far the learning of English language involved the reconciling of different cultural values.

On the matter of educational technology, there seemed to be a rather too exclusive concern with the computer. What other devices were available? And how far are technological aids in general practicable across different teaching circumstances? Again, would methodological innovations stimulated by the computer be adaptable to situations where no such technological aids were available?

The relationship between ESP and general English teaching was noted as a problematic one. How far, for example, did ESP presuppose previous instruction in general English, how far could general English teaching be carried out from an ESP perspective?

The issue of teacher training was seen as one of great importance. Both ESP and general English teaching which followed a communicative approach made demands on the knowledge and proficiency of teachers which they would frequently find difficult to meet. Proposals were often made without taking into account the conditions of their implementation, particularly in regard to the competence expected of teachers.

It was noted that testing and evaluation had not been given focal attention. There were issues here of pressing importance, particularly with regard to literary study, with or without an explicit association with the learning of language.

It was pointed out that participants at the Conference necessarily interpreted certain issues from the perspective of their own English teaching situations. It would have been preferable, it was suggested, for the comparisons between such situations (English as a native language, English as a second language, English as a foreign language) to have been more systematically explored so that the particular conditions of relevance could have been made more clear.

# 2 Selected issues

John Sinclair

1   In this personal perspective, I shall pick out three issues that seemed to dominate the Conference, and then consider three themes which, although they were not excluded, did not arise, but whose omission is indicative of the present state of the profession.

**1.1**   The first issue was a matter of prerogative. Although it was news to no one, it was important for Conference to be told, gently but firmly, that English was no longer the exclusive province of the native speaker; that was but one of the many categories of English User. The English language was much too valuable around the world for it to remain in the control of any one special group; the native speakers had, it would appear, exported their language only too successfully. Whereas a previous Conference might have worried about the range of models available among native speakers, this Conference accepted a much more pluralistic view, more readily perhaps on the literary side than on the purely linguistic. The shift in perspective solves no problems, because the pattern of standards and usage becomes much more complex, but it helps to identify the problems that need solving. Everyone present was impressed by the sheer range and variety of situations where English is useful, and the need for greater understanding of the various circumstances. There is a need for research, co-ordination and monitoring of developments in this field, as the previous paper in this chapter makes clear.

**1.2**   The second issue took the form of a warning from some participants that English Studies is still not integrated, and that there is real substance in the broad distinction between linguistic and literary work.

There are now plenty of scholars whose perspectives are broad enough for them to approach the language/literature question with sympathetic understanding and a preference for freedom to discuss literary texts without first declaring an ideological commitment. They should be convened, and asked to study the question in depth and resolve it.

Of all the matters raised this is the trickiest, and the most difficult to report upon because of the various viewpoints. Perhaps a broad consensus view would be that nothing much is to be gained by re-engaging in a controversy which many people feel is sterile. However, I am not the only one to believe that this problem should be pursued until resolved, and that the main ingredients of a resolution are now available.

The message which I took from the Conference is that this is a problem which will not just go away. Many people want to explore matters like the teaching of literature, from a number of approaches, but cannot feel secure in this if the literary establishment is in a position to condemn all such enterprises. One got the impression that we were nearly there, but there were certain formal steps still to be taken.

**1.3** The third issue of the Conference was undoubtedly methodology. It was an interest rather than an issue, and it emerged in a number of papers. Clearly the profession as represented at the Conference gave perhaps their highest priority to hearing about and discussing trends and innovations in methods of teaching. The impression which I received was of a state of flux, with a number of interesting approaches put on offer, and a more open attitude to change than has been the case in previous gatherings of this kind.

**1.4** It was slightly worrying that one or two themes did not seem to me to integrate with the rest, but were pursued – most usefully – in relative isolation. One was the new concern with computing, where the excitement about current work was intense, but the sessions did not link in with the rest of the Conference activity. It still does not touch the profession as a whole.

Two things can be drawn from this for the future. The first is that there is a danger of alienation, of teachers taking against the machines. This can only be relieved by serious attention to orientation courses and hands-on experience. The other point is that computer-assisted learning needs to be securely integrated with the methodology of a course as a whole, and that in turn means that it must be allowed to affect the overall methodology. So it should become a priority that the powerful mainstream development of methodology should concern itself with the pros and cons of CALL and be prepared to accommodate it.

In passing it should be noted that there was disquiet in some quarters that the enthusiasm for computing had squeezed out other equally relevant technological developments, particularly video-disc.

Another theme which seemed to me to remain distinct from the others was English for Special Purposes. This was all the more surprising since it was clearly implied in examples and illustrations in other sessions. The distinctiveness was not a failure to communicate, but a matter of different problems and priorities. ESP has such a life of its own that it has begun to move in different directions from what might be called 'General English'.

The main problem in ESP was the yawning gap which has appeared between the demands of the subject and the capabilities of the teachers. The gap has always been present, of course, and has been referred to routinely in the literature. But the deepening understanding of ESP shows how specialized, how subtle and complex an area it is. Meanwhile the difficulties of preparing teachers to cope with even the simplest manifestations of ESP remain serious.

2    It is important to ask why there is no such gap apparent in English language teaching at large, and this point makes a suitable transition between what the Conference said and what it didn't say. Research into ESP results in a syllabus which is drawn from text structure and needs analysis, and it can be uncompromising. In ESP the teachers are constantly faced with external demands.

**2.1**    Outside ESP, however, we seem to have managed to avoid uncomfortable situations like that. Perhaps the most surprising omission from the work of the Conference was attention to the study of the English language. There were very few occasions indeed where some new evidence about English was presented, and hardly ever was the Conference invited to consider it in relation to the theory and practice of teaching.

I should say that this was not an intentional omission; the title of the Conference was 'Progress in English Studies' and it is significant that the title was not retained for this book. It is not so much that English Studies have not progressed, but that the Conference was not much interested in them. Without any collaboration, the people who took all the hundreds of decisions that led to the final shape of the Conference all tended to choose something other than the language as their focus.

It is as if we now take for granted the facts of the language, and concentrate on the teaching of it. The 'it' does not seem to be in question. Linguistics has all but disappeared, confirming the view in many language-teaching circles that the very term is now almost taboo.

I think it is a shame that interest has shifted from the actual description of languages, and that the language-teaching profession has become resistant to linguistics. No doubt the regular inoculations provided by postgraduate courses over the last twenty-five years have developed the resistance. There is now a received 'view of the language' which is held in various forms among language teachers, and which is distinct from current models in linguistics.

Any apologist for modern linguistics would have to concede that, in computer jargon, it is not nearly as 'user-friendly' nowadays as it used to be. It is often highly technical, fragmented and frequently deals with very fine detail. It could be argued that the typical concerns of the linguists are not germane to the major issues of language teaching. Nevertheless, there are many who make a conscious effort to keep in touch, and we should be grateful to them; for if the more abstract branch of the subject is having a somewhat introverted decade or two, it is all the more important that those who lead the language teachers should remain firmly in touch with developments in theory and description.

The danger, in the 1960s and 1970s, was the spread of watered-down and inadequate models. This nowadays may seem preferable to an absence of interest in the models at all. An absence of interest in what one is teaching is surely a perilous condition; an assumption that everything relevant is known and securely known is surely complacent in the extreme, and on the brink of decadence.

Yet such is the position implied by the balance and preoccupation of the contributions to the Conference.

It would seem that we know most of what there is to know about the English language. The study of it in recent years has been intense to the point of overkill. 'The facts', it is often said, 'are not in dispute.' The spirit of complacency is pervasive. Interest has shifted to new ways of teaching, new attitudes to technology, new views of the position of English in the intellectual map of the world.

Even if the serious study of the language was somewhat stagnant, I think this would be a vulnerable position for a profession to adopt. If practitioners in other professions, say medicine or law, came to a similar view, the public might become quite alarmed. I would urge practitioners to reassert the importance of the foundations of English Studies in the autonomous study of the language and its literature. The structure of the Conference envisaged little to report on this front, and the concerns brought out in the papers seem to confirm that point of view.

I think that we are on the verge of a major re-orientation in language description – one that will create problems for anyone who thinks that the facts are known. I am compelled to take this view by the early results of computer processing of language text. The picture is quite disturbing. On the one hand, there is now ample evidence of the existence of significant language patterns which have gone largely unrecorded in centuries of study; on the other hand there is a dearth of support for some phenomena which are regularly put forward as normal patterns of English. For some years I tended to assume that the computers would merely give us a better documented description of the language, but I do not think that that position remains tenable. Now that we have the means to observe samples of language which must be fairly close to representative samples, the clear messages are:

a) We are teaching English in ignorance of a vast amount of basic fact. This is not our fault, but it should not inhibit the absorption of the new material.
b) The categories and methods we use to describe English are not appropriate to the new material. We shall need to overhaul our descriptive systems.

c) Since our view of the language will change profoundly, we must expect substantial influence on the specification of syllabuses, design of materials and choice of method.

Let us hope, then, that this Conference represents the calm before a very interesting storm, and prepare ourselves for quite substantial movement in the coming years.

So the first major omission is the falling away of interest in the language itself. Much the same could probably be said for literature and criticism, though there are more signs among the papers of changing positions, incipient controversies, and a lively interest in how the subject is studied. One senses that people are still discovering things about literature, but not about language.

2.2    There is another point to which I would like to draw attention – a point which is not brought out substantially in the run of papers. It concerns the status and career of the English teachers, both in and out of institutions all over the world. It seems to me that one of the major achievements of the ELT profession is that it has become a profession. The British Council must be particularly proud that its efforts have led to this result. From a UK perspective, the ELT profession is now considerably in advance of other groups of language teachers. The flow of expertise and ideas tends to be one way.

Thus far I suspect that most Conference delegates would agree; the type and degree of professionalization has been different in different circumstances, but substantial progress has been made, often in considerable haste. The problem which I want to identify is also, I think, widespread, but manifests itself in many different ways. It is, broadly speaking, a worry about the career structure for English language teachers. From what intellectual background are they drawn? How are they initially trained, if indeed there is provision for initial training? How do they gain early experience? How are they supported by in-service training? How are promotions determined? What career paths are offered? How is staff development provided at the more senior levels? How do teachers relate to policy-makers? Is it healthy to separate the more academic side of the profession from the rest?

Of these questions, the one about in-service training is attended to in the Conference papers in some detail, the others hardly at all. My concern focuses particularly on senior staff development, and I see staff development in broader terms than the purely academic. Much English language teaching nowadays is project-based and demands all sorts of organizational skills: and even the ordinary curriculum is becoming more complex, more dependent on technology, intricate time-tabling and the provision of a wide range of resources. Successful classroom teachers are not prepared for the type of work that comes their way on promotion. There are no Staff Colleges.

I do think that progress in English Studies, since it cannot be separated from the teaching of English, is also dependent on further moves towards professionalization. I think we must recognize that although big and basic steps have been taken, it is a new and relatively untried profession. It has no statutory bodies, no stable reference points. It is pretty seriously under-capitalized and underfunded and is often seen as a cinderella subject.

If we take this point with my first one – that the study of English no longer occupies centre-stage – we can expect that teaching groups are more and more resting on their laurels. There is less impetus to change, experiment, except in methodology. Yet the profession must sustain a good pace of development if it is to improve conditions and carry the burdens that will be placed on it. I hope that everyone concerned with the profession will recognize it is only just viable, far from resilient, and that it needs much more explicit attention to itself. There is a growing number of relevant organizations with interests in English language teaching, but which require co-ordination.

**2.3** My third and final point of omission is an extension of the same basic argument. One way of viewing language teachers shows them as having an almost impossible job. They must have an articulate and explicit command of linguistic complexity, including many points that have not yet been described. They must use a language (the target language, or a common language) to teach a language. They must be psychologists, sociologists, technologists and managers, and they must control the whole process in real time. Some groups are not native speakers of the language they teach, yet they are expected to have an understanding and a competence which matches that of the native speaker. If they have this competence they certainly didn't get it from the published descriptions. Some groups are expected to be expert at teaching the language of texts they do not understand (this is called ESP). Some groups have various combinations of these disadvantages.

The Conference papers draw attention to some of these, indeed, but not to the scale of help and support that I think is needed, and can gradually be provided. We are putting our teachers into almost impossible predica-ments, and relying on their ingenuity and dedication to make up for the lack of an adequate support system. The speed of change, the constant pressure to improve, has left little or no time for proper documentation of each successive view of the language. By proper documentation I don't mean a provocative essay or two, or even a book-length descriptive treat-ment. The teacher ultimately has to face up to the *whole* array of facts of the language, and is currently without adequate reference tools.

It would be difficult to imagine members of other professions in similar situations — lawyers without a very extensive knowledge of the law, and without detailed reference books, but with a good sense of natural justice; bankers without full information on rates and costs, or detailed accounts, or clearly laid down procedures, but with a general set of injunctions about how to do their business.

Language teachers urgently need some very full documentation about the language, frequently updated and as reliable as possible. If it can be made available, they should have it. Their job is difficult enough.

It can be argued that students of the English language have in fact a magnificent array of informative works and reference works — second to none. An investigation of teachers' perception of their needs would probably reveal a quiet satisfaction with what is available; there is at present no demand for more detailed and relevant information systems. But these arguments do not constitute good reasons for not doing what can be done.

It is already possible to imagine a database and retrieval system which would supply a teacher with accurate, up-to-date and detailed information about the usage of words. There are general rules and the individual words, and grammars and dictionaries make brave attempts respectively at these two extremes. In between is the area of usage, idiom, phraseology, style. It is this vast area that the mass of language teaching directs itself to, and there is, apparently, very little actually set down about it. Perhaps the native speaker can pick his way, but uncomprehendingly. To the non-native speaker it is a jungle.

Who knows what patterns we waste time in teaching because they do not occur? Why are so many of our model sentences, dialogues and texts clearly artificial? What tells us instantly that a model is fabricated? I end up with questions, questions which can be answered, and which may lead to better information and guidance for those who pursue English Studies.

# 3    General issues

Roger Bowers

1    It is possible to discern in the variety of topics discussed certain under-lying themes which can be expressed in terms of oppositions.

1.1    The first and most pervasive theme, it seems to me, has been the balancing of *freedom* and *authority*. Our discussions around this theme have posed the following questions:

a) What are the boundaries of our freedom, as *users* of the language, to interpret it as we wish, to make it our own?
b) How, as *learners* of the language, can we exercise our individuality in order to acquire it as we see fit?
c) As *teachers* of the language and its literatures, what freedom do we have and what constraints of authority do we labour under? And what authority do we cite, or lean upon, in our turn in order to justify what we teach and how we teach it?
d) As *trainers* and *advisers*, *academics* and *administrators*, what justification can we assert for our normative or destabilizing roles, what liberties can we foster?
e) As representatives of the *systems* which we serve, what freedoms do we have and proffer? What social controls do we suffer and exercise?
f) Finally, as a *practising profession* within the totality of speakers of English, working within our own societies marked by social and linguistic, geographical and economic distinctions, what freedoms do we jointly lay claim to and what common authority can we reasonably wield within the total fellowship?

These are questions without answer, or without an end to answering, questions which we can approach only in the context of our own objective dispositions and subjective predispositions.

1.2    Our second set of 'honourable mentions' rests upon the potentially conflicting notions of *instrument* and *sentiment*, notions which have been contested in some heat. In brief:

a) Is language a tool, or a treasure trove?

b) If tool, can we learn to treasure it – to travel through sentimental journeys of appreciation towards mastery of its functions?
c) If it is treasure, are there instruments by which we can weigh its worth?
d) And if there is room for both perceptions (as I believe there is), how best can we accommodate our personal predilections within the task of our joint profession, which is to promote *literacy* in its fullest sense – both efficiency in usage and sensitivity in use?

**1.3**   A third area, less of dispute than of different emphasis, has been the relation between *illumination* and *operation*.

a) If our intention is to illuminate, where are the areas of darkness, and for whom – apart from ourselves – do we offer enlightenment? What mirrors do we hold up, to what reality?
b) If our emphasis is on the operational issues, what are our answers, and where the empirical justification for them, to the many specific questions which fall within the superordinate one: Are we teaching the right thing rightly?
c) What constraints must we set upon our own skills and perceptions in developing the skills and perceptions of others in this less than ideal world?
d) Where, indeed, do we draw the line between speculation and prediction, research and development, academic dispute and practical concern, experiment and exploitation, realism and complacency?

**1.4**   A final set of concerns warmly recurrent in the conference discussions, centres upon the engagement between *man and machine*.

a) Are we, as a profession, technology-driven, or are we driving the technology?
b) In conditions of unequal resource – we may speak of rich and poor, of North and South, of this World and that World, of this circle and that (and perhaps we should further clarify such terms) – are we using technology to eradicate inequality, or is it a symbol of that separation?
c) As information becomes increasingly dependent on technological process, is that information freely available or is it eked out, whether between cultures or within them, by the knowing to the uninitiated?

**2**   As we toy with these words and argue our positions along these universal parameters, it is hard to resist the feeling that as individuals and as institutions we dance to inner tunes, raising cacophonies that deafen rather than delight, progressing in circles to the point from which we came.

We all live and work, nevertheless, in the real world, and do our best to follow our profession within it – professing, I have some confidence, that we conduct our research, run our projects, teach our classes, write our books, attend our conferences not simply because we like to do so but because, in some confluent variety of senses, it is in the common good that we do so.

What then are the learning outcomes indicated by our discussions, for the profession at large and for an institution which seeks, with sometimes insufficient humility and varying success, to act as (I quote) 'a support agency, assembling and disseminating information to serve the inter-cultural context'?

At the end of this Conference, I have a fuller awareness of the common needs we share:

1 To know more about the English language and its use; so, *research*.
2 To know more about learning and teaching through testing and through systematic observation; so, *evaluation*.
3 To recognize a multilingual world in which English plays a non-ethnic role; so, *a global view*.
4 In recognizing our contemporary ethnic values and practices, to mediate between these and alternative ethics and ways of acting, both generally and in educational terms; so, *respect*.
5 To make common our knowledge and share our uncertainties; so, *communication*.

It was not objective, nor is it the outcome, of this Conference to offer a blueprint for the future, for the British Council or for any part of that profession which we represent. We are neither mandated nor, I would respectfully suggest, equipped to do this. But the sense and sensitivity dis-played and the exhortations and warnings performed by this week's colloquy may serve to moderate and at the same time motivate our joint endeavours.

# List of Conference participants

(*Note*: Locations given are those which apply at the time of going to press.)

James E. Alatis
Georgetown University, USA

Richard L. Allwright
University of Lancaster, UK

Ayo Banjo
University of Ibadan, Nigeria

Roger G. Bowers
The British Council

Odette Boys Michell
The British Institute, Teacher Training
 College, Chile

Gillian Brown
University of Essex, UK

Christopher Brumfit
University of Southampton, UK

Adriana Calderón de Bolívar
Central University of Venezuela

Christopher N. Candlin
University of Lancaster, UK

Fernando Castaños
National Autonomous University,
 Mexico

Maria Antonieta A. Celani
Catholic University of São Paulo,
 Brazil

Kenneth Churchill
The British Council

Anthony P. Cowie
University of Leeds, UK

Dennis R. Craig
University of the West Indies, Jamaica

David Crystal
University of Reading, UK

Abdel M. Daoud
Ain Shams University, Egypt

Mahmoud Daoud
University of Sana'a, Yemen

Alan Davies
University of Edinburgh, UK

Blanca A. de Escorcia
Universidad del Valle, Colombia

Husain Dhaif
University College of Bahrain

Patrick B. M. Early
The British Council

Christoph Edelhoff
State Institute for Teacher In-service
 Education and Training, Germany

Nils E. Enkvist
Åbo Akademi, Finland

Lloyd Fernando
Association of Commonwealth Literature and Language Studies, Malaysia

Jan Firbas
University of Brno, Czechoslovakia

Jacek Fisiak
A. Mickiewicz University, Poland

Herbert Foltinek
University of Vienna, Austria

R. N. Ghosh
Central Institute of English and
 Foreign Languages, India

Sidney Greenbaum
University College London, UK

Ali H. S. Hajjaj
Ministry of Education, Kuwait

Khalil I. Hamash
Ministry of Education, Iraq

John Haycraft
English International, UK

Henri Holec
University of Nancy II, France

Anthony P. R. Howatt
University of Edinburgh, UK

Raymond Janssens
Imelda-Instituut, Belgium

Timothy F. Johns
University of Birmingham, UK

Keith Jones
The British Council

Braj B. Kachru
University of Illinois, USA

Graeme D. Kennedy
Victoria University of Wellington,
  New Zealand

Svetozar Koljević
University of Sarajevo, Yugoslavia

Li Xiaoju
Guangzhou Foreign Languages
  Institute, China

Ramón López-Ortega
University of Extremadura, Spain

Luis Enrique López Quiroz
Ministry of Education, Peru

Colin MacCabe
University of Strathclyde, UK

Alan D. Moller
The British Council

Elizabeth Moloney
The British Council

Keith E. Morrow
The Bell Educational Trust, UK

Tony O'Brien
The British Council

Elite Olshtain
University of Tel-Aviv, Israel

Martin Phillips
The British Council

Hans-Eberhard Piepho
University of Giessen, Germany

Jina Politi
Aristotelian University of Salonika,
  Greece

N. S. Prabhu
The British Council

Terence J. Quinn
University of Melbourne, Australia

Randolph Quirk
University of London, UK

Peter Roe
The British Council

Kari Sajavaara
University of Jyväskylä, Finland

Maurits Simatupang
University of Indonesia

John McH. Sinclair
University of Birmingham, UK

Peter Strevens
The Bell Educational Trust, UK

Jan Svartvik
University of Lund, Sweden

Merrill K. Swain
University of Toronto, Canada

John M. Swales
University of Aston, UK

Edwin Thumboo
National University of Singapore

Katsuaki Togo
University of Waseda, Japan

John L. M. Trim
Centre for Information on Language
  Teaching and Research, UK

Raymond E. Underwood
The British Council

Henry G. Widdowson
University of London Institute of
  Education, UK

Yang Huizhong
University of Shanghai Jiao Tong,
  China

Maria T. P. Zagrebelski
University of Turin, Italy

Arne Zettersten
University of Copenhagen, Denmark

259

# Bibliography

Allwright, R. L. 1976, 'Putting cognitions on the map', *TESL–UCLA Work-papers*, Vol. X, June: 1–14.

1977, 'Language learning through communication practice', *ELT Documents*, 76/3, London, The British Council: 2–14.

1982, 'The importance of interaction in classroom learning', Honolulu, TESOL, mimeo.

Andrews, Stephen 1984, 'The effect of Arabicization on the role of service English', in Swales and Mustafa, 1984.

Apel, Karl-Otto 1976, 'The transcendental conception of language communication and the idea of a first philosophy', in Parret, 1976: 32–61.

Atkinson, Max 1984, *Our Masters' Voices*, London, Methuen.

Bailey, Richard W. and M. Görlach (eds.) 1982, *English as a World Language*, Ann Arbor, Mich., University of Michigan Press.

Baldauf, R. B. and B. H. Jernudd 1983a, 'Language of publications as a variable in scientific communication', *Australian Review of Applied Linguistics*, 6, 1.

1983b, 'Language use patterns in the fisheries periodical literature', *Scientometrics*, 5, 4.

Bamgboṣe, Ayọ 1982, 'Standard Nigerian English: issues of identification', in Kachru 1982c.

Banjo, Ayo 1970, 'A historical view of the English language in Nigeria', *Ibadan*, 28.

Barber, C. L. 1982, 'Some measurable characteristics of modern scientific prose', *Contributions to English Syntax and Phonology*, Gothenburg Studies in English, 14, Gothenburg.

Barmada, Warka, 1983, 'Ten English language centres in the Arab world: an investigation into their macro ESP/ELT problems', M.Sc. dissertation, University of Aston in Birmingham.

Baron, Dennis E. 1982, *Grammar and Good Taste: Reforming the American Language*, New Haven, Yale University Press.

Bazerman, Charles 1983, 'Scientific writing as a social act: a review of the literature of the sociology of science', in Paul Anderson and John Brockman (eds.) *New Essays in Technical and Scientific Communication: Research Theory and Practice*, New York, Baywood.

Beinashowitz, J., R. Ingria and K. Wilson 1981, 'Generative tutorial systems', Paper presented at the 1981 Annual Meeting of the Association for the Development of Computer-Based Instructional Systems, Atlanta, Georgia, 3–5 March 1981.

Bernstein, Basil 1971, *Class, Codes and Control*, Vol. 1, *Theoretical Studies towards a Sociology of Language*, London, Routledge & Kegan Paul.

Blickenstaff, J. and M. J. Moravcsick 1983, 'The profile of an international meeting', *Scientometrics*, 5, 3.

Bloor, Meriel 1984, 'English language needs in the University of Cordoba: the report of a survey', University of Aston in Birmingham, mimeo.

Bokamba, Eyamba G. 1982, 'The Africanization of English', in Kachru, 1982c.

Bourhis, R. Y. and Howard Giles 1977, 'The language of intergroup distinctiveness', in Giles, 1977: 119–35.

Bradbury, Malcolm 1983, *Rates of Exchange*, London, Secker & Warburg.

Breen, M. P. 1983, 'How would we recognize a communicative classroom?',
*Dunford House Seminar 1982: Teacher Training and the Curriculum*, The
British Council.

Breen, M. P. and C. N. Candlin 1980, 'The essentials of a communicative
curriculum in language teaching', *Applied Linguistics*, 1, 2, Summer:
89–112.

    1981, 'Basic principles of communicative language teaching and learning',
Workshop handout, Boston, TESOL, mimeo.

Breen, M. P., C. N. Candlin and L. Dam 1981, 'The flower', Workshop handout,
Greve, mimeo.

Breen, M. P., C. N. Candlin and A. Waters 1979, 'Communicative materials
design: some basic principles', *RELC Journal*, 10, 2: 1–13.

The British Council 1981, *The ESP Teacher: Role, Development and Prospects*,
*ELT Documents*, 112.

    1982, *Humanistic Approaches: an Empirical View*, *ELT Documents*, 113.

The British Council and University of Cambridge Local Examinations Syndicate,
1984, *English Language Testing Service: An Introduction*.

Brumfit, C. J. 1979, 'Communicative language teaching: an educational perspective', in C. J. Brumfit and K. Johnson (eds.) 1979, *The Communicative
Approach to Language Teaching*, Oxford University Press.

    1984a, *Communicative Methodology in Language Teaching*, Cambridge
University Press.

    (ed.) 1984b, *General English Syllabus Design*, *ELT Documents*, 118, Oxford,
Pergamon Press.

Brumfit, C. J. and J. T. Roberts 1983, *A Short Introduction to Language and
Language Teaching*, London, Batsford Academic and Education Ltd.

Buttjes, D. (ed.) 1980, *Landeskundliches Lernen im Englischunterricht: Zur
Theorie und Praxis des inhaltsorientierten Fremdsprachenunterrichts*,
Paderborn u.a.: Schöningh.

    1982, 'Landeskunde im Fremdsprachenunterricht, Zwischenbilanz und
Arbeitsansätze', *Neusprachliche Mitteilungen*, 1: 3–16.

Canale, Michael and Merrill Swain 1980, 'Theoretical bases of communicative
approaches to second language teaching and testing', *Applied Linguistics*,
1, 1, Spring: 1–47.

Candlin, C. N. (ed.) 1981a, *The Communicative Teaching of English: Principles
and an Exercise Typology*, London, Longman.

    (ed.) 1981b, *Second International Workshop on Communicative Curricula in
Modern Languages*, Lancaster, University of Lancaster, Institute for
English Language Education.

    1983, 'Applying a systems approach to curriculum innovation in the public
sector', (RELC Seminar, April 1983), in Read, J., 1984.

    1984, 'Syllabus design as a critical process', in Brumfit, 1984b.

Charles, D. 1984, 'The use of case studies in business English', *The ESP Classroom*, Exeter Linguistic Studies, University of Exeter.

Chinweizu, O. Jemie and I. Madubuike 1975, 'Towards the decolonization of
African literature', *Transition*, 48.

*Bibliography*

Chishimba, Maurice 1983, 'African varieties of English: text in context', Ph.D. dissertation, University of Illinois at Urbana-Champaign.
Chomsky, Noam 1964, *Current Issues in Linguistic Theory*, The Hague, Mouton.
  1965, *Aspects of the Theory of Syntax*, Cambridge, Mass., MIT Press.
  1968, *Language and Mind*, New York, Harcourt Brace & World.
Coffey, Bernard 1984, 'ESP – English for specific purposes', *Language Teaching Abstracts*, 17, 1.
Cole, P. and J. Morgan (eds.) 1975, *Syntax and Semantics*, Vol. 3, *Speech Acts*, New York, Academic Press.
Cooper, Robert L. 1984, 'Fantasti! Israeli attitudes towards English', in Greenbaum, 1984.
Corder, S. Pit 1981, *Error Analysis and Interlanguage*, Oxford University Press.
Council of Europe 1981, Council for Cultural Co-operation, *Modern Languages, 1971–1981*, Strasbourg, 1981.
Council of Europe 1983, 'Across the threshold towards multilingual Europe – vivre le multilinguisme européen', Council for Cultural Co-operation Conference, February 1982, Strasbourg, 1983.
Cox, C. B. and A. E. Dyson 1963, *Modern Poetry: Studies in Practical Criticism*, London, Edward Arnold.
Crocker, Anthony 1982, 'LSP and methodology: some implications for course design and implementation in EALP', *English for Specific Purposes*, 67.
Dakin, J. 1973, *The Language Laboratory and Language Learning*, London, Longman.
Davidson, Donald 1984, 'On the very idea of a conceptual scheme' in Donald Davidson (ed.) *Enquiries into Truth and Interpretation*, Oxford, Clarendon Press.
Davies, C. H. 1983, 'Institutional sectors of "mainstream" science production in sub-Saharan Africa 1970–1979: a quantitative analysis', *Scientometrics*, 5, 3.
Davies, G. D. and J. Higgins 1982, *Computers, Language, and Language Learning*, London, Centre for Information on Language Teaching and Research.
de Escorcia, Blanca A. 1984, 'Team-teaching for students of economics: a Colombian experience', in Raymond Williams *et al.*, 1984.
Dewey, J. 1916, *Democracy and Education: an Introduction to the Philosophy of Education*, New York, Textbook Series in Education.
Dhaif, Husain 1983, 'Learning English for science and technology . . . an alternative approach', Ph.D. thesis, University of London.
Dubois, Betty Lou 1982, 'The construction of noun phrases in biomedical journal articles', in J. Hoedt (ed.), *Pragmatics and LSP*, Copenhagen, The Copenhagen School of Economics.
Eble, Connie E. 1976, 'Etiquette books as linguistic authority', in Peter A. Reich (ed.), *The Second LACUS Forum*, Colombia, S.C., Hornbeam Press.
Edelhoff, C. 1973, 'Probleme der fremdsprachlichen Landeskunde im kommunikativen Curriculum', in *Beiträge zu den Sommerkursen 1973*, München, Goethe-Institut: 116–23.
  (ed.) 1978a, *Trends in Language Syllabus Design*, Singapore, Singapore University Press.
  (ed.) 1978b, *Kommunikativer Englischunterricht: Prinzipien und Übungstypologie*, München, Langenscheidt-Longman.

262

1980, 'Kommunikative Lernziele im Fremdsprachenunterricht: Vom Verstehen zum Außern', in *Sprache und Beruf*, 2: 61–74.

(ed.) 1983a, *The Communicative Teaching of English, Analysing and Building Discourse, Applying Communication Principles to the English Language Classroom*, Report on two Danish/German Teachers' Conferences at Skarrildhus/Jutland 1981 and 1982, Gesellschaft zur Förderung des Englischunterrichts an Gesamtschulen, Grebenstein.

1983b, 'Internationalität und interkulturelle Ziele des Fremdsprachenunterrichts in Europa, Verstehen und Verständigung', in L. Arabin and V. Kilian (eds.) *Deutsch in der Weiterbildung, Orientieren – Verstehen – Verständigen*, München, Lexika, Hueber: 75–92.

1984, 'Landeskunde zum Anfassen, The Lancaster Outing, Lehrerfortbildung zum Erfahrungen machen', in M. Schratz (ed.), *Englischunterricht im Gespräch*, Bochum, Kamp.

*The Especialist* No. 9, Pontifícia Universidad Católica de São Paulo, Brazil.

*EST/ESP Chile Newsletter*, 1979, Special Number, June.

Ewer, Jack 1981, 'Nine problem areas in ESP', *English for Specific Purposes*, 54: 1–7.

Faerch, C. and G. Kasper (eds.) 1983, *Strategies of Interlanguage Communication*, London, Longman.

Farrington, B. 1982, 'Computer based exercises for language learning at university level', *Computers and Education*, Vol. 6: 113–16.

Ferguson, Charles A. and Shirley Brice Heath 1981, *Language in the USA*, Cambridge and New York, Cambridge University Press.

Finegan, Edward 1980, *Attitudes toward English Usage: the History of a War of Words*, New York, Teachers College Press.

Firth, John Rupert 1959, 'The treatment of language in general linguistics', in F. R. Palmer (ed.) 1968, *Selected Papers of J. R. Firth*, Bloomington, Indiana, Indiana University Press.

Gattegno, Caleb 1963, *Teaching Foreign Languages in Schools: The Silent Way*, New York, Educational Solutions Inc. (2nd edn 1972).

Geertz, Clifford 1973, *The Interpretation of Cultures*, New York, Basic Books. 1983, *Local Knowledge*, New York, Basic Books.

Gilbert, G. Nigel 1977, 'Referencing as persuasion', *Social Studies of Science*, 7.

Gilbert, G. Nigel and M. Mulkay 1984, *Opening Pandora's Box, A Sociological Analysis of Scientific Discourse*, Cambridge University Press.

Giles, H. (ed.) 1977, *Language, Ethnicity and Intergroup Relations*, London, Academic Press.

Goethe Institut, The British Council, AUPELF 1982. *Approaches, Methodik, Enseignement*, Triangle, 2.

Gower, R. 1984, 'Review of B. Lee, *Poetry and System*', *ELT Journal*, 38/1: 63–6.

Greenbaum, Sidney (ed.) 1985, *The English Language Today*, Oxford and New York, Pergamon Press.

Grice, H. 1975, 'Logic and conversation', in Cole and Morgan, 1975: 41–58.

Habermas, J. 1970, 'On systematically distorted communication', *Inquiry*, 13, 3, Autumn: 205–18.

Haft, H. 1981, 'In-service training in the Federal Republic of Germany: The general situation, contents, needs of participants and relations to curriculum development', in Nissen *et al.*, 1981: 51–101.

Halliday, M. A. K. 1975, *Learning How to Mean*, London, Edward Arnold.
Harding, A. *et al.* 1980, *Graded Objectives in Modern Languages*, CILT.
Hartig, Paul (ed.) 1965, *Englandkunde*, (Handbücher der Auslandskunde), Frankfurt, Diesterweg.
Hawkes, Terence 1977, *Structuralism and Semiotics*, London, Methuen.
Higgins, J. 1981, 'How real is a computer simulation?', Paper given at the IATEFL Conference, London, December 1981, in Goethe Institut, 1982.
Higgins, J. and Tim Johns 1984, *Computers in Language Learning*, London and Glasgow, Collins.
Holliday, A. R. 1984, 'Research into classroom culture as necessary input into syllabus design', in Swales and Mustafa, 1984.
Holliday, A. R. and T. Cooke 1982, 'An ecological approach to ESP', in A. Waters (ed.) *Issues in English for Specific Purposes*, Oxford, Pergamon Press.
Holmes, J. and B. de Escorcia 1984, 'Report on the first national ESP seminar', Bogotá, April, mimeo.
Hornby, A. S. 1954, *Guide to Patterns and Usage in English*, Oxford University Press.
Huckin, Thomas N. and Leslie A. Olsen 1984, 'On the use of informants in LSP discourse analysis', in A. Pugh and J. Ulijn (eds.) *Reading for Professional Purposes*, London, Heinemann.
Huddleston, R. D. 1971, *The Sentence in Written English*, Cambridge University Press.
Hutchinson, T., A. Waters and M. Breen 1979, 'An English language curriculum for technical students', *Lancaster Practical Papers*, 2.
Hymes, D. 1967, 'Models of the interaction of language and social setting', *Journal of Social Issues*, 23, 2: 8–28.
    1971, *On Communicative Competence*, Philadelphia, University of Pennsylvania Press.
Ituen, Stephen A. U. 1980, 'Special needs and expectations for the teaching of international languages: a case study of French in Nigeria and English in Ivory Coast', Ph.D. dissertation, University of Toronto.
Iyengar, K. R. Srinivasa 1962, *Indian writing in English*, Bombay, Asia Publishing House.
Izevbaye, Dan 1968, 'The relevance of modern literary theory in English to poetry and fiction in English-speaking West Africa', Ph.D. thesis, University of Ibadan.
James, K. 1984, 'The writing of theses by speakers of English as a foreign language: the results of a case study', in Raymond Williams *et al.*, 1984.
Johns, Tim 1981a, 'Exploratory CAL: an alternative use of the computer in teaching foreign languages', Paper given at the British Council Conference on Computers in Language Teaching, Paris, December, 1981.
    1981b, 'The uses of an analytic generator: the computer as teacher of English for specific purposes', in The British Council, 1981.
    1983, 'Generating Alternatives', in D. Chandler (ed.), *Exploring English with Microcomputers*, London, National Association for the Teaching of English on Behalf of the Microelectronics Education Programme.
    1984, 'Small machines with big ideas', *Proceedings of Man and the Media Seminar*, Frankfurt, June, 1984.
Johns, Tim and A. Dudley-Evans 1980, 'An experiment in team-teaching of

overseas postgraduate students of transportation and plant biology', *ELT Documents*, 106, The British Council.

Johns, Tim and J. Higgins 1983, 'Approaches to CALL for English as a foreign language: a survey of work in progress', mimeo.

Johnson, Alex 1981, 'Language and society in West African literature: a stylistic investigation into the linguistic resources of West African English', Ph.D. thesis, University of Ibadan.

Jones, C. 1982, 'Teachers, authoring systems, and computer assisted language learning', mimeo.

Kachru, Braj B. 1976, 'Models of English for the Third World: white man's linguistic burden or language pragmatics?', *TESOL Quarterly*, 10: 221–39.

　1981, 'American English and other Englishes', in Ferguson and Heath, 1981.

　1982a, 'Language policy in South Asia', *Annual Review of Applied Linguistics*, 1981, Rowley, Mass., Newbury House: 60–82.

　1982b, 'South Asian English', in Bailey and Görlach, 1982.

　(ed.) 1982c, *The Other Tongue: English Across Cultures*, Urbana, Ill., University of Illinois Press.

　1982d, 'Models for non-native Englishes', in Kachru, 1982c.

　1983a, *The Indianization of English: The English Language in India*, New York and Delhi, Oxford University Press.

　1983b, 'The bilingual's creativity: discoursal and stylistic strategies in contact literatures in English', *Studies in the Linguistic Sciences*, 13, 2: 37–55.

　1984a, 'Regional norms for English', in Sandra Savignon and M. Berns (eds.) *Initiatives in Communicative Language Teaching: A Book of Readings*, New York, Addison-Wesley.

　1984b, 'The alchemy of English: social and functional power of non-native varieties', in Cheris Kramarae, Muriel Schulz, and William O'Barr (eds.) *Language and Power*, Beverly Hills, Calif., Sage Publications.

　1985a, 'Institutionalized non-native varieties of English', in Greenbaum, 1985.

　1985b, *The Alchemy of English: The Spread, Functions, and Models for Non-Native Varieties of English*, Oxford, Pergamon Press.

Kachru, Braj B. and Randolph Quirk 1981, 'Introduction', in Smith (ed.), 1981.

Kachru, Yamuna 1983, 'Cross-cultural texts and interpretation', *Studies in the Linguistic Sciences*, 13, 2: 57–72.

Keller, G. 1983, 'Grundlegung einer neuen Kulturkunde als Orientierungsrahmen für Lehrerausbildung und Unterrichtspraxis, *Neusprachliche Mitteilungen*, 4, 3: 200–9.

Kennedy, Chris and Rod Bolitho 1984, *English for Specific Purposes*, London, Macmillan.

King, Bruce 1974, *Literatures of the World in English*, London, Routledge & Kegan Paul.

　1980, *The New English Literatures: Cultural Nationalism in a Changing World*, New York, St Martin's Press.

Knab, D. 1981, 'Curriculum reform and in-service training: problems of a coalition', in G. Nissen *et al.*, 1981.

Knorr-Cetina, Karin D. 1981, *The Manufacture of Knowledge*, Oxford, Pergamon Press.

# Bibliography

Krashen, S. D. 1982, *Principles and Practice in Second Language Acquisition*, Oxford, Pergamon Press.

Krashen, S. D. and T. D. Terrell 1983, *The Natural Approach: Language Acquisition in the Classroom*, Oxford, Pergamon Press.

Labov, W. 1972, *Sociolinguistic Patterns*, Philadelphia, University of Pennsylvania Press.

Leech, G. N. 1983, *Principles of Pragmatics*, London, Longman.

Levinson, S. 1983, *Pragmatics*, Cambridge University Press.

Long, M. 1983, 'The design of classroom second language instruction: towards task-based instruction', University of Hawaii, mimeo.

Long, M. and C. Sato 1984, 'The present state of interlanguage: methodology', Paper presented at a conference in honour of S. P. Corder, Edinburgh, mimeo.

Lowenberg, Peter 1984, 'English in the Malay archipelago: nativization and its functions in a sociolinguistic area', Ph.D. dissertation, University of Illinois at Urbana-Champaign.

Lyons, John and R. J. Wales (eds.) 1966, *Psycholinguistics Papers*, Edinburgh University Press.

McDonough, Jo 1984, *ESP in Perspective*, London, Collins.

Magura, Benjamin 1984, 'Style and meaning in southern African English', Ph.D. dissertation, University of Illinois at Urbana-Champaign.

Maley, Alan and Alan Duff 1978, *Drama Techniques in Language Learning*, Cambridge University Press (2nd edition, 1982).

MAVO Project 1983, *Report: The Communicative Teaching of Foreign Languages*, Second Dutch-German workshop for teachers of English, German and French as foreign languages, LPC-MAVO, 's-Hertogenbosch, Kerkrade, 1982.

Mohammed, A. A. 1984, 'Problems in the management of ESP programmes', in Swales and Mustafa, 1984.

Moorhouse, Geoffrey 1984, *India Britannica*, London, Paladin.

Mukherjee, Meenakshi 1971, *The Twice Born Fiction: Themes and Techniques of the Indian Novel in English*, New Delhi, Arnold-Heinemann.

Munby, John 1978, *Communicative Syllabus Design*, Cambridge University Press.

Murphy, D. and C. Candlin 1979, 'Engineering lecture discourse and listening comprehension', *Lancaster Practical Papers*, 2.

Naiman, N., M. Frölich, H.H. Stern and A. Todesco 1978, *The Good Language Learner*, Research in Education Series, No. 7, Toronto, Ontario Institute for Studies in Education.

Narasimhaiah, C. D. 1976, *Commonwealth Literature: A Handbook of Select Reading Lists*, Madras, Oxford University Press.

1978, *Awakened Conscience: Studies in Commonwealth Literature*, New Delhi, Sterling Publishers.

Nelson, Cecil L. 1982, 'Intelligibility and non-native varieties of English', in Kachru, 1982c.

1984, 'Intelligibility: the case of non-native varieties of English', Ph.D. dissertation, University of Illinois at Urbana-Champaign.

Newman, Edwin 1974, *Strictly Speaking: Will America be the Death of English?*, Indianapolis, Bobbs-Merrill.

1976, *A Civil Tongue*, Indianapolis, Bobbs-Merrill.

Newmark, Leonard 1966, 'How not to interfere with language learning', in C. J.
Brumfit and K. Johnson (eds.) 1979, *The Communicative Approach to
Language Teaching*, Oxford University Press.

Nissen, G., W. P. Teschner, S. Takala and H. Haft (eds.) 1981, *Curriculum
Change Through Qualification and Requalification of Teachers*, Lisse,
Swets & Zeitlinger.

Noss, Richard (ed.) 1983, *Varieties of English in Southeast Asia*, Singapore,
Regional English Language Centre.

*Oregon ESP Newsletter*, Nos. 79, 80, 81.

Osundare, O. 1979, 'Bilingual and bicultural aspects of Nigerian prose fiction',
Ph.D. thesis, Toronto, York University.

Palmer, H. E. 1922, *The Principles of Language Study*, London, Harrap, reissued
1964, Oxford University Press.

Parret, Herman (ed.) 1976, *History of Linguistic Thought and Contemporary
Linguistics*, Berlin, Walter de Gruyter.

Phillips, M. K. 1983, 'Intelligent CALL and the QWERTY phenomenon: a
rationale', Paper presented at the 16th annual meeting of the British Association of Applied Linguistics, Leicester Polytechnic, 16–18 September, 1983.

Pickett, G. D. 1978, *The Foreign Language Learning Process*, ETIC Occasional
Paper, London, The British Council.

Platt, John T. and Heidi Webber 1980, *English in Singapore and Malaysia:
Status, Features, Functions*, Kuala Lumpur, Oxford University Press.

Porter, P. 1983, 'How learners talk to each other: input and interaction in task-
centred discussions', Toronto, TESOL, mimeo.

Prabhu, N. 1984, 'Procedural syllabuses', RELC Seminar, 1983, in J. Read, 1984.

Prator, Clifford 1968, 'The British heresy in TESL', in Joshua A. Fishman,
Charles A. Ferguson and Jyotirindra Das Gupta (eds.) *Language Problems
in Developing Nations*, New York, John Wiley & Sons, Inc.

Prendergast, T. 1864, *The Mastery of Languages*, London, Longman.

Pride, John 1981, 'Native competence and the bilingual/multilingual speaker',
*English World-Wide: A Journal of Varieties of English*, 2.2: 141–53.
(ed.) 1982, *New Englishes*, Rowley, Mass., Newbury House.

Quirk, Randolph, S. Greenbaum, G. Leech and J. Svartvik 1972, *A Grammar of
Contemporary English*, London, Longman.

Rautzenberg, J. 1982, *Erlebte Landeskunde, Dokumentation eines Fort-
bildungsseminars am Goethe-Institut Berlin*, München, Goethe-Institut.

Read, Allen Walker 1933, 'British recognition of American speech in the
eighteenth century', *Dialect Notes*, 6: 313–34.

Read, J. (ed.) 1984, *Trends in Language Syllabus Design*, Singapore, Singapore
University Press.

Reeve, A. J. 1982, *Business Games*, Cambridge, Acornsoft.

Renouf, A. J. 1983, 'Corpus Development at Birmingham University', in J. Aarts
*et al.* (eds.) *Corpora Linguistics*, Amsterdam: Rodopi, 1984: 3–39.

Richterich, R. 1972, *A Model for the Definition of Language Needs of Adults
Learning a Modern Language*, Strasbourg, Council of Europe.

Rivers, Wilga M. 1979, 'Learning a sixth language: an adult learner's daily
diary', *Canadian Modern Language Review*, 36, 1, October: 67–82.

Robert-Bosch-Stiftung (ed.) 1982, *Fremdsprachenunterricht und internationale
Beziehungen, Stuttgarter Thesen zur Rolle der Landeskunde im
Französischunterricht*, Deutsch-Französisches Institut, Ludwigsburg.

# Bibliography

Robinson, I. 1973, *The Survival of English: Essays in Criticism of Language*, Cambridge University Press.
Roe, Peter 1977, *Scientific Text*, *ELR Monographs*, No. 4, University of Birmingham.
Rorty, Richard 1983, 'Solidarité ou objectivité?', *Critique*, December.
Rutherford, W. 1982, 'Functions of grammar in a language teaching syllabus', *Language Learning and Communication*, 1, 1: 21–37.
Safire, William 1980, *On Language*, New York, Times Books.
Sager, J. C., D. Dungworth and P. F. McDonald 1980, *English Special Languages*, Wiesbaden, Brandstetter.
Sanders, D. and R. Kenner 1983, 'Whither CAI? the need for communicative courseware', *System*, 11, 1: 33–9.
Savignon, Sandra J. 1972, *Communicative Competence: an Experiment in Foreign Language Teaching*, Philadelphia, Center for Curriculum Development.
Schmidt, Maxine F. 1981, 'Needs assessment in English for specific purposes: the case study', in L. Selinker *et al.*, 1981.
Schneider, E. W. 1983, 'Veni, vidi, vici via videodisc: a simulator for instructional conversations', *System*, 11, 1: 41–6.
Schubert, A. *et al.* 1983, 'Scientometric analysis of attendance at international scientific meetings', *Scientometrics*, 5, 3.
Searle, John 1969, *Speech Acts*, Cambridge University Press.
Sebeok, T. A. and D. J. Umiker-Sebeok 1983, ' "You know my method": a juxtaposition of Charles S. Peirce and Sherlock Holmes', in U. Eco and T. A. Sebeok, (eds.) *The Sign of Three*, Bloomington, Indiana University Press.
Seletzki, M. *et al.* 1982, *Job Satisfaction and the Effects of Unemployment, Teaching Materials for Intermediate and Advanced Classes*, Hessisches Institut für Lehrerfortbildung, Hauptstelle Reinhardswaldschule (No. 1439), Fuldatal.
Selinker, L. 1979, 'On the use of informants in discourse analysis and language for specialized purposes', *International Review of Applied Linguistics*, 27, 3.
Selinker, L., E. Tarone and V. Hanzeli (eds.) 1981, *English for Academic and Technical Purposes*, Rowley, Mass., Newbury House.
Selinker, L. and S. Gass 1983, *Language Transfer*, Rowley, Mass., Newbury House.
Sinclair, J. McH. 1980, 'Computational text analysis at the University of Birmingham', in Johansson, S. (ed.), *Newsletter of the International Computer Archive of Modern English*, 4, September, Bergen, The Norwegian Computing Centre for the Humanities.
    1982, 'Reflections on computer corpora in English language research', in Johansson, S. (ed.), *Computer Corpora in English Language Research*, Bergen, The Norwegian Computing Centre for the Humanities.
Sinclair, J. McH., S. Jones and R. Daley 1970, *English Lexical Study*, OSTI Report, Department of English, University of Birmingham.
Sinclair, J. McH. and R. M. Coulthard 1975, *Towards an Analysis of Discourse*, Oxford University Press.
Smith, Larry E. (ed.) 1981, *English for Cross-Cultural Communication*, London, Macmillan.
    (ed.) 1983, *Readings in English as an International Language*, Oxford and New York, Pergamon Press.
Solmecke, G. 1982, *Landeskunde in Fremdsprachenkursen, Arbeitstexte zur*

*Berufseinführung*, 2, Bonn, Pädagogischen Arbeitsstelle des Deutschen Volkschochschulverbandes.

Soyinka, W. 1975, 'Neo-Tarzanism: the poetics of pseudo-traditionalism', *Transition*, 48.

Stevick, Earl W. 1980, *Teaching Languages: A Way and Ways*, Rowley, Mass., Newbury House.

Stichting voor de Leerplanontwikkeling (SLO) 1982, *Report*, First Dutch-German workshop for teachers of English, German and French as foreign languages, Enschede, 1982 (Vierhouten, 1981).

Strevens, Peter 1982a, 'The localized forms of English', in Kachru, 1982c.

    1982b, 'World English and the world's English – or, whose language is it anyway?', *Journal of the Royal Society of Arts*, June: 412–28.

Svartvik, J. and B. Oreström 1982, *Survey of Spoken English*, Lund, Wallin & Dalholm Broktr AB.

Swales, John 1983, 'Developing materials for writing scholarly introductions', in R. R. Jordan (ed.) *Case Studies in ELT*, London, Collins.

    1984a, *Episodes in English for Science and Technology*, Oxford, Pergamon Press.

    1984b, 'A review of ESP in the Arab world 1977–1983: trends, developments and retrenchments', in Swales and Mustafa, 1984.

    1984c, 'Thoughts on, in and outside the classroom', in Charles, 1984.

    1985, 'English language papers and author's first language: preliminary explorations', *Scientometrics*.

Swales, John and Hassan Mustafa (eds.) 1984, *ESP in the Arab World*, Language Studies Unit, University of Aston in Birmingham.

Tarone, E., S. Dwyer, S. Gillette and V. Icke 1981, 'On the use of the passive in two astrophysics journal papers', *The ESP Journal*, 1, 2: 123–40.

Trudgill, Peter 1974, *Social Differentiation of English in Norwich*, Cambridge University Press.

van Ek, J. 1975, *The Threshold Level*, Strasbourg, Council of Europe.

von Hofe, H. H. 1955, *Im Wandel der Jahre: ein deutsches Lesebuch für Anfänger*, New York, Holt, Rinehart & Winston.

Wales, R. J. and J. C. Marshall 1966, 'The organization of linguistic performance', in Lyons and Wales, 1966: 29–80.

Wallin, E. 1981, 'Curriculum realization and teacher training', in G. Nissen *et al.*, 1981.

Ward, Ida C. 1929, *The Phonetics of English*, Cambridge, Heffer.

Widdowson, H. G. 1978, *Teaching Language as Communication*, Oxford University Press.

    1979, *Explorations in Applied Linguistics*, Oxford University Press.

    1981, 'English for specific purposes: criteria for course design', in L. Selinker *et al.*, 1981.

    1983, *Learning Purpose and Language Use*, Oxford University Press.

    1984, *Explorations in Applied Linguistics*, 2, Oxford University Press.

Wilkins, D. A. 1976, *Notional Syllabuses*, Oxford University Press.

Williams, Raymond 1973, *The Country and the City*, London, Chatto & Windus (cited from Paladin edition, St Albans, 1975).

Williams, Raymond, J. Swales and J. Kirkman (eds.) 1984, *Common Ground: Shared Interests in ESP and Communication Studies*, Oxford, Pergamon Press.

# Index

## Index of names